PERSPECTIVES IN SOCIAL INQUIRY

PERSPECTIVES IN SOCIAL INQUIRY
CLASSICS, STAPLES AND PRECURSORS IN SOCIOLOGY

Advisory Editors
ROBERT K. MERTON
ARON HALBERSTAM

STUDIES IN SOCIAL PSYCHOLOGY
IN WORLD WAR II

Volume 3

ARNO PRESS
A New York Times Company
New York — 1974

Reprint Edition 1974 by Arno Press Inc.

Copyright, 1949 by Princeton
   University Press
Reprinted by permission of
   Princeton University Press

Reprinted from a copy in
   The Newark Public Library

PERSPECTIVES IN SOCIAL INQUIRY
ISBN for complete set: 0-405-05490-4
See last pages of this volume for titles.

Manufactured in the United States of America

———◆———

Library of Congress Cataloging in Publication Data

Main entry under title:

Studies in social psychology in World War II.

   (Perspectives in social inquiry)
   Reprint of vols. 1-3 of the ed. published by
Princeton University Press, Princeton, N. J.
   1. Soldiers--United States. 2. Social
psychology. I. Series.
U22.S82 1974   355.1   73-14180
ISBN 0-405-05523-4

EXPERIMENTS ON
MASS COMMUNICATION

STUDIES IN SOCIAL PSYCHOLOGY
IN WORLD WAR II

The four volumes in this series were prepared and edited under the auspices of a Special Committee of the Social Science Research Council, comprising

The data on which these volumes are based were collected by the Research Branch, Information and Education Division, War Department, during World War II. In making the data available, the War Department assumes no responsibility for the analyses and interpretations contained in these volumes, which are the sole responsibility of the authors.

These volumes were prepared under a grant from the Carnegie Corporation of New York. That corporation is not, however, the author, owner, publisher, or proprietor of this publication, and is not to be understood as approving by virtue of its grant any of the statements made or views expressed therein.

VOLUME III

EXPERIMENTS
ON MASS
COMMUNICATION

BY

CARL I. HOVLAND

ARTHUR A. LUMSDAINE

FRED D. SHEFFIELD

PRINCETON, NEW JERSEY

PRINCETON UNIVERSITY PRESS

1949

Printed in the United States of America by
The Colonial Press Inc., Clinton, Mass.

PREFACE

THE present volume is the third of a series describing the work of the Research Branch of the Army's Information and Education Division. The function of the Research Branch as a whole is described in Chapter 1 of the first volume. Briefly, the Branch's mission was to collect and analyze data on soldiers' attitudes and opinions. These data, obtained primarily through anonymous questionnaires answered by enlisted men, were for general use by Army policy makers—particularly by those responsible for planning the information, orientation, and education programs. Much of the work of the Research Branch consisted of large-scale cross-sectional surveys, carried out by the Survey Section of the Branch. Other studies, involving controlled experimentation, were the primary responsibility of the Experimental Section. A number of these experimental studies, dealing with the effectiveness of films and other mass-communication devices, are described in the present volume. The studies reported here are the ones thought to be of general interest to persons concerned with the use of mass-communication methods and those engaged in research on the effectiveness of these media.

The main mission of the Experimental Section was to make experimental evaluations of the effectiveness of various programs of the Information and Education Division. The first study of this type was done soon after Pearl Harbor to provide data on the effectiveness of the existing lecture system when compared with documentary films as a means of imparting information concerning the events leading up to America's participation in the war. Subsequently extensive experimental studies were carried out on the first four of the "Why We Fight" series of orientation films prepared for the Division to explain the background of the war, as well as briefer studies of a series of educational and general interest films.

In addition to these studies of films, a number of experimental and nonexperimental studies were made of other media used by the Information and Education Division. These were quite diverse in character. One of them was an extensive study for the Information Branch of readership interest in *Yank*—the Army weekly magazine —conducted in four overseas theaters as well as in the United States. A similar study of book readership, based on library card records and other indices of use, was made for the Library Branch. Studies concerned with the optimal phonetic representation of foreign language words were conducted for the Education Branch. At the request of the Radio Branch, listening habits and program preferences of Army hospital patients were studied by direct observational methods. Extensive studies were conducted to evaluate various unit orientation programs, materials for which were supplied by the Division's Orientation Branch. Some of these results are presented in Chapter 9 of Volume I. In still another study, comparisons were made of commentator and documentary radio presentations. Some results obtained from this study are described in Chapters 4 and 8 of this volume.

The research of the Experimental Section was not, however, confined to studying the program of the Information and Education Division. Almost from the outset, requests for assistance in psychological research were received by the Experimental Section from other Divisions of the War Department lacking suitable personnel or research facilities of their own. Thus, one of the first experiments performed was a comparison of the effectiveness of the standard Army physical conditioning program with a new program proposed as an alternative by a committee of athletic coaches. Another study, requested by the Office of the Surgeon General, investigated combat veterans' reports of the relative fear-producing effects of various kinds of enemy weapons and tactics. An extensive series of psychological studies was undertaken at the invitation of the Paratroop School at Fort Benning, including an experiment to determine the optimal time for trainees' first training jump from a practice tower. In another study, personnel from the Experimental Section were called upon by the Air Corps to carry out intensive interviews with returnees as a basis for policy decisions concerning redeployment from the European Theatre to the Pacific.

Partly because the Information and Education Division was originally charged with responsibility for reporting on the status of Army morale and the factors affecting it, a continuing interest in this area led to several studies on various aspects of "morale." These included studies of leadership practices among commissioned and non-commissioned officers in both training and operational situations. A general interest in training problems led to the undertaking of several collaborative research projects on military training films, requested by the Military Training Division of Army Service Forces. Results from some of these studies of training films are reported in the present volume.

The members of the Experimental Section who had major responsibilities for the planning, conduct, or analysis of experimental studies over an extended period of time were the following:

Frances J. Anderson   Arthur A. Lumsdaine
John L. Finan   Nathan Maccoby
Carl I. Hovland   Fred D. Sheffield
Irving L. Janis   M. Brewster Smith

Others in the Section whose work covered a briefer period included John M. Butler, David A. Grant, Donald Horton, Eugene H. Jacobson, Ansel Marblestone, Alice H. Schmid, and Adeline Turetsky.

Throughout, there was a very close link between the Experimental Section, which was composed mainly of psychologists, and the Survey Section, which was staffed mainly by sociologists. Not only was there constant interchange of ideas, but borrowing of personnel frequently occurred, sometimes for extended periods of time. Robert Ford, Edward A. Suchman, and Paul Wallin were the three members of the Survey Section who spent the most extended periods of time working on Experimental Section studies. In overseas operations there was no clear distinction between Experimental Section and Survey Section personnel and, since the feasibility of conducting controlled experimentation was much more limited than in the United States, Experimental Section personnel engaged mainly in survey and other nonexperimental work. Both in the United States and overseas a common pool of officers functioned in making arrangements for the administration of studies in the field for both survey and experimental studies. Similarly, pooled facilities and staff services for processing of data and for editing and printing of reports and questionnaires were employed in the conduct of both types of studies.

Special appreciation is expressed to a number of consultants who contributed to the work of the Branch. Those who consulted most frequently on Experimental Section studies were John Dollard, Paul F. Lazarsfeld, Quinn McNemar, and Robert K. Merton. In the studies of training films, valuable assistance was rendered by Lester F. Beck and Major Arthur Weimer of the Military Training Division. Needless to say, the research reported in this volume could not have been accomplished without the constant support of Samuel A. Stouffer, civilian head of the Research Branch professional staff, Lt. Col. Charles Dollard and others who served as officers in charge of the Branch, and Major General Frederick H. Osborn, Director of the Information and Education Division.

The diversity of topics covered by the research of the Experimental Section made it unfeasible to publish a single cohesive account of all of the studies. However, it did appear possible to integrate the group of studies on the effects of motion pictures, film strips, and radio programs into a systematic treatment concerning the effectiveness of mass communication media which would be of general scientific interest. Results of most of the other Experimental Section studies are available in Washington to qualified investigators in the form of summary War Department reports and IBM punch cards, and some of the findings are included in Volumes I and II of this series.

The writing of the present report was the joint work of the undersigned. The planning and writing of the original draft and revision were done in such close collaboration that it is difficult to allocate credits on an individual chapter basis. The writers wish to express their appreciation to the other members of the Experimental Section who participated in the conduct and analysis of some of the studies on which this report is based. Special acknowledgment is due to the following: Frances Anderson, Mary Arnold, and Robert Grose for assistance in organizing the files and tabulations in New Haven; Ruth Hays for aid in reading proof and preparing the index; Dean Manheimer, for editorial assistance, particularly in the graphical presentations; Leland C. DeVinney, for general editorial supervision; Frederick C. Mosteller, for a careful reading of the final draft of several portions of the Appendix; and Leonard Doob, Charles Dollard, Quinn McNemar, Paul F. Lazarsfeld, and Robert K. Merton, for a reading of the first draft in the fall of 1946.

CARL I. HOVLAND
ARTHUR A. LUMSDAINE
FRED D. SHEFFIELD

New Haven, Conn.
November, 1948

CONTENTS

EXPERIMENTS ON
MASS COMMUNICATION

CHAPTER 1

INTRODUCTION

THE Army's unprecedented utilization of films and similar mass
communication media during World War II provided a favorable opportunity for experimental studies on the effectiveness of
these devices. This volume describes a series of such studies conducted by the Experimental Section of the Research Branch in the
War Department's Information and Education Division. The
films studied included the "Why We Fight" series, designed for indoctrination of members of the Armed Forces concerning the events
leading up to American participation in the war, and a number of
training films studied in cooperation with other divisions of the War
Department. The methods used in these studies and the results
obtained are described here in the belief that there will be increasing
use of such procedures both for determining whether motion pictures and similar media really do succeed in attaining their objectives and for modifying the products in accordance with the results
obtained by research.

These experimental studies comprised a large-scale attempt to
utilize modern socio-psychological research techniques in the evaluation of educational and "indoctrination" films. In nearly all cases,
however, the studies had an immediate practical purpose and did
not constitute a systematic research program. The present volume
is, therefore, essentially a report on those by-products of the applied
research that are thought to be of scientific interest. In preparing
the report, an attempt has been made to give some systematization
to the results and to present a rationale of the general field of research on mass educational media.

In the majority of the studies motion pictures were used as the
communication medium. For this reason the discussion that follows is phrased mainly in terms of films. However, the primary
interest throughout is not restricted to films as such, but rather is
in principles which would apply more generally to any mass communication medium. It is to be expected that ultimately the re-

sults of film studies will become part of a more general body of principles concerning mass communication. Mass communication principles in turn will presumably become integrated into a larger body of principles concerning the manner in which ideas and ways of reacting are acquired through learning. A systematic treatment of educational film research therefore should ultimately include principles at three different levels of generality:

1. *Basic learning principles*—common to all educational devices.
2. *Mass communication principles*—applying to films and similar educational media.
3. *Film principles*—related specifically to the medium of films.

The *basic learning principles* would be phrased in terms of very general concepts, such as "repetition," "response," "motivation," "interference." *Mass communication principles* would translate these principles into the terms of more specialized learning situations —"participation," "interest," "initial attitude," "attention," etc. *Film principles* would be generalizations at the most specific level, translating from the two more general levels into a specialized terminology for films. This might include terms like "dramatic presentation," "animation," "voice-over narration," "discussion breaks," etc.

The research to be described is mainly restricted to analysis of *the effects of films on the audience*. Therefore many types of research connected with films will not be covered here: problems of film distribution, methods of maximizing voluntary attendance, library "research" on background material, curriculum analysis, etc., are excluded. Even with this restriction to analysis of the educational effects, a number of different kinds of film research may be classified, each with its own requirements and restrictions as to conclusions that may be drawn.

Objectives of Film Research

A basic distinction can be made between studies where the purpose is to evaluate a completed product and those where the purpose is to investigate variables by controlled variation. These two kinds of research may each in turn be divided into two subtypes, giving four general classes of film study:

1a. Evaluation of a single film.
 b. Evaluation of a class of films.
2a. Experimental investigation of a single variable by controlled variation.

b. Experimental analysis of two or more variables in combination.

Each of these classes of film research is briefly characterized below. The studies described in Part I of this volume are *Evaluative* (1a and 1b) while those of Part II employ *Controlled Variation* (2a and 2b). In both kinds of studies the main emphasis was on the measurement of changes in knowledge, opinion, or behavior produced by a film or other communication device. This contrasts with most commercial film research, which is limited to polling the audience to determine what they think of the film.

1a. *Evaluation of a single film.* A film may be produced to achieve a particular educational objective and a purely practical research project can be carried out to determine the extent to which this objective is achieved. The adequacy of the research is determined by the representativeness of the sample audience, the representativeness of the conditions of testing, and the validity of the measuring instrument. The sample of people must represent the population for which the film is designed, the experimental presentations must approximate the actual conditions of use of the film, and the measurements made must reflect the behavior changes desired of the film as an educational device. The measurements need not reveal all of the behavior changes produced by the film but may be primarily focused on designated objectives. For example, a film may have the purpose of explaining the structure of the American government and it would be unnecessary to measure any American history that might be taught by the film. Or, a film may be designed solely to stimulate discussion on a subject, in which case only the effects of discussion stimulated need appropriately be measured, although the audience may incidentally have learned a number of facts from the film.

It is important to note that conclusions from an evaluative study of a single film apply to *that particular film;* generalizations to other films have the status of untested hypotheses. Some film studies may not actually have the purpose of evaluating a single product but nevertheless may conform to the pattern of such a study and have the same limitations on generalizability. Thus a test of the effects of a single film may be conducted "to determine the utility of films as educational devices"; obviously the conclusion from such a study would normally have little generality.

Aside from their limited scientific value in contributing testable hypotheses which may lead to the development of principles, evalu-

ative studies are useful as a form of *applied* research.   If the evaluations are made when the films are finished products, the most the
results can tell the film producer is whether he has succeeded or
failed in attaining specified educational objectives.   If he has failed
in major respects, the only recourse is to reject the film or design
supplementary materials to reinforce its weak points.   Further
application of the results is possible only to the extent that the implications of the findings can be generalized to future films of a
similar nature.

However, if a "rough cut" or preliminary try-out version is used
in the evaluative study, prior to the completion of the finished product, the results can be more useful to the producer.   They may then
be utilized in modifying the film, or if need be in redesigning it, so
as to try to correct or reinforce the weak points in its presentation.
Ideally such evaluations should be carried out as early in the stage
of production as feasible, and repeated after each major stage of
revision.   By successive correction and re-evaluation one might
achieve a far more effective communication than if the product had
been carried through to completion as originally designed.

1b. *Evaluation of a class of films.*   A research project may seek to
evaluate a class of films rather than a single product.   In this case,
besides the problems of adequate audience sampling, representative
conditions for testing, and validity of the measuring instrument,
there is the additional problem of adequate sampling of the class of
products about which the conclusions are to be made.   The conclusions have to apply to the *average* film of a particular kind—a consideration which greatly multiplies the size of the project as compared with evaluation of a single film.

For example, a study may be done to determine the effectiveness
of films in teaching a particular subject, such as general science.
Even if an adequate sample of existing films of this type were used
and compared with an adequate sampling of other instructional devices, the conclusion would apply only to *existing* films of this type
and would not determine how effective such films *could* be.

This form of research has also been used in attempts to get at the
effect of a particular film variable.   For example, the question may
be, "Which is more effective for educational purposes—silent film or
sound film?"   The variable here would be sound accompaniment in
educational films.   A number of examples of sound and silent films
—comparable in varying degrees in other respects—are compared
to determine their "relative effectiveness."   The results of this

mode of attack have doubtful generality. At best they could give only the typical effects of the variable as usually employed; when the sampling of films is small, even this conclusion cannot be drawn.

2a. *Experimental investigation of a single variable by controlled variation.* A more efficient mode of attack on the type of question discussed in the preceding paragraph is one in which the variable under consideration (in this case, the use of sound) is studied by means of controlled variation. Here all factors are held constant except the one being investigated. For instance, in the case of sound vs. silent films controlled variation would involve comparing the effectiveness of sound and silent films having the *same subject and pictorial content.* This would require the use of two films (or of pairs of films) differing only in the particular of having representative sound accompaniments for the pictorial material in one film (or set of films), with the appropriate portions of the sound replaced by visual titles in the parallel film or films. Thus instead of trying to "average out" differences due to noncomparability, the experimental and control forms of the film presentation are constructed so as actually to be comparable.

Even where this form of research is undertaken, there may be difficulties in achieving comparability with respect to irrelevant variables. To use the above example of the effects of sound accompaniment, this factor might be controlled by using a sound film with the sound omitted, or a silent film might be used with sound "dubbed in." But if the techniques of sound and silent film differ, the result might be quite different when the sound is omitted from a sound film and when the sound is added to a silent film. Sound accompaniment might turn out to be an important factor in the former case and a detriment in the latter case. With other types of variables, the problem of achieving comparability of control and experimental conditions might readily be solved. For example, a comparison of a color film and an achromatic print of the same film would probably involve no similar difficulties, nor would the measurement of the effects of showing a film twice as contrasted with a single showing.

Probably one of the greatest difficulties in the way of drawing useful conclusions from this type of film study is the problem of generality. An inherent feature of such research is that it seeks a conclusion about a single variable without respect to other variables with which it might interact. Thus sound accompaniment might be an aid to learning under some conditions and a detriment in others. An unqualified conclusion derived from a single-variable study would ordinarily have to be checked with a variety of films and under a variety of conditions before its generality could be determined.

2b. *Experimental analysis of two or more variables in combination.* As suggested above, it seems likely that with the complexity of variables present there would be few empirical generalizations that would hold up for all educational films, all audiences, and all conditions for using the films. Variables would be expected to interact so that the effects of any one variable would have to be differentially designated according to the accompanying variables. Accordingly, the result of an attempt to determine the generality of a conclusion about a single variable would lead to a series of principles rather than a single principle.

Because of this likelihood, the type of research that will probably result in the broadest generalizations for the field of educational films and related media is research studying the controlled variation of several variables in combination. The qualifications on the generalizations are thus determined, and generalizations may be stated in the form: "Under condition A, result 1 is obtained, whereas under condition B, result 2 is obtained."

Multi-variable experimentation will be needed to establish such principles, and the research will be benefited greatly by being based upon adequate theory. A "shotgun" empirical approach would necessitate studying any number of variables in combination, whereas the development of a successful theoretical structure makes it increasingly likely that the experimenter can select in advance the proper variables—both those which most influence the effects of a communication and those which modify that influence. In addition, there is more likelihood that the correct generalization will be made from findings proceeding from a theoretical statement, which is already couched in general rather than specific terms. A purely empirical generalization, on the other hand, may often generalize in terms of the wrong variables. For example, in early research on memory, the "law of forgetting," was formulated on the assumption that forgetting was due to the lapse of time. Subsequent theoretical developments deriving from other experiments led to the prediction that time was a false variable in this generalization and that it was the nature of the activity intervening between learning and recall, rather than lapse of time per se, which was primarily

responsible for forgetting. This prediction was subsequently verified experimentally.

These advantages of a theoretical structure emphasize again the
desirability of integrating scientific research on the educational
effects of films with research on other educational methods and with
the psychology of learning in general. Wherever possible, the concepts and variables of film study should be related to those of a general theoretical structure which is applicable to the entire field of
education.

Of course research does not necessarily have such broad scientific
aims; it may sometimes have a purely practical purpose. For example, it may be desired to determine which of several available
films should be selected for use in a given course of instruction. The
answer could make an important difference in the success of the
course, but it would have no implications for general principles
about films except to suggest hypotheses useful in subsequent scientific research. But even for practical purposes the decisions one
can make on the basis of principles are often more effective—because
of their known generalizability—than those based on conclusions
from specific evaluative studies. The ultimate objective in developing general principles is, in fact, to improve our ability to make
wise practical decisions.

Kinds of Variables Related to Effects of Films

The discussion so far has taken "variables" for granted and has
not discussed different types of variables that may influence the
effects of a film. Such variables could be classified in a variety of
ways. The classification that follows is simply in terms of *locus* of
the variable, but at least serves to identify, in broad categories, the
areas in which film research problems might exist.

1. *Population variables.* One of the first considerations of the
producer of an educational film is the nature of the audience which
a film or other communication is designed to affect. Thus one
group of variables determining a film's effects are the *population
variables.* Important examples of such variables in most educational films would be *age* (general maturity), *intelligence,* and *previous knowledge* of the subject matter. For example, a film for children would be designed differently from one for adults; a film for an
audience composed of individuals differing widely in learning ability
might require a greater range of kinds of presentation than one for a

homogeneous audience; and a film for specialists would be pitched
at a different level than a film for laymen. In educational films
with special purposes, other population variables might also become
particularly important. Thus, in a film with a broad educational
purpose such as one designed to overcome prejudices, the initial
attitudes of the audience might be particularly important.

2. *Film variables.* With the nature of the audience in mind, a
film producer must decide what to put into the film in order to
achieve its educational purpose. The total field of what may be
included in the film or other communication may be referred to as
film variables, or content variables, and the producer must include
some things and exclude others according to their probable effects
on the intended audience for which the film is designed. To a certain extent, of course, the contents of the film are determined by the
educational purpose, but principles relating content variables to
effects on the audience would also be an important guide, particularly to mode of presentation.

3. *External variables.* Once a film has been produced, the educator must decide the most effective way of using it. Variables other
than properties of the film and properties of the audience may be
called *external variables.* For example, the effects of a film may
differ according to what supplementary material is presented, either
prior to or after the film. Or, effects of the film may be studied as a
function of "discussion breaks," interpolated quizzes, and other
procedures involving interrupting the film and using devices designed to maximize its effectiveness.

It should be pointed out that the three kinds of variables cannot
be considered independently; rather, research on any one of these
variables is best carried out in relation to the interactions with other
variables. Furthermore, a given psychological variable may occur
in more than one of the three categories outlined above. Thus motivation, as a variable in learning, will be a *population* variable in
that some audience members will possess more motivation to learn
than others; it may be a *film* variable if techniques to motivate the
audience are incorporated into a film; or it may be an *external* variable if a supplemental technique of motivation—such as announcing
in advance that a quiz on the film will be given—is used in conjunction with showing a film.

The relation of film effects to *population variables* and *external
variables* can be analyzed in any kind of film research. For example,
an evaluative study of a single film can show how the effects vary

as a function of intelligence, or age, initial bias, or other character- istics of the individuals in the audience. Here some replication of effects is possible even in evaluating a single film, since the film may have a number of discrete effects which can be individually related to a given population variable. Similarly, the evaluation of a single film under two or more external conditions of presentation consti- tutes a study of the effects of an external variable, although the gen- erality of the conclusion may be limited. In the study of *film vari- ables*, on the other hand, it is usually necessary to have two or more controlled versions of the film. The only exception to this would be a single film in which controlled variation was accomplished in the treatment of different parts of the film; but this approach lacks complete control without another version in which the treatment of different parts is reversed. For this reason studies of film variables are usually more difficult and expensive than studies of population or external variables.

Kinds of Effects of Films

So far little consideration has been given to kinds of *effects* pro- duced—the dependent variable in the science of educational films and related media. It is important to distinguish two broad cate- gories.

1. *Interest and evaluative reactions of the audience.* In the pro- duction of Hollywood features the main criterion of an effective film is the "box-office"—that is, the attendance at the film. With this criterion, one relevant concern for research is to measure the immediate reactions and evaluations of the audience. Whether or not the audience showed interest in the film would probably be the film's most important "effect." Subsidiary measures would be the audience's opinions and comments about specific aspects of the film.

Such evaluations on the part of the audience may frequently be a useful part of research on educational films. Part of the purpose of the film may be to initiate interest in a subject, and interest shown in the film might serve as one measure of its motivational value. In any case, interest in the film would be important from the standpoint of maximizing attention, and thereby the amount learned, during the showing. Other aspects of the audience's evaluations of au- thenticity, fairness, and coverage of relevant facts may also be use- ful indices of factors influencing what is learned, particularly in a film on a controversial issue.

There is, however, a tendency for many individuals who are not familiar with experimental research on educational films to think in terms of audience evaluations as the sole measure of the effectiveness of films. Although evaluations by the audience are usually of importance in educational films, the real purpose of the film is to *teach* something, and the effectiveness of the film in this sphere must be determined by some measure of what has been learned. It is even possible that much might be learned from a film that was intensely disliked.

2. *Measurement of what the audience has learned.* The kind of measurement usually most relevant to determining the effects of an educational film or of particular variables in the field of mass communications is measurement of the extent to which the film or other communication device actually teaches the material to be learned. If a film is designed to teach history, the critical question is the amount of history learned by the audience as a consequence of seeing the film. This cannot be determined by asking the audience how much they learned—it can be determined only by giving a history test with and without exposure to the film. Similarly, if the purpose of the film is to reduce a particular prejudice, the relevant measure is a measure of the extent of this prejudice with, as compared to that without, exposure to the film.

In some cases it is relatively easy to measure the actual behavior a communication is designed to influence. A film on history would probably be a good case in point, since history is a verbal subject and it should not be difficult to prepare the relevant verbal test. On the other hand, a film for infantrymen on the subject of hand-to-hand combat is designed to affect men's ability to take care of themselves in combat, which would be a difficult ability to measure, either in training or in combat. An indirect measure might be obtained from *simulated* hand-to-hand combat, but a verbal test would be very indirect and of unknown validity as a measure of the teaching effects of the film on performance at the actual task.

Nature of the Film Research Done by the Experimental Section

As indicated earlier, all of the studies carried out by the Experimental Section had a practical purpose rather than a purely scientific one. In most cases, film materials studied were prepared independently by film-makers to achieve desired effects rather than to establish principles of film construction or use. Even where a clear-cut test of a factor was possible in a study there was little or no opportunity to determine the generality or the limits of the findings by replication with a variety of materials.

Three general categories of kinds of films were studied. These are described below.

Orientation films. A preliminary study undertaken by the Experimental Section was to get information on the desirability of using documentary films instead of a series of orientation lectures then being given by local camp personnel in the Army. Following this study, a series of "Why We Fight" documentary films was initiated by the Information and Education Division. As a sequel to the earlier study the Experimental Section was called upon to evaluate the first four films in the series. One purpose of this research was to evaluate the effectiveness of the films in imparting information about the background of the war and in effecting changes in attitudes toward the war that were related to the objectives of the Army's orientation program. Another purpose of the research was to insure against the possibility of any undesirable effects that might result from the films. Partly for this reason the studies of each film were carried out prior to the general release of that particular film for Army distribution.

The content of the orientation films was primarily factual material, but there was a considerable amount of interpretation of the factual material. The films were shown during training hours, but they were not presented as part of any courses of training on which the men would be tested. These films may therefore be distinguished from instructional films that are integrated into a regular teaching program in that little or no external motivation is applied as an incentive for learning the material presented. The films were more like voluntary education—they had to "sell themselves." Little expectation of immediate application—either in an "exam" or in putting the material into practice—was present as a stimulus for paying close attention. For these reasons, together with the fact that some of the content was controversial material, considerable emphasis was placed on stimulating interest and getting acceptance of the interpretive material.

Three general types of measurements were made in connection with orientation films: (1) measurement of experimentally produced changes in knowledge of factual material; (2) measurement of experimentally produced changes in interpretations, opinions, and "morale"; and (3) the audience's evaluation and acceptance of the films. The last type of measurement was, of course, not experimental; men were questioned after seeing the film for the stated purpose of finding out what they thought of it. However, in the experimental measurement of film-induced changes in interpretations, opinions, and "morale," it was necessary to measure the effects of the film without awareness on the part of the men that an experiment was in progress. This was necessitated by the type of effect being studied—if the men knew they were being tested some might give what they thought were "correct" answers rather than answers expressing their own feelings in the matter. Thus *learning* the content and *accepting* the content must be distinguished. In the case of changes in knowledge of material accepted by the audience as factual, on the other hand, measurement may be made with full knowledge that a test is being given.

Training films. During the course of the studies of orientation films, a series of investigations was requested by personnel concerned with visual aids in the Military Training Division of Army Service Forces. This organization had no research facilities for studying the training value of their films and other visual aids, and wished to use research methods as an aid in improving the effectiveness of their products. In line with this request, several experimental and nonexperimental studies were carried out on training films, film strips, and other visual aids. These were practical studies with the purpose of testing the training value of factors which on a priori grounds seemed possible sources of product-improvement. In some cases the studies took the form of controlled variation of one or more variables.

With instructional films of this type there is for the most part no problem of authenticity or acceptance of the material. Also, the use of such a film is usually integrated into a general course of instruction in which there exists external motivation to learn the material shown in the film. This motivation is in terms of an expectation of early application of the material, either for some useful purpose or at least in examinations on the subject of instruction. Thus such a film does not usually place much emphasis on "selling" itself; rather it is usually assumed that an external source of motivation is present and effort is concentrated on other aspects of effective teaching methods. Correspondingly there is usually no need to test for effects without awareness on the part of the audience that a test is in progress. Normally no test would be announced in advance of the film showing, unless this was a factor being studied; but no attempt would be made to conceal the connection between film and test once the test was about to be administered. In fact at this point it might even be desirable to maximize test motivation, to permit measuring the amount of learning that occurred without dilution of effects because of lack of effort.

Films designed to satisfy general interests. Having been stamped as "film testers" by experimental studies on orientation films and other films, the Experimental Section was also called upon to carry out a number of nonexperimental studies of films sponsored by the Information and Education Division. In some of these studies chief concern centered about what the men thought of the product. For example, a study was carried out to determine whether a film describing Army educational opportunities overseas during the redeployment period would "boomerang" because it was "too Hollywood" to make a convincing presentation. Similar audience-evaluation studies were carried out on a number of films in a series designed to satisfy overseas men's desires to know about what was going on back home, in other theaters of operations, other branches of service, etc. Studies of these films were designed primarily to determine what kinds of topics, presentation methods, etc., were liked or disliked by the men. Thus measurements with these films were in terms of audience evaluations of the products.

Scientific Status of Present Investigations

As stated earlier, the present studies do not comprise a systematic program of research in the field of educational films. Most of the studies were evaluative and all were dominated by practical rather than theoretical considerations. However, the studies covered a fairly wide range of designs, variables, types of films, and kinds of effects measured, and they illustrate many of the methodological problems that are encountered in research on films and similar mass communication media. No specifically methodological studies were possible within the scope of the purpose of this program, but some evidence was accumulated on methodological problems and in several instances new techniques were utilized.

In some respects the studies were carried out under advantageous conditions not usually possible in film research with civilian subjects during peacetime. Although the audiences were restricted to the male population and to the age range of those eligible for military service, they had a wide range with respect to intellectual ability and various regional and socio-economic factors. Moreover, it was possible to avoid a problem sometimes regarded as insoluble in the study of films designed for general consumption—namely, the fact that the audience members attend voluntarily, and there is often no way to control this "self-selection" factor without biasing the results by the psychological effects of forced attendance. In the Army compulsory attendance is the norm, so the problem was automatically eliminated. This advantage is particularly relevant in the case of orientation and general interest film studies, because these films were of the type that would be used in attempts to achieve broad educational purposes among members of the general public, where the self-selection problem is most acute. Another favorable condition in the Army studies was that in most instances it was possible to carry out the studies with exact duplication of the conditions under which the films were to be used. Thus there was no problem of degree of applicability of "laboratory" findings to the real life situation.

Some of the material to be presented is in the form of pure hypothesis, since some of the results were obtained on a particular film with no opportunity to check them in further studies. Where such findings seemed important if proved generally true, or where they seemed reasonable on theoretical grounds, they have been mentioned as likely factors for future study. All of the results suffer from one of the faults common to a great deal of existing research on films and other communication media: they are results obtained in a single study or a few studies and therefore have unknown generality. However, they are presented as contributions to the accumulation of single studies from which generalizable principles will eventually be possible.

PART I
FILM EVALUATION STUDIES

INTRODUCTION TO PART I

THE considerations discussed in the preceding chapter point to the necessity of developing a body of scientific principles to assist producers of educational films in achieving products with maximum educational effectiveness. The final demonstration of these principles will require controlled experimentation with varied types of content and methods of presentation. Studies to be reported in Part II approximate this type of research. The studies to be reported in Part I, on the other hand, are evaluative studies carried out as part of a program of applied research. These evaluative studies are in most cases controlled experiments, but they do not involve controlled variation in film content or in technique of presentation.

However, they illustrate many aspects of the methodology required in film experimentation and experimentation with other communication media. Moreover, it is likely that the initial discovery of general principles is greatly facilitated by the examination of the effectiveness of specific contents and presentations, and comparison of the relative effectiveness of different contents and types of presentation. A hypothesis that is subsequently proved correct may have its origin in noting that a film with one treatment appears to be more effective than another with a different treatment, or from noting that a point made in one way is better learned than another made in a different way within the same film.

It is in this sense that the study of the effects of particular products presented in this portion of the book adds to our scientific knowledge. The main purpose of Part I is to present the methods used in evaluating the effectiveness of particular finished film products in achieving their objectives.

In some of the present studies the focus of attention was upon the evaluation of a single product. In others the main interest was in the class of products represented by the particular film tested.

Studies in which two media are compared are prime examples of the latter type of study.   The results reported are illustrative of studies of three types of educational films: (1) orientation films, (2) training films, and (3) general interest films.

CHAPTER 2

THE ORIENTATION FILM, "THE BATTLE OF BRITAIN"

C HAPTER 2 presents the procedures used and the findings obtained in the experimental study of one orientation film. The procedures described serve to illustrate the methods used throughout the series of orientation film studies. Readers whose primary interest is in research on the general principles of communication may wish to omit reading the detailed findings presented in the latter portions of the chapter.

A great deal of interest attended the experiments carried out to evaluate the Army's orientation films. These "Why We Fight" films constituted probably the largest-scale attempt yet made in this country to use films as a means of influencing opinion. The films were of especial interest to people concerned with mass education because their purpose was not purely instructional in the manner of a training film, but was rather to get across particular interpretations of facts, overcome prejudices, arouse motivations, and in general to modify attitudes rather than merely to convey factual information.

In the present chapter research on "The Battle of Britain," the fourth film in the "Why We Fight" series, will be described. This film was more extensively studied than any of the others and in some ways appeared to achieve the greatest effects. However, before describing this study, it is well to indicate more specifically the nature and purpose of the film and the criteria of effectiveness that were used.

The Objectives of the Film

1. NATURE OF THE ORIENTATION FILM SERIES

The orientation films were a series of seven 50-minute films that traced the history of World War II from the rise of Fascism in Italy and Germany and the Japanese attack on Manchuria in 1931 through America's mobilization and participation after Pearl Harbor. The general title of the series was "Why We Fight." The films were designed for showing to new recruits during basic training, and their purpose is indicated by General Marshall's statement in the opening title of the first film:

"This film, the first of a series, has been prepared by the War Department to acquaint members of the Army with factual information as to the causes, the events leading up to our entry into the war, and the principles for which we are fighting. A knowledge of these facts is an indispensable part of military training and merits the thoughtful consideration of every American soldier."

The style of the films was for the most part objective and documentary, with direct quotations, references to official sources, animated diagrams, cuts from domestic newsreels, and cuts from foreign newsreels and propaganda films. The visual presentation was drawn together by a running narration which told the story of the war and explained the scenes. While the general tenor of the films was "the facts speak for themselves," they were not dryly factual. Foreign speech was frequently translated into English with a "foreign accent," "production" shots using actors were employed to tie the documentary material together, the films were scored throughout with background music, and montages and trick photography were used in trying to achieve vivid and dramatic presentation.

2. CRITERIA OF EFFECTIVENESS

Two basic assumptions appeared to underlie the preparation of these films.

1. That a sizable segment of the draftee population lacked knowledge concerning the national and international events that resulted in America's entrance in the war.

2. That a knowledge of these events would in some measure lead men to accept more willingly the transformation from civilian to Army life and their duties as soldiers.

In line with these assumptions, the experimental evaluation of these films involved three aspects: first, the measurement of the extent to which the film produced changes in factual knowledge about the events concerning the war; second, measurements of changes in interpretation of these events (opinions concerning the war effort, the allies, and the enemy); and, third, measurements of changes in acceptance of the military role and willingness to serve.

A distinction should be made at this point between the effects *intended* for a film and the effects *actually produced*. A film might be very effective at getting across material that was not part of the initial purpose. From the standpoint of teaching ability such a film would be very successful, but from the standpoint of achieving its particular educational purpose, the film would be unsuccessful. This distinction was crucial in the decision as to what should be tested for in studying the effectiveness of the orientation films, since they could fail in their intended effects either because the presentation did not get across the material or because even getting across that particular material might turn out to have no effect on the desired response.

In the evaluative studies done on the "Why We Fight" films, the attempt was made to study simultaneously the effectiveness in terms of the *intended effects* of the films and in terms of the *material covered* in the films. The criteria for testing the former were derived from the stated objectives of the films; the criteria for testing the latter were derived from content analyses of the film coverage. However, because of the wide coverage of material in these 50-minute films and the practical limitations on the number of areas that could be tested in an experiment, no attempt was made to cover all possible effects of a given film. First priority was given to intended effects, second priority to any possible "boomerangs" or undesirable effects, third priority to the basic material in the film thought most likely to be a source of the intended effect, and lowest priority to possible effects relevant only to presentation technique or film study in general.

In the case of the orientation films the intended effects were not specifically designated for each film, and the artists in charge of production had considerable leeway in determining the content of the films. Therefore, since the films were part of the total orientation program, the objectives of this program, insofar as they were relevant to a particular film, were used as criteria of the degree to which a particular film achieved its "intended" effects. An overall objective of the orientation program, as indicated above, was the increase of willingness to serve, and the effects in this area were determined for each film. In addition, the orientation program had a number of subobjectives which were regarded as means by which the above overall objective would be achieved. These subobjectives, as stated in a directive to the Information and Education Division, were to foster the following:

1. A firm belief in the right of the cause for which we fight.
2. A realization that we are up against a tough job.
3. A determined confidence in our own ability and the abilities of our comrades and leaders to do the job that has to be done.
4. A feeling of confidence, insofar as is possible under the circumstances, in the integrity and fighting ability of our Allies.
5. A resentment, based on knowledge of the facts, against our enemies who have made it necessary for us to fight.
6. A belief that through military victory, the political achievement of a better world order is possible.

In a sense each film had these objectives in view. Material relevant to all of these objectives was not included in each film, but none of the films was to include material running counter to any of the objectives.

3. THE NATURE AND OBJECTIVES OF "THE BATTLE OF BRITAIN"

"The Battle of Britain" was aimed primarily at objective 4 in the preceding list—it sought to establish confidence in the integrity and fighting ability of our ally, Britain. It dealt with the dramatic British resistance to the German air attacks on England during the fall of 1940, and covered the period starting with the fall of Dunkirk in June 1940 to the last major bombing raid of the Luftwaffe, which set fire to large areas of London in December.

The story told by the film may be briefly outlined as follows: Hitler had a plan for world conquest which had moved forward without a hitch through the conquest of France and the evacuation of the British at Dunkirk. If Hitler could have conquered England and taken over the British Isles and the British fleet, America would have been placed in a very dangerous position. Hitler did attempt to conquer England but failed because he could not get control of the air over Britain. This failure, which gave America precious time in which to prepare for war, was due to the almost superhuman efforts of the British people and of the RAF and to the unwillingness of the British to give up even in the face of apparently hopeless odds.

Although "The Battle of Britain" thus had as its chief objective the strengthening of confidence in America's ally, Britain, the experimental study also took the other orientation objectives into account in measuring the effects of the film.

THE EXPERIMENTAL PROCEDURE

The experimental test involved an *experimental* group that saw the film, a *control* group that did not see the film, and the administration of an anonymous check-list questionnaire to both groups, ostensibly as a War Department "survey" but actually as a measure of knowledge and opinions on subjects related to the film. The effects were determined from a comparison of the experimental and control groups, any statistically significant differences in their responses being assumed to be due to the film. The details of the experimental design will be described shortly.

As was pointed out in the preceding chapter, the learning of factual material presented in a film can be measured with full awareness on the part of the subjects that they are being tested, but effects of the film on interpretations, opinions, etc., must be measured without the subjects' awareness that they are being tested. In testing the orientation films, however, *both* factual knowledge and interpretations were measured *without awareness* on the part of the men that they were being tested. This was done partly for greater efficiency, in that only one experiment was thereby required, partly because it was desired to get both types of measures on the same men, and partly because it was not certain that all men would accept all of the factual material without reservation. The methods of achieving lack of awareness were inherent partly in the measuring instrument, partly in the design, and partly in the administration of the experiment, and will be explained in connection with each of these aspects of the study.

1. THE MEASURING INSTRUMENT

The check-list questionnaire used contained two types of items that formed the measuring instrument per se: multiple-choice *fact-quiz* items of the type used in the *Time* magazine current-events quiz, and *opinion* items that obtained the individual's interpretations and opinions on nonfactual items and his personal feelings on matters related to his role in the war. The opinion items were predominantly of two types: (1) multiple-choice—expressing varying shades of opinions; and (2) "agree-disagree" statements made up of quotations with which the individual expressed agreement or disagreement. Free-answer and other types were less frequently used. In addition, the questionnaire contained *personal-history* items for obtaining information about the individual's education, age, etc., and what might be called "camouflage" items that were not necessary for the test but were used to give scope to the "survey" and reduce the concentration of items dealing with material covered in the film.

a. *Qualitative "pretesting" of items.* In preparing the items that formed the measuring instrument proper, one of the important steps was the *qualitative pretesting* of the wording and meaning of the items. Qualitative pretesting consisted of face-to-face interviewing of soldiers, with the questions asked verbally by the interviewer in some cases and read by the respondent in others. In these interviews the interviewer, usually a civilian or enlisted man, identified himself as an official War Department "pollster" but kept the interview informal, encouraging the respondent to discuss the general topic of each question and to qualify his answers. In this way, misinterpretations of the questions and misunderstood words were uncovered and at the same time natural wording and natural categories of response were revealed. After the first few interviews suggestions for rewriting were accumulated and the items were revised and pretested again, the whole process being repeated until difficulties were reduced to a minimum. In the orientation film studies more pretesting was given to attitude items than fact-quiz items, but there was ample evidence that even simple completion-items of the fact-quiz type require qualitative pretesting.

b. *Quantitative pretesting of items.* In addition to the qualitative pretest of items a *quantitative* pretest was conducted. The purpose of the quantitative pretest was the advance determination of the approximate distribution of answers to each question and the relationships between questions. For this purpose a sample of two hundred men was used.

The analysis of the relations between questions consisted mainly in an analysis of the attitude items in terms of their conformity to scales of the type to be discussed in Volume 4 of this series. The assumption in this analysis was that if a group of items in a given area were found not to "scale" in the quantitative pretest, the area, as defined a priori, was not a single content variable and the items had to be treated as specific and separate areas of response. If on the other hand a group of items did "scale" in the pretest, it was assumed that they could all be treated as representatives of a single content area. In cases where individual items did form a scale in the pretest, only two or three items from the scale were used in the experiment, and effects on these items were assumed to be evidence of effects in the entire area.

The approximate distribution of responses to the check-list categories, as determined in the quantitative pretest, also served as a basis for selecting or revising items to use in the experimental test of the film. In such cases one consideration was the initial split of opinion on the item. For example, an item in which 90 per cent of the population endorsed the favorable category was considered undesirable for measuring increases in favorable opinion since the number of individuals who can be shifted to the favorable response is very small. Another reason for considering the initial split arose in connection with items to be used in analyzing the film's effects as a function of initial response. In such cases response categories that made for subgroups too small to analyze were undesirable.

c. *Avoidance of items that suggested the film.* One factor that had to be considered in preparing the measuring instrument was the possibility that the items would be so specific to the material in the film that they would remind the men of the film. This was avoided in line with the general motive mentioned earlier of preventing the men from divining that their reaction to the film was being studied. But even if this suspicion were not aroused, a question that specifically suggested the film might get an unrepresentative measure of the film's effect merely because the individual would not normally be viewing his response in the light of the film. Thus, he might have more respect for Britain's participation in the war when he happened to be reminiscing on episodes from "The Battle of Britain," but such occasions might be rare occurrences. Ideally the individual should be "taken unawares" by the question and give his typical response.

This latter problem was more important in the case of opinion questions than fact-quiz questions, where specificity is an inherent aspect of the content and less variability of response is to be expected. In order to prevent the specificity of the fact-quiz questions from affecting the responses to the opinion questions, the fact questions were placed at the end of the questionnaire where they would be read only after the other responses had been made. Fact questions relating to material covered in the film were distributed among an equal number of "camouflage" fact questions unrelated to the film. Even with these precautions, a certain amount of specificity was sacrificed in order to prevent a tie-up with the film.

2. THE DESIGN OF THE EXPERIMENT

Two different experimental designs were used in the study of "The Battle of Britain." One design involved measuring at a specified time after the film showing the factual knowledge and opinion in a *film* group (which saw the film) and a *control* group (which did not

see the film). This design was termed the "after-only" design because measurements were not made for the same group of men both
before and after the film showing. The other design had the additional feature of getting a measurement on the same men before the
film showing. This was termed the "before-after" design because
measurements were taken on the film and control groups both *before
and after* the introduction of the experimental variable.

Each of these two designs has its advantages and disadvantages.
In general, the before-after design is superior from the standpoint
of problems of analysis and sampling, whereas the after-only design
is better from the standpoint of being easier to administer and less
subject to the possibility that the measuring process will bias the
measurements obtained. The relative advantages and disadvantages of the two designs are taken up in more detail in Appendix C.

It should be pointed out that in the before-after design it was
possible to match the before and after questionnaires of the same
individuals and still maintain anonymity. The responses to personal-history questions (age, education, region, etc.) in the "before"
and "after" surveys provided a basis for matching the two surveys
of a given individual in most cases, and handwriting was sufficient
additional evidence to permit the matching of practically all the
men in the sample who filled out both questionnaires. The matching process was greatly facilitated by the fact that the men filled out
both questionnaires in platoon groups. The platoon could be identified, so that matching was initially narrowed down to groups of
around fifty men each.

The time interval between the film showing and the administration of the survey after the film was set at approximately one week
in the case of all of the experimental studies of orientation films and
always involved an intervening week end. While the effects might
have been greater immediately after the film, it was desired to determine the more lasting effects, so the interval of about one week
was selected as an appropriate point for testing. In the study of
"The Battle of Britain," however, an additional feature was the
determination of effects after a lapse of about nine weeks from the
showing of the film. Only the short-time effects (just under a week)
will be described in the present chapter. A comparison of the effects
of the film after the short-time interval and after nine weeks is reported in Chapter 7.

The experimental studies of the film were conducted at two different camps, one during February and one during April of 1943. The

total sample on which the data presented in this chapter are based is 2,100 cases. Half of these were men who saw the film, and half were controls who did not. The after-only design was used at one camp (N = 1,200) and the before-after design was used at the other (N = 900).

3. SAMPLING PROCEDURE

It would have been desirable from the standpoint of sampling to have the experimental and control groups composed of men selected at random from the total available group. But such a procedure could easily have biased the results because it would have been contrary to all precedent in the training centers. Assembling a random audience from many different outfits to see a movie would have been a most mysterious event and would have led to numerous speculations as to why it was done. Moreover, this procedure would require the same mysterious assemblage in taking the survey. From the standpoint of getting a realistic and unbiased estimate of the effects of the film as it was to be used by the Army, therefore, it was considered necessary to show the film by company unit, with the consequence that the sampling was unit sampling rather than individual sampling.

The effect of this unit sampling procedure would be expected to increase the sampling error as compared with a random sampling of individuals. The difference would be a function of the variables that had been used to assign the men to a particular company and the correlation between these variables and questionnaire responses. It was usually alleged that men were assigned without any system, but fairly large variation in composition of companies was occasionally found in the film studies.

It will be noted that the increase in sampling error that may occur with unit sampling applies mainly to the after-only design and exemplifies the sampling advantage of the before-after design. Varied composition of companies would increase the chance of obtaining sizable after-only differences between experimental and control groups due merely to initial differences in the two groups. But in the before-after design such differences are revealed in the "before" survey.

It should be pointed out that even in the after-only design relatively large differences in composition are required before the sampling error of the group is noticeably different from a random sample. And even fairly large differences in composition will have little effect on the sampling error unless fairly large correlations exist between responses being measured and the composition variables on which the groups differ. (See Appendix C.)

4. EQUATING OF EXPERIMENTAL AND CONTROL GROUPS

Partly to compensate for the effects of unit sampling, it was considered desirable to *equate* the experimental and control groups as far as possible on the major variables that might be related to the responses of the men. This was done both in the course of setting up the experiment at the camps, and in the construction of the final sample after the survey responses had been punched onto IBM cards. At the camps, distributions of Army General Classification Test scores, education, age, and census region of birth were obtained for each company, and two "most comparable" groups were selected by grouping of the companies. "Comparability" not only involved the personal history variables mentioned above, but also the balancing of stage of training, previous exposure to orientation material, and any other local factors which affected company units and were considered relevant. Thus the only random factor was the decision as to which of the two groups so selected would be experimental and which control, and this was decided by tossing a coin after the two groups were selected.

The equating of the two groups was further refined after all the questionnaires had been coded and punched onto cards. AGCT information was not available at this stage because the questionnaires were anonymous, but the other background information listed above, plus additional information such as marital status, rural-urban origin, etc., had been filled in by the men and was used for further equating on IBM machines. This was done simply by discarding, on a random basis, men of a given background type in whichever group—film or control—had an appreciably larger number of that type.

5. ADMINISTRATION OF THE EXPERIMENT

For proper administration of the experiment it was important to present the film under realistic conditions, to prevent the men in the sample from realizing that an experiment was in progress, and to obtain honest answers in the questionnaires. For realism in presentation, the film showings for the experimental group were incorporated into the training program and scheduled during the weekly orientation hour exactly as the films were to be used. This not only insured realistic presentation but also avoided any evidence that the film was being tested, films being a standard part of the men's training.

The questionnaires were presented as being part of a War Department survey to find out how a cross section of soldiers felt about various subjects connected with the war, with examples being given of previous Research Branch surveys and how they were used. Questionnaires were filled out by all the men in a platoon at once, the men being assembled in mess halls for the purpose. The questionnaires were administered by "class leaders" selected and trained for the job from among the enlisted personnel working in the camp orientation office and in the camp classification office. In the introductory explanation of the survey, the class leader stressed the importance of the survey and the anonymity of the answers. The purpose of this emphasis was to get the men to take the survey seriously and to give honest answers. No officers were present at these meetings and the men were assured that the surveys went directly to Washington and that no one at the camp would get a chance to see what they had written.

6. SPECIAL PROBLEMS IN THE ADMINISTRATION
   OF THE REPEAT SURVEY

In the case of the before-after design a special rationale must be prepared to explain the fact that a second survey is made. In a repeat survey with a long intervening time interval (e.g., two months or more) probably no precautions are required to explain the similarity of the two surveys. Many respondents will then have forgotten the content of the preceding survey, and the previous experience probably only makes the "after" survey seem less out of the ordinary. If anyone does comment on the similarity, "checking on trends" is a convenient rationale. But when the time interval is only two or three weeks, some reasonable explanation must be provided.

The rationale used with the before-after design in evaluating "The Battle of Britain" was that the questionnaire had been revised on the basis of preliminary results. The class leaders were rotated so that the same men did not administer the questionnaire to the same platoons, and the new class leader mentioned in passing that "some of you men may have filled out a questionnaire like this a while back" and went on to explain that a similar survey had been made but that the questionnaire had been revised and was being administered again. The format of the repeat questionnaire was conspicuously altered, and it carried a "REVISED" in large type next to the survey number on the front page. Items for which retest answers were not needed were included in only one of the questionnaires, so their addition or deletion provided some of the "revision." The addition of the fact-quiz items, which were not included in the "before" questionnaire, also increased the extent of revision, together with omitted, added, or revised "camouflage" questions.

As an added precaution in the administration of the repeat survey the class leader never allowed anyone in the class the opportunity to ask a question before the group. After his introductory explanation, he instructed the men to start filling out the questionnaire and to raise their hands if they had any questions. This procedure prevented the possibility that some one man might express suspicion as to the true nature of the "survey" before the entire class and thereby raise suspicions in the minds of the others.

It should be pointed out that these precautions and some of the others described above were taken mainly on a priori grounds and they do not indicate that evidence for a frequent tendency to be suspicious was ever obtained. Actually, only a very small percentage of men were ever found to indicate suspicion of the purpose of the surveys in the film studies, even when questions were specifically directed toward this point.

RESULTS OF THE EXPERIMENTAL EVALUATION

The results of the experiment are presented in terms of the percentages of men in the film and control groups who chose various responses after the film showing. The difference between the film and control percentages for each questionnaire item indicates the effect of the film on responses to that question.

In using this procedure it is recognized that the effect of the film is not being completely described. For example, positive effects cannot be detected among those who initially select the key response on a question: such men are already as positive as the measuring instrument can record. Similarly, the above procedure does not detect changes among those who are influenced in a positive direction but not sufficiently to shift to the key response of the question. Furthermore, the only kind of effect that is detected is a shift of response to a questionnaire item. Other kinds of effects are likely to be present, or some effects may be latent and emerge only at a later time in combination with causal factors other than the film.

Thus the difference between film and control percentages choosing the key response must be regarded only as a standardized indicator of the complete effect that is present as a result of the film. A discussion of some of the problems of describing and measuring effects will be found in the Appendix.

In combining the results of the two camps only the "after" responses are used for the camp at which the before-after design was employed. The "before" differences between answers given to questions by the experimental and control groups at this camp were slight (none greater than 4 per cent and most close to zero) so that the results are not materially altered by using only the "after" differences between film and control.

The fact that sampling was on a unit basis, plus the counteracting factor of equating of the groups, makes it difficult to evaluate precisely what constitutes a statistically significant difference between the responses of the film group and the control group. However, differences of 6 per cent or more between the percentages choosing a particular response in the film and control groups may fairly safely be regarded as significant beyond the 1 per cent level of confidence, and were so regarded in evaluating the film.[1] It is worth pointing out that borderline cases are not particularly important in any case since, even if a six per cent difference were *statistically* significant, it will usually be of little practical significance from the standpoint of achieving the film's objectives.

The experimental findings will be presented first in terms of the content areas covered in the film and then in terms of more general effects upon attitudes related to orientation objectives, including possible adverse effects of the film ("boomerangs").

1. EFFECT OF THE FILM'S PRINCIPAL CONTENT THEMES
   ON MEN'S OPINIONS

a. *There was an actual "Battle of Britain."* One of the main themes of the film was that the air raids by the Nazis were an all-out attempt to knock Britain out of the war. The inferred plan of the Nazis for taking England after the fall of France was described in the early part of the film. Animated maps were used to illustrate

---

[1] A 6 per cent difference would occur about one time in a hundred by chance with the N's involved if sampling had been random and if the initial frequency of a response is 50 per cent. The fact that control and film groups were equated and that most responses had a frequency greater or less than 50 per cent tends to make this a conservative estimate of the 1 per cent level of confidence.

the plans and German shots were interspersed showing Hitler and his staff in conference and German forces in readiness. The outcome of the air warfare over England was presented as a distinct German defeat, in which the plan to conquer England was upset because the Nazis could never accomplish the first phase of gaining control of the air over the British Isles. This interpretation of the Battle of Britain was presumably in contrast to the conception previously held by the soldiers, for whom the Battle of Britain was a relatively forgotten phase of the war and was thought of more as merely a series of bombing raids than as a prelude to a projected invasion.

The film produced a substantial change in the men's interpretation of the Nazi bombing of Britain. This is illustrated by the responses to the following item, which was presented to the men as part of a fact-quiz series.

Question: "The heavy bombing attacks on Britain were part of an attempt by the Nazis to . . . CHECK ONE" (of the four possible answers)

Percentage of men checking "key" answer:[2] i.e., "invade and conquer England."

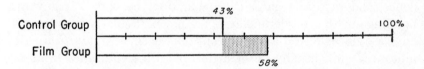

The other alternatives presented in this particular question were "get even with the British for bombing German cities"; "keep them from helping Russia"; and "break down their morale so they would surrender."

b. *Heroic British resistance.* Closely related to the foregoing theme was one depicting the effort and spirit of the British people in blocking the invasion attempt. Facing great odds, the British people refused to give up and, despite the terrible bombing of their homes and cities, were willing to go on with their efforts as the only nation fighting against the Nazis. This theme emphasized what little the British had with which to defend themselves, the terrible

---

[2] The "key" answer is the critical one, the response which the film was calculated to change. It is the one used in the measurement of the film's effectiveness; in the case of a fact-quiz item this is of course the *correct* answer to the question. Questions presented in the text will quote only the "key" answers—or the "correct" answers in the case of information questions—unless it is felt that the other answers may be helpful in interpreting the findings.

punishment they had to take, and the extent to which everyone in Britain was integrated into an all-out war effort. Evidence of the effect of the film in this area is furnished by answers to a question asking for the probable reason why the Nazis did not invade Britain after France fell. Interpretations implying that the Nazis did not attempt an invasion of England were much less common as a result of the film, and there was a corresponding increase in the number of men interpreting the Battle of Britain as an unsuccessful invasion attempt which was thwarted by the determined resistance of the British.

Question: "What do you think is probably the real reason why the Nazis did not invade and conquer Britain after the fall of France?" (three alternatives)

Percentage of men checking "key" answer: i.e., "the Nazis tried and would have succeeded except for the determined resistance of the British."

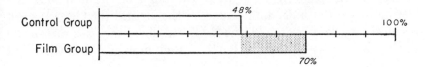

The all-out effort of the British and their strong spirit despite their hopeless position was documented with a considerable amount of material: the Home Guard, factory workers putting in long hours, women taking over men's jobs, excerpts from Churchill's famous "we shall never surrender" speech, workers continuing at their jobs through the bombings, volunteer firemen and rescue workers, Londoners "taking" the blitz all night but getting back to their jobs in the morning, and so forth. Several agree-disagree items were used to test for effects of this material on the men's evaluation of the efforts of the British people. As can be seen, very little effect was obtained on these items.

	Control Group	Film Group	Difference
Percentage of men who *agree* with statement:			
"The British stood up under bombing better than Americans probably would."	28%	36%	8%
Percentage of men who *disagree* with statement:			

"The British are taking it easy in their
war effort in the hope that America will
win the war for them."   75   79   *4*

Percentage of men who *disagree* with statement:
"If the Germans had kept up the bombing of London a little longer the British
might have given up and asked for peace."   76   79   *3*

c. *Contribution of the Royal Air Force.* Linked to the theme of
the attempted invasion was the magnificent job of the RAF in staving off the German attack. The RAF occupied a fairly central role
throughout the film, which contained many striking action shots of
planes in combat. The outstanding performance of the RAF was
documented with figures showing their disadvantage in numbers,
figures showing the greatly disproportionate plane losses of the
Luftwaffe, and action shots of British fighters skillfully shooting
down German planes. In general, the tenor of the film was that
German conquest hinged on control of the air and the Germans lost
because they were beaten by the RAF. A sharp increase was shown
in the per cent crediting the RAF with giving the Nazis their first
real defeat.

Question: "In your opinion who gave the Nazis their first real defeat?"
(four alternatives)

Percentage of men checking "key" answer: i.e., "the British Royal Air
Force."

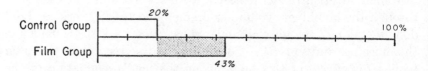

This change not only underscored the importance of the RAF but
was further evidence that the men who saw the film perceived the
air attack of the Germans as constituting a major battle and a for-
midable military defeat—comparable to the Russian victory at
Stalingrad and the Allied victory in North Africa which were included in the other choices to the question.

The answers to another question also combining the themes of
attempted conquest and credit to the RAF show the effectiveness
of the film in getting across this message.

Question: "Which of the following would you say was the *most important* reason why the Germans were not able to conquer England?" (four alternatives)

Percentage of men checking "key" answer: i.e., "they were stopped by the RAF."

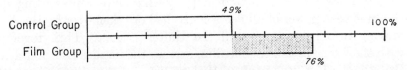

The other alternatives presented to the men on this question were: "the Germans were afraid of having to fight a war on two fronts" (which decreased from 24 per cent to 9 per cent); "the British Navy kept them from crossing the English Channel"; "the British Home Guard prevented them from landing any troops."

Increased recognition of the outstanding performance of the RAF was also shown from the answers to the agree-disagree item shown below.

Percentage of men who *agreed* with statement:

"About the best job of fighting that has been done in this war has been done by the British Royal Air Force."

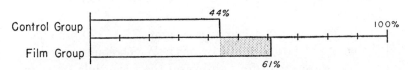

d. *British resistance gave us time to prepare.* A fourth important theme of the film was that the British, in staving off a German invasion of England, gave America and the rest of the world precious time to get prepared for the struggle against Germany. This was explicitly stated in the final sentences of the narration and was implied in other portions of the film. The results of an agree-disagree item on this theme are shown below.

Percentage of men who *agreed* with statement:

"By refusing to surrender to Hitler, the British people probably kept American cities from being bombed by the Germans."

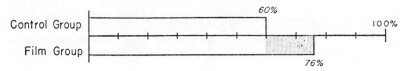

In the introductory portions of the film in which Hitler's dreams of world conquest were discussed, the point was made that if Hitler could conquer Britain and get control of the British fleet, he would be in a position to "phone his orders to Washington." This was accompanied by an animated map showing ships representing the combined sea power of all fleets controlled or taken over by the Axis moving into position around the United States. This, together with the later portions of the film, carried the implication that after Britain, the U.S. was next on Hitler's list and that Britain's resistance, therefore, saved us from attack. A write-in question was included as a test of whether the men concluded from the film that America would have been attacked next if Britain had been conquered.

Question: "If Hitler had been able to invade England and defeat the British, what country do you think he probably would have attacked next?" (write in answer)

Percentage of men writing in the answer "United States."

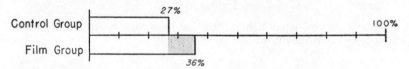

A third question was asked at one camp (N = 1200) on the general theme of obligation to the British: "Which country do you feel deserves the most credit for fighting off the Axis while we were getting better prepared?" The three alternatives were "Russia," "Britain," and "China." Initially the majority of the men in the sample favored Russia rather than Britain or China. (During the two years preceding the study, the major scenes of action had been in Russia.) However, some effect of the film in increasing the per cent choosing Britain is seen in the results below.

Question: "Which country do you feel deserves the most credit for fighting off the Axis while we were getting better prepared?" (three alternatives)

Percentage of men checking "key" answer: i.e., "Britain."

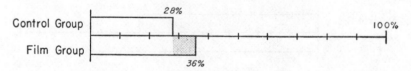

Another version of the question restricted to countries fighting the Nazis was asked at the other camp and yielded similar results. The four themes outlined so far—real invasion attempt, all-out effort of the British, outstanding performance of the RAF, and winning precious time for the rest of the world—constituted the major content of the film. The remaining content not coming under one of these headings dealt primarily with military information concerning the strategy and tactics of the British and the Nazis.

2. EFFECTIVENESS OF FILM IN IMPROVING KNOWLEDGE OF MILITARY EVENTS

In connection with the British defense, the film pointed out that the RAF had learned "the lesson of Poland" and had scattered their planes at the edges of airfields to prevent their being destroyed on the ground. The large effect of the film in getting across this point is shown below.

Question: "The reason Germany was not very successful in bombing British planes *on the ground* was that . . ." (four alternatives)

Percentage of men checking "correct" answer: i.e., "the British kept their planes scattered at the edges of the fields."

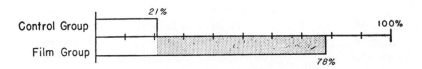

That the film was effective in getting across the numerical disadvantage of the RAF relative to the size of the Luftwaffe is seen in the results of a fact-quiz item concerning the extent to which the RAF was outnumbered.

Question: "When the Germans began mass bombing attacks on Britain, the Nazi Air Force was . . ." (four alternatives)

Percentage of men checking "correct" answer: i.e., "ten times as large as the British Air Force."

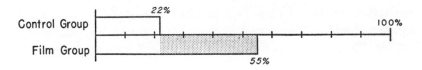

(The other alternatives presented in this question were: "five times as large"; "about the same size"; and "one-half as large.")

As a test of their knowledge of the role of the British Navy, the men were asked to check one of four alternative statements about the British fleet's part in the Battle of Britain. The results show that a sizable proportion learned that the fleet was of little use to the British as a defense against invasion.

> *Question:* "At the time of the battle of Britain, the British Navy . . ." (four alternatives)
>
> Percentage of men checking "correct" answer: i.e., "could not operate in the English Channel because it would be too easy to bomb."

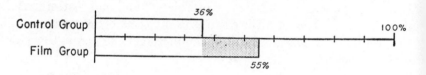

Another fact-quiz item was concerned with the lack of military equipment after the fall of Dunkirk. In the film were shown shots of the evacuation, German shots of ruined British equipment covering the beaches, and shots contrasting the well-equipped Germans with Britain's inadequately equipped forces. The statement was made in the film that "in all of Britain there was not enough equipment for one modern division." The extent to which the film was effective in getting this point across is shown below.

> *Question:* "At the time of the fall of France, the British Army had enough modern guns and other equipment to arm a force of about . . ." (four alternatives)
>
> Percentage of men checking "correct" answer: i.e., "1 division."

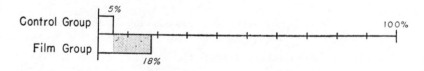

The other alternatives presented in the above question were 10, 30, and 100 divisions. In addition to this increase of 13 per cent in the number choosing the correct choice there was an increase of 8 per cent in the number choosing "10 divisions," indicating that some men probably revised their estimates downward without having adopted the figure given in the film.

Two information questions used in the study dealt solely with Goering's strategy and tactics. In explaining the changing strategy of the Luftwaffe, it was shown that the original plan called for gaining control of the air as a prelude to invasion. The film portrayed the events leading to the final strategy of trying to force surrender by indiscriminate bombing of cities and civilians. One fact-quiz item dealing with Goering's strategy was included to determine not only the extent to which the film got across the original plan, but also the extent to which the film avoided confusion between the original and final plans. The men were asked to check one of four alternative statements about the original Nazi plan of conquering Britain.

Question: "The way the Nazis originally planned to conquer Britain was to . . ." (four alternatives)

Percentage of men checking "correct" answer: i.e., "destroy the RAF, then invade England with paratroops and panzer divisions."

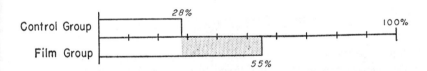

The other three alternatives were: "starve the British into surrender by blockade"; "destroy the British Navy, then attack Britain from all sides at once"; and "bomb the British civilians until they surrendered without a fight." Not only was a sizable effect of the film obtained on the "correct" choice, but also there was a decrease in the per cent choosing Goering's final plan, "bomb the British civilians until they surrendered without a fight," which might have been a source of confusion with the original plan. The per cent choosing "bomb the British civilians until they surrendered without a fight" dropped from 38 per cent (among men who did not see the film) to 20 per cent (among men who did see the film).

The other fact-quiz item dealing with Nazi strategy and tactics tested men's recognition of the targets and time of day of the first German bombing attacks against England. The film, showing the first bombing to be daylight attacks against convoys and harbors in the Channel and along the Thames Estuary, was found to be effective in getting this information across to the men.

> *Question:* "The first major bombing attacks on Britain in this war were . . ." (four alternatives)
>
> Percentage of men checking "correct" answer: i.e., "daylight attacks on ports and ships."

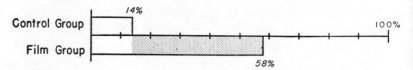

The other alternatives presented in the question were: "night attacks on RAF bases"; "daylight attacks on London"; "night attacks on London." Most of the increase in the percentage of men checking the "correct" answer came from the category "night attacks on London," which dropped from 63 per cent (for men who did not see the film) to 19 per cent (for men who saw the film).

3. EFFECTIVENESS OF FILM IN IMPROVING GENERAL ATTITUDES
TOWARD THE BRITISH

Since one of the principal intended effects of "The Battle of Britain" was to establish a feeling of confidence in the integrity and fighting ability of one of our allies, a number of items were included which were less specifically related to the film content but concerned general attitudes toward the British. In contrast to the large effects afforded above, where the items were tied to specific phases of the British war effort covered in the film, *the effects were small or unreliable on the more general questions dealing with confidence in the British effort.* The responses to several questions in this category are presented below.

> *Question:* "Do you feel that the British are doing all they possibly can to help win the war?" (two alternatives—"yes" or "no")
>
> Percentage of men checking "key" answer: i.e., "yes."

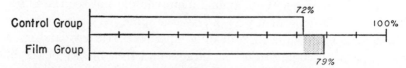

> *Question:* "Do you think the British are trying to get others to do most of their fighting for them in this war, or do you think they are doing their fair share of the fighting?" (two alternatives plus "undecided")

Percentage of men checking "key" answer: i.e., "British are doing their fair share of the fighting."

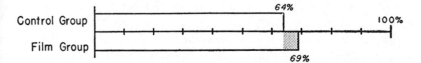

Question: "Do you think Britain may try to make a separate peace with Germany before the war is over, or do you think Britain will keep on fighting to the end?" (two alternatives plus "haven't any idea")

Percentage of men checking "key" answer: i.e., "will fight on to the end."

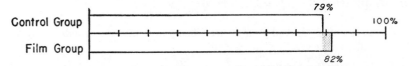

Other questions were included to determine any positive transfer of the effects of the film to general "pro" and "anti" British sentiment. Here the questions did not refer to the war effort of the British but were regarded as indices of general friendliness or unfriendliness toward the British people. The findings, which are illustrated below, indicated little or no transfer of the effects of the film to overall attitude toward the British people.

Question: "Some people say that the British are largely to blame for our being in this war. Do you agree with this, or disagree?" (two alternatives plus "undecided")

Percentage of men checking "key" answer: i.e., "disagree."

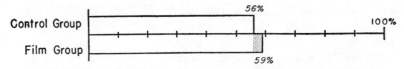

Question: "Do you think we ought to send food to England, even if it means rationing a lot more foods for civilians here in the United States?" (two alternatives plus "undecided")

Percentage of men checking "key" answer: i.e., "should send food, even if it means more rationing here."

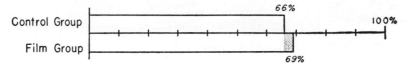

4. EFFECT OF "THE BATTLE OF BRITAIN" ON MEN'S MOTIVATION

While the film's chief objective was to strengthen confidence in the integrity and fighting ability of the British, it presumably also had the general objective, common to the entire "Why We Fight" series, of influencing men's motivation. Accordingly, the film's effects with regard to willingness to serve, attitude toward unconditional surrender, and resentment against the enemy were examined.

a. *Willingness to serve.* Did the film bring about an increased willingness to serve? This was considered to be one of the principal objectives in showing the orientation films. However, no reliable changes were found in this area as a result of seeing the film. The main question used was:

> *Question:* "If you had your choice when you finish your training, which would you choose?" (Check one)
>
> ☐ Duty in an outfit overseas or
>
> ☐ Duty in an outfit in the United States
>
> Why? _____
>
> Percentage of men checking "key" answer: i.e., "duty in an outfit overseas."

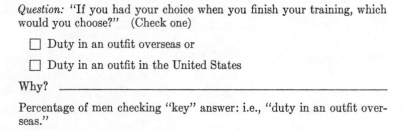

Thus the results showed no reliable effect of "The Battle of Britain" on the men's answers to this question. The results on another question in this area asked at one camp (N = 1200) are shown below.

> *Question:* "In your honest opinion, do you feel you can do *more to help win the war* here in the Army, or do you feel you were doing more to help win in the job you had before you came into the Army?" (three alternatives plus "don't know")
>
> Percentage of men checking "key" answer: i.e., "can do more in the Army."

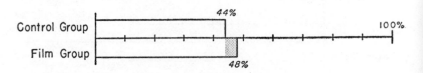

b. *Insistence on "unconditional surrender."* Similar results were obtained in a closely related area, namely agreement with the unconditional surrender policy of continuing the war until the complete defeat of the Axis powers. This question provided men who did not want to serve a convenient rationalization for their position and an opportunity to express their willingness to stop short of complete victory. As can be seen, no reliable change was produced by the film.

Question: "If Hitler offered to stop fighting right now and discuss peace terms do you think we should consider the offer seriously to prevent loss of American lives and money?" (two alternatives plus "undecided")

Percentage of men checking "no, should reject the offer."

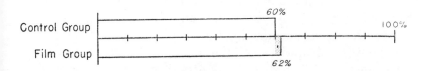

c. *Resentment against the enemy.* Supposedly one of the important motivations making men willing to serve in the Army was resentment against the enemy. At the time of the study, mass bombing of cities had not yet become a regular part of Allied methods, and it was thought that resentment against the Nazis might be increased by such scenes as those of the indiscriminate bombing of civilians and the mass burials after the destruction at Coventry. However, no evidence was obtained for a reliable increase either in belief in Nazi brutality or in expression of aggression against the Germans. Relevant results are shown below.

	Did not see film	Saw film	Difference
Percentage of men who *disagree* with statement:			
"The Nazis probably do not treat the people they conquer as badly as American newspaper and radio stories say."	66%	70%	4%
Percentage of men who *agree* with statement:			
"We should see to it that the Germans and Japs suffer plenty for all the trouble they are causing us."	78	78	*less than 1*

5. CHECKS ON POSSIBLE "BOOMERANGS"

There is always a possibility that some of the ideas emphasized in any film may produce "boomerangs"—adverse effects resulting from emphasis upon certain points with consequent distortion of related ideas. Accordingly, checks of these possibilities were usually made in each film study. In "The Battle of Britain" the following points were investigated as areas in which "boomerangs"; seemed possible.

a. *"American help not really needed in war."* A potential source of adverse effect upon the orientation objective of the necessity of our entering the war was the film presentation of the inability of the Germans to defeat England. It was thought that this might be used by the men in support of the belief that Germany was weaker than had been supposed and American help was not needed to prevent the Nazis from conquering the world. The film also explained how the British had withstood the enemy from across "that 21 miles of Channel . . . that short 8 minutes of water." It seemed possible that the men's reaction to this might be that if this was the case with England, we could certainly protect ourselves across 3,000 miles of ocean and so need not have sent our troops to Europe after all. However, the results showed no such effects on the items in this area.

Question: "How much help from the United States do you think Britain and Russia *needed* in order to beat Germany?" (three alternatives)

Percentage of men checking "key" answer: i.e., "Britain and Russia would not be able to beat Germany without our sending both men and materials."

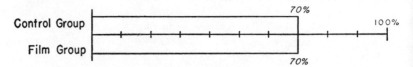

Percentage of men who *disagree* with statement:

"Since the Germans couldn't even get across the 20 miles of the English Channel in 1940, they certainly could never have attacked American shores across 3,000 miles of ocean."

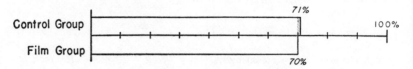

b. *"The Nazis will be easy to defeat."* It was also thought that the film might have an adverse effect in connection with the objective of bringing about a realization of the difficulty of defeating the Axis. Thus it could be expected that the portrayal of an unprepared Britain successfully warding off an invasion attempt would lead to the men's concluding that the Nazis would be easier to defeat than they had previously supposed. Answers to an agree-disagree question, however, relating to the difficulty of the job show no increase in overoptimism.

Percentage of men who *agree* with statement:

"America and her allies can still lose this war."

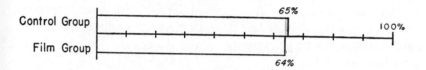

c. *"Civilians back home are not backing us up."* Another potential "boomerang" was that the men's confidence in their own civilian support might be adversely affected by the film's showing the outstanding efforts of the British civilians. A question was included on the relative war effort of the American and British civilian workers. The results are shown below.

Percentage of men who *agree* with statement:

"America would be producing more planes, tanks, and guns if only American civilians would work as hard as the British have done in this war."

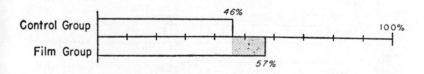

Thus, there was a sizable increase in the number of men agreeing with the idea that America would be producing more war materials if American civilians would only work as hard as the British civilians.

However, this effect of the film did not appear to carry with it any criticism of the war efforts of American civilians. A general item dealing with evaluation of the American civilian effort showed no increase in unfavorable attitude. The results were as follows:

Percentage of men who *agree* with statement:

"Most of the civilians in the United States are trying to do everything they possibly can to back up the armed forces."

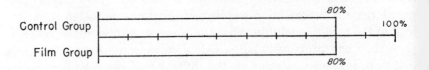

An explanation for the apparent inconsistency between this result and the one mentioned above was suggested by the comments of men who were given special film showings and interviewed about the film. While they recognized that the efforts of the British were greater than those of the American civilians, a frequent interpretation was that the British *had* to work that hard whereas America's situation was far less desperate so the American civilians did not need to work so hard.

d. *"American leaders did not fulfill their responsibility in preparing us for war."* A theme of the film already mentioned was that Britain's victory saved a precious year in which America could prepare. It was thought that the film might have made the men wonder why America needed a year to prepare—why America was not already prepared to whatever extent was required. An agree-disagree item was included to check on this possibility. The results give no evidence of a "boomerang" effect.

Percentage of men who *agree* with statement:

"Our military leaders did everything they possibly could to try to get us well prepared for the war."

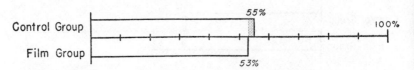

e. *"The Air Force is the only important branch."* The possibility was investigated that the film's emphasis on the RAF and the dependence of the British on their fighter planes might cause the men to underestimate the importance of branches of service other than the Air Corps. The main question used to check this possibility was one asking the men which arm or branch of service they considered most important in present-day warfare. The choices were

Artillery, Armored Force, Infantry, and Air Force. The per cent choosing Air Force as most important was high in both film and control groups, but only 2 per cent higher in the film group, nor were there any reliable changes in men's evaluation of the other branches of service.

f. *"The Russians can't be depended upon."* A final possibility of a "boomerang" was in the relative confidence in our allies. While Russia was not at all included in the film content, it was possible that the presentation of Britain's outstanding effort in holding off the Nazis might lessen the feeling of obligation to Russia. There might be a release of the men's former suspicions of Russian integrity—suspicions that had been inhibited by respect for and obligation to Russia since she had currently been doing the bulk of the fighting. Questionnaire items dealing with Russian integrity indicated that the film had some adverse effect in this area.

Question: (Immediately following the parallel question about Britain) "What about Russia—do you think she may try to make a separate peace or will she keep on fighting?" (two alternatives plus "haven't any idea")

Percentage of men checking "key" answer: i.e., "will fight on to the end."

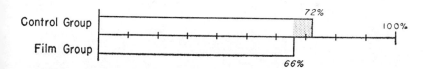

Except for the above question, which was asked at both camps, different items dealing with Russian integrity were asked at each camp. However, the results obtained at the individual camps were similar to those for the item used at both camps. At one camp (sample equals 1,200) the following results were obtained.

Percentage of men who *disagree* with statement:

"After we help Russia beat the Germans the Russians are liable to turn around and start fighting us."

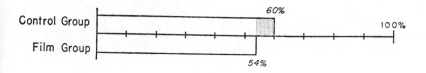

At the other camp (sample equals 900) several Russian-integrity items were used and all showed a slight negative difference between groups of men who had and had not seen the film. Results based on a representative item are shown below.

Percentage of men who *agree* with statement:

"If Germany is beaten before Japan, the Russians will probably help us fight the Japanese."

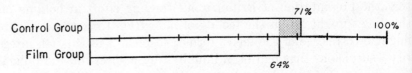

The consistency of the results on the various items and between the two camps makes it appear that a small but significant decrease was obtained in favorable evaluation of Russia as an ally. This constitutes the only "boomerang" revealed by the study.

CHAPTER 3

GENERAL IMPLICATIONS DERIVED FROM THE ORIENTATION FILM EXPERIMENTS

THE preceding chapter presented a fairly comprehensive account of the evaluation of an orientation film, "The Battle of Britain," showing the experimental measurement of changes in knowledge, opinions, and motivation. Similar studies were carried out on three other orientation films in the "Why We Fight" series: (1) "Prelude to War," (2) "The Nazis Strike," and (3) "Divide and Conquer." The first film, "Prelude to War," was studied with procedures almost identical to those described in the foregoing account of the study of "The Battle of Britain," with the use of both the after-only and the before-after designs. The study of Films 2 and 3 involved the departure of investigating experimentally the *cumulative* effects of two films in combination rather than testing each film singly. Film 3 was shown two days after Film 2, and the combined effects were then measured.

The question may be raised as to what general conclusions came out of these fairly large-scale and intensive evaluative studies of four of the "Why We Fight" films. Did the films accomplish their objectives in the orientation program? Did they benefit the morale of the men, that is, did they make the soldiers more willing to serve in the Army? Or, one might ask the still more general question: "Can motivations of this sort be influenced by documentary films —i.e., films with a purely educational approach?" Such questions are especially likely to arise in the minds of those interested in the possibility of using documentary films as a mass educational medium for producing desired changes in motivations—as, for example, overcoming racial or national prejudices.

It will be the purpose of this chapter to summarize those findings from the orientation studies which are relevant to the problem of how effectively attitudes and motivations can be altered by an educational or instructional program. It is apparent that the results of these evaluative studies are useful mainly in providing hypotheses rather than in establishing dependable generalizations.

CONTENT OF FILMS 1, 2, AND 3

Before discussing the question of how well the films achieved their objective, the content of the three films tested in addition to "The Battle of Britain" will be briefly summarized.

"Prelude to War" traced the background of the war from the Japanese attack on Manchuria in 1931 through the conquest of Ethiopia by Italy in 1935. It also went back in time to present the rise of Mussolini and Fascism in Italy, and related this to the rise of Hitler and Nazism in Germany and to the control of Japan by a military clique. The film contrasted the slogans, practices, and philosophy of the Axis countries with those of America and the other democracies. It documented the growth of aggressive militarism and the amassing of armed might in the Axis countries, together with the trends of thought and action in the United States that led to our noninterventionist policy and lack of preparedness for global war. The thesis of the film was that war was inevitable for the United States because the three Axis countries had teamed up to conquer the world and divide it up among themselves. Sooner or later America would necessarily become involved in defending itself —and unfortunately was in a tight spot because she had not realized this soon enough.

"The Nazis Strike" began with a historical summary of past German aggressions, presenting Hitler's conquests as a repeat performance of those of Bismarck and Kaiser Wilhelm. The military rearmament under Hitler was portrayed, and events were traced from the Austrian *Anschluss* through the series of territorial acquisitions and Franco-British appeasements, ending with the attack on Poland and the declaration of war by Britain and France. The Polish campaign was depicted in considerable detail, offering a vivid illustration of Nazi ruthlessness and efficiency. A theme running through the film was the futility of the various attempts to appease Hitler.

"Divide and Conquer" was a sequel to "The Nazis Strike" and continued the story of the Nazi "grand strategy" of using a "pincers

movement" against England, showing the strategic need for Norway. The film described the overrunning of Denmark and the conquest of Norway, aided by the Quislings, and the unsuccessful attempt of the Allies to help the Norwegians. Finally, the capture of the Low Countries and the breaking through the Ardennes and Sedan were shown, leading to the collapse of France. A considerable amount of footage was devoted to the German campaign in France, with emphasis on strategy and tactics and the failure of the Allied reliance on defensive warfare.

How Well Did the Films Accomplish Their Objectives?

The general findings for the entire series of films studied follow closely the pattern of those already presented in Chapter 2 for "The Battle of Britain." Relevant findings from Chapter 2 will be briefly summarized before discussing the results from the other films.

"The Battle of Britain" was effective in presenting factual information, materially improving men's knowledge of events concerning the air war over Britain in 1940. The film was also quite effective in changing opinions in some areas—that is, the film altered the men's *interpretations* of the facts as well as giving them new facts. However, these changed opinions were nearly all closely related to material specifically covered in the film. Also, these "opinions" were not particularly distinguished from the factual material in the film's presentation—that is, an interpretation such as that the air attack was a real invasion attempt warded off by the British was presented in the film virtually as an accepted fact.

While this film produced relatively large effects on material it specifically covered and while opinions were markedly changed about the performance of the British during the Battle of Britain, reliable effects were not obtained on questions of a general nature dealing with the war effort or integrity of the British. There seemed to be no transfer of the specific material to more general attitudes toward the British. For example, there was an increase in the proportion of men who thought the RAF gave Germany "its first real defeat," yet only a barely significant increase in the number who believed that Britain was doing all it could in the war effort or that the British were doing their fair share of the fighting. These results, excerpted from Chapter 2, are as follows.

	Control	Film	Diff.
Specifically covered Question: "In your opinion who gave the Nazis their first real defeat?"			
Percentage checking "the British Royal Air Force"	20%	43%	23%
Generalization Question: "Do you think the British are doing all they possibly can to help win the war?"			
Percentage checking "yes"	72	79	7
Question: "Do you think the British are trying to get others to do most of their fighting for them in this war or do you think they are doing their fair share of the fighting?"			
Percentage checking "British are doing their fair share of the fighting"	64	69	5

Another interesting example is seen in the sizable increase (16 per cent) in the number of men who believed that the British refusal to surrender saved American cities from German bombs (p. 37), without any corresponding increase in a sense of obligation to the British, as reflected in willingness to send more food to England (p. 43).

These two examples illustrate the general result in the experimental evaluation of "The Battle of Britain"—that the sizable effects on specific points in the film were not accompanied by changes in the more general attitudes toward the British. Since these latter more general attitudes were more nearly the target of the orientation program than the specific details of factual information, it would appear that the film's effects on its orientation objectives were slight or lacking.

Similarly, no effects were obtained on the stated orientation objective of increasing resentment toward the enemy nor on the motivation of the men from the standpoint of willingness to serve and to continue the war to unconditional surrender. Thus the film also appeared to have no appreciable effect on the ultimate target of the orientation program—increasing soldiers' motivations.

The question might be raised as to whether "The Battle of Britain" could have been expected to increase willingness to serve. Since it dealt solely with the British effort, perhaps its only "intended" effect was to build respect for America's allies. Did the other orientation films tested show effects on the men's motivation? A brief answer to this question is that the same pattern of results was obtained on the other films tested. In each case marked effects were obtained on items of factual information, some sizable changes were obtained on opinions closely related to the material covered, and no appreciable changes were found in the more general attitude areas comprising the orientation objectives or in the area of willingness to serve.

1. EFFECTIVENESS IN IMPARTING FACTUAL INFORMATION

The general effectiveness of the films in imparting the factual material presented is summarized in the following table, which gives the average effect and the range of effects on the information tests used. In each case the average is based on a battery of ten or more questions about factual points covered in the film.

TABLE 1

FILM EFFECTS ON FACTUAL INFORMATION ITEMS

Orientation film	AVERAGE PERCENTAGE CHECKING CORRECT ANSWER			RANGE OF DIFF. BETWEEN FILM AND CONTROL ON INDIVIDUAL TEST ITEMS
	Control	Film	Av. Diff.	
1. "Prelude to War"	34.8%	49.3%	14.5%	1% to 52%
2. & 3. "The Nazis Strike" and "Divide and Conquer" (studied in combination)	32.8	52.0	19.2	−3 to 46
4. "The Battle of Britain"	29.4	51.4	22.0	3 to 57

Not all of the points of factual knowledge included in the batteries of fact-quiz items were equally important, and for various reasons some items were included in the questionnaires to test for effects on facts of little consequence, some of which showed no significant effect.

2. EFFECTIVENESS IN CHANGING OPINIONS

Appreciable changes in questions of opinion where the interpretation involved was fairly specifically covered were obtained in all the films tested.

a. *"Prelude to War."* "Prelude to War" produced relatively few reliable opinion changes. Of a large number of opinion items that were included in the "Prelude to War" questionnaire, only six showed statistically significant effects of the film.[1] These fell into three categories:

(1) *Axis military strength:* The film described the Luftwaffe as "the world's largest air force," and documented the huge extent of German military expenditures, together with shots of the Wehrmacht in mass maneuvers. Two questions were affected in which the men ranked their estimates of the relative strengths of the air and ground forces of the five chief combatants—Japan, Germany, Britain, Russia, and the United States.

	Control	Film	Diff.
Percentage rating German *Air Forces* as one of the two strongest.	44%	56%	*12%*
Percentage rating German *Ground Forces* as one of the two strongest.	47	54	*7*

(2) *Nazi menace to freedom:* In documenting the restrictions of personal freedom under Nazism, the film covered, among other things, the topics of religious intolerance and the influence of the Nazi state in the raising of children.

	Control	Film	Diff.
Percentage checking "yes" to "Close all our churches and make everyone worship Hitler" (as what the Nazis would attempt if they could conquer America).	75%	83%	*8%*
Percentage who *agree* with statement: "In Germany all children are taken away from their parents shortly after they are born, and are raised by the government."	51	62	*11*

(3) *A "better world" after the war:* In two questions from several about a better world after the war, the men were asked if they thought soldiers and civilians would be better off, worse off, or about the same after the war as they were before. The small effects obtained are shown below:

---

[1] In the study of "Prelude to War" the final equated sample from three different camps contained 1,678 cases, half experimental and half control. Using the same method of determining statistical significance as applied in the case of "The Battle of Britain" in Chapter 2, a 6 per cent difference between control and film was considered reliable.

	Control	Film	Diff.
Percentage checking "Better off" for soldiers	34%	40%	6%
Percentage checking "Better off" for civilians	28	35	7

b. *"The Nazis Strike" and "Divide and Conquer."* The cumulative effects of "The Nazis Strike" and "Divide and Conquer" showed more opinion changes than did "Prelude to War." Twelve opinion items showed differences of 6 per cent or more between the experimental and control groups with these two films in combination.[2] Predominantly these effects fall into four categories:

(1) *German military efficiency:* A large portion of the content of these two films was devoted to German footage of their war machine in training and in action during the period covered, a period of rapid conquest for the Germans.

	Control	Film	Diff.
Percentage of men who *agree* with following statements:			
"We may not like the Nazis, but we have to admit that in most of their attacks they work out every detail just about perfect."	71%	83%	12%
"Whether we like it or not, we have to admit that the German Army has about the best trained officers in the world."	37	48	11
Percentage of men who *disagree* with the statement:			
"American soldiers who are sent overseas to fight the Germans are probably just as well trained as the Nazis they will be fighting against."	31	38	7

(2) *Interpretation of Allied appeasement:* "The Nazis Strike" took up each of the Allied appeasement attempts and showed how poorly Hitler kept his promises. The point was therefore emphasized that the appeasement attempts failed, but the film's interpretations concerning the motivations of the Allies in the Munich pact and the Russian nonaggression pact were rather vague. The men concluded that the appeasement policy was a mistake, but made lenient interpretations in each case: that Britain and France hoped

[2] Here the sample was 1,140 cases and a difference of 8 per cent was regarded as significant. However, for comparability with the other films, any differences of 6 per cent or more are shown in the present section. This approximates the 5 per cent confidence level rather than the 1 per cent level for these films.

to prevent war entirely and that Russia was stalling for time rather than being temporarily in league with the Axis.

	Control	Film	Diff.
Percentage checking "No, they only made things worse in the long run" (to a question about whether Britain and France did the right thing "in letting Hitler have his way for a while").	61%	72%	11%
Percentage checking "They disapproved of Hitler but hoped that they would prevent war entirely in this way" (to a question on Britain and France's motivation in appeasing Germany).	47	58	11
Percentage checking "To get time to prepare for defense against Nazi attack" (as the Russian motivation for the nonaggression pact).	60	71	11

(3) *Allied defensive strategy:* "Divide and Conquer" took two stands in connection with Allied defensive strategy in the battle for France. On the one hand it discussed the weakness of the Maginot defense because it was not extended clear to the coast and because of the reliance on the impassability of the Ardennes Forest; on the other hand it criticized the Allied dependence on defense rather than offense. This material was presented in the context of a fairly technical military discussion, with animated war maps to portray the various military maneuvers of both sides. Both ideas were strengthened despite their apparent inconsistency:

	Control	Film	Diff.
Percentage who *agree* with the statements:			
"If the French had built their Maginot Line defenses along their *entire* border, the Nazis probably would not have been able to invade France."	30%	38%	8%
"Defensive fighting is old-fashioned; the only way to win in modern warfare is by always attacking."	58	71	13

(4) *Resentment for Nazis:* These two films provided the only instance of reliable increase in aggressive responses toward the Nazis. No significant effects were obtained on questions asked in terms of resentment toward the Nazis alone. But with questions phrased in terms of comparative resentment against the Nazis and the

Japanese, significant increases in relative resentment expressed toward the Nazis were obtained.

	Control	Film	Diff.
Percentage checking *either* "Hate Nazis more" or "hate both about equally" (on question about which they hate more of the two).	39%	49%	10%
Percentage who *agree* with the statement: "The Nazis have been every bit as cruel and brutal as the Japs in their treatment of conquered people."	66	76	10

It would be desirable to be able to present some form of summary of the effectiveness in changing opinions of the four films, comparable to the earlier summary of their average effects on the information tests. However, a completely comparable summary is not possible. The main reason for this is that while one can definitely specify whether or not a point of fact was presented in a film, it is more difficult to specify whether or not the material in the film could be expected to change a particular opinion. Factual material may vary in coverage, but a fact either is or is not stated or shown. On the other hand, it is a matter of *judgment* whether or not the material will be interpreted in a particular way. A highly skillful judge who uses only those opinion items for which he anticipates a change will get a higher average effect on all opinion items included than a poor judge who because of lack of skill fails to test for likely effects and at the same time has many "deadwood" items for which he expects effects when actually they are unlikely.

Thus a straight average on all opinion items included in a film questionnaire is not very meaningful as a test of the overall effectiveness of the film in changing opinions, at least unless standardization of the factors determining inclusion of a particular item is involved. The "shotgun" approach used in the present studies was to use a fairly low criterion of likelihood in deciding whether or not to include an opinion item. That is, some items were included even though there was low anticipation of effects. This was particularly true in some of the opinion items included to test for potential boomerangs. For these reasons an average of the results for all opinion items included would come out very low and would not at all be a fair basis for evaluating the films.

The following summary of the findings should be viewed with these factors in mind. The summary shows the total number of opinion items used in each experiment, the number for which a difference of 6 per cent or more was found between the control and film groups, the average results for such items, and the range of the difference between control and film groups for each average. In all three studies the same personnel prepared the items to be used in testing the films.

TABLE 2

FILM EFFECTS ON RELIABLY AFFECTED OPINION QUESTIONS

Film	Total opinion items used	Number reliably affected	Average checking key response in control group	Average checking key response in film group	Av. diff.	Range of differences
"Prelude to War"	46	6	46.5%	55.0%	8.5%	6% to 12%
"The Nazis Strike" and "Divide and Conquer"	69	12	52.3	60.5	10.2	7 to 13
"The Battle of Britain"	44	13*	44.2	57.7	13.5	6 to 27

* This does not include the two items described in Chapter 2 on which "boomerangs" against the Russian allies were found.

Since this summary table is likely to invite comparisons, some cautions that might be overlooked should be emphasized. In comparing the different films it should be borne in mind that the initial average (the control average) sets a limit on the maximum size of difference possible. Thus a high initial level generally means that only a small proportion of the sample is able to change to the key response because most of the men would choose this response even before seeing the film. The differences in initial level are fairly small in the foregoing table, so this factor is not too important in comparing the different films—however, it is more important in comparing the above summary table for significantly affected opinion changes with that shown previously for fact-quiz items, where the initial level is lower for all films than for the opinion items shown.

Attention should be drawn to the fact that the table of average opinion changes is a selection of only those items that showed reliable changes. This should be in mind if comparisons with the fact-quiz averages are made. In the latter case, averages are based on all items used, including those with zero effects, whereas the averages for opinion change are a selection, from those used, of the minority on which a 6 per cent or greater change was obtained. The extent of this selective factor can be judged in part from the comparison of the number of opinion items used with the number that showed the required size of effect.

For this last reason it seems justifiable to conclude that while opinions were definitely changed in many cases they were considerably less affected in general than factual knowledge.

3. EFFECTIVENESS WITH SUBOBJECTIVES
   OF THE ORIENTATION PROGRAM

Earlier in the chapter, attention was called to the fact that in the study of "The Battle of Britain" no appreciable effects were obtained on general questions in the areas related to the subobjectives of the orientation program. It was further stated that this was the typical result of all the studies of the "Why We Fight" films.

In view of the numerous opinion changes just shown, most of which were in line with orientation objectives, something should be said about the nature of the "general" items used in the studies. At the outset of the film studies, an attempt was made to construct attitude scales for each of the specified orientation objectives, independently of any consideration of film content. This attempt was not very successful, largely because the areas designated by the orientation objectives appeared, on the basis of empirical analysis of the interrelations of responses, to break up into subareas rather than to form single content dimensions. Thus "confidence in our allies" could not be treated as a single variable but had to be broken down into subareas for the separate allies, and "confidence in Britain" could not be treated as a single variable but had to be subdivided into "British integrity," "British war aims," "British war effort," "British fighting strength," and so forth.

The chief characteristics of the items finally selected as "scale items" in each orientation area were that they were derived independently of film contents and were concerned with topics of a much more general (i.e., inclusive) nature than opinion items specifically written to test for a film effect anticipated on the basis of content analysis. Thus these items defined the "intended" effects of the films—they stated the objectives, independent of the film procedures adopted to achieve them—and at the same time they tended to be broad generalizations rather than interpretations of specific facts.

Of the reliable opinion changes shown in Chapter 2 and the present chapter, very few involved the general "scale items" that had been prepared independently of film contents—even though a considerable number of such items were included in all of the orientation-film studies. Only two clear-cut cases can be cited, and the effects on these were not striking. The two cases are shown below, one from the study of Film 4 and one from the study of Films 2 and 3.

	Control	Film	Diff.
Question: "Do you think the British are doing all they possibly can to help win the war?"			
Percentage checking "Yes"	72%	79%	7%
Question: "Which do you feel you really hate more—the Nazis or the Japs?" (including "don't hate either")			
Percentage checking either "Hate Nazis more" or "Hate both about equally."	39	49	10

Two less clear-cut cases may also be cited, from the study of "Prelude to War." These are the opinion changes concerning the strength of the Nazi air forces and the Nazi ground forces. As shown in the preceding section, a 12 per cent and a 7 per cent difference respectively, due to the film, was found on these items. These two items were less clear examples because they did not "scale" with each other or with a number of items that did "scale" in the content area of difficulty of the task of winning the war. The items were, therefore, regarded as fairly specific subareas of opinions about enemy strength. Whereas these enemy strength areas, which were specifically covered in the film, showed reliable effects, no effects were obtained on items in the more general area dealing with the difficulty of the task of winning the war. An interesting progression of results is seen in comparing the effects on a fact question about German armament, on the rating of the relative strength of the Luftwaffe (which was named "The world's largest air force" by the film), on the rating of the relative strength of the German ground forces, and on the results for questions from the general area of difficulty of winning the war. The progression is the same as in the illustrations excerpted from the study of "The Battle of Britain" at the beginning of the chapter.

Type of Item	Content	Control	Film	Diff.
Fact	Percentage checking "80 billion dollars" as the amount spent for German rearmament between 1933 and 1939.	43%	57%	14%
Specific opinion (stated as fact in film)	Percentage rating the German *air forces* as one of the two strongest.	44	56	12
Specific opinion (not explicitly stated)	Percentage rating the German *ground forces* as one of the two strongest.	47	54	7
General Orientation	Percentage who *disagree* with the statement: "the war will probably be over within the next twelve months."	44	41	−3
	Percentage checking "It will take a long hard fight to win the war even after our war production hits its peak" (on a question about the difficulty of the task ahead).	49	47	−2

It may be seen in this series of results that on a fact-quiz item the film shifted a sizable proportion of men to a higher estimate of German war expenditures. Also, as in the case of "The Battle of Britain," specifically covered opinions were reliably changed. That is, the men's estimates of the strength of the German air and ground forces definitely went up relative to the other four countries compared. But this increase in respect for specific aspects of enemy strength did not at all transfer to the general area of the difficulty of the task, which was one of the orientation objectives listed in the preceding chapter. Thus, the overoptimistic response of believing the war would be over in twelve months (it actually took 33 months from the time of the study) was held by the majority of both groups and was slightly greater in the film group. The last two questions in the preceding table were from a "scale" of items about the difficulty of the job which were specifically designed to measure effects of orientation films on this attitude. Several additional questions in this scale were also included in the questionnaire for testing "Prelude to War" and all showed the same result as the examples above: a slight and unreliable negative difference between the experimental and control groups.

4. EFFECTIVENESS IN INFLUENCING MOTIVATION

The scales of items initially devised for measuring effects on the overall orientation objective of increasing men's motivation in terms of expressed willingness to serve proved unsatisfactory, and items in this area were revised in the course of the orientation film studies. A battery of five items was used in the first study ("Prelude to War"), all concerned with willingness to go overseas and willingness for combat service. In the subsequent studies, three general areas were utilized: (1) motivation to be a soldier rather than a civilian, (2) motivation for overseas and combat service, and (3) motivation to see the war through to unconditional victory rather than to accept a negotiated peace. Items from these areas are exemplified in the study of "The Battle of Britain" reported in Chapter 2. Items with much the same wording were used in the study of "The Nazis Strike" and "Divide and Conquer."

In no instance was a reliable effect obtained on willingness-to-serve items. At least three such items were included in each of the film studies; the range of differences between film and control on all such items for all films was from $+4\%$ to -4%, with a mean of $+1\%$, about what would be expected by chance.

Thus, to the extent that the items used were adequate measures, neither Film 1 nor Film 4 had any effect on willingness to serve as single presentations, and Films 2 and 3 had no cumulative effects when presented successively (two days apart).

5. SUMMARY OF EFFECTIVENESS

The "Why We Fight" films had marked effects on the men's knowledge of factual material concerning the events leading up to the war. The fact that the upper limit of effects was so large—as for example in the cases where the correct answer was learned well enough to be remembered a week later by the *majority* of the men—indicates that highly effective presentation methods are possible with this type of film.

The films also had some marked effects on opinions where the film specifically covered the factors involved in the particular interpretation, that is, where the opinion item was prepared on the basis of film-content analysis and anticipated opinion change from such analysis. Such opinion changes were, however, less frequent and in general less marked than changes in factual knowledge.

The films had only a very few effects on opinion items of a more general nature that had been prepared independently of film content but which were considered the criteria for determining the effectiveness of the films in achieving their orientation objectives.

The films had no effects on the items prepared for the purpose of measuring effects on the men's motivation to serve as soldiers, which was considered the ultimate objective of the orientation program.

HYPOTHESES CONCERNING LACK OF EFFECTS ON ORIENTATION OBJECTIVES

The question arises as to the explanation for the pattern of results summarized above. It is not possible to answer this question, but a number of possible contributory factors may be suggested, some of which are problems for future research in the field of communications.

1. PREVIOUS INDOCTRINATION AS CIVILIANS

One important possibility is that the men may already have been subjected to such an extensive information program from civilian sources that about the maximum effect had already been achieved in molding their opinions related to orientation objectives. The Army orientation objectives were similar to the objectives of the Office of War Information, and civilians were exposed to newsreels, documentary films, documentary radio programs, newspaper and magazine articles, etc., which provided material similar to that presented in the orientation films. Since the men used in the study were nearly all trainees with only a few weeks' service in the Army, they would be expected to show the effects of all the civilian information media. For example, religious intolerance under Hitler was highly publicized, and in the study of "Prelude to War," 75 per cent of the men believed at the outset that Hitler would "close all our churches" if he could conquer America. Similarly, 82 per cent believed Hitler would "persecute and torture Jews and other minority groups," another highly publicized topic. It is obvious in these examples from the "Prelude to War" questionnaire that the great majority of the men had already been convinced of the point of view the film was trying to put across, and little further effect could be expected.

The high initial frequency limits the size of effect which is numerically possible. If 82 per cent of the men are already sold on the idea that Hitler would persecute minority groups, the maximum difference between control and experimental group that it is possible for the film to produce is 18 per cent, that is, only 18 per cent of the men could change their opinions in the desired direction. This is quite a different situation from the case of a fact question for which only 10 per cent initially check the correct answer, leaving room for 90 per cent of the men to change to the correct answer.

The actual difference obtained between control and film groups on the question about persecution of minorities was +2%, which was too small to be reliable with the size of samples used. Nevertheless it was 1/9 of the total change possible. But a change of 1/9 of the total possible change would, on our hypothetical fact question, be an increase from 10 per cent to 20 per cent checking the correct answer, a difference of 10 per cent which would be highly reliable with the size of control and experimental samples used in the study. Thus if we think not in terms of the total sample but rather in terms of that portion of the sample which has the undesirable opinion—which is the group to which the film is actually directed—a reason for the lack of effects on orientation objectives could be that civilian indoctrination made that group so small that even if a sizable portion of these men changed it would still be an insignificant proportion of the total sample. Even where the difference is reliable, it is not likely to be impressive in size. Thus the item in the questionnaire about Hitler "closing our churches" showed a difference of +8% between control and film, which was a reliable difference but not very large. However, from the standpoint of the small group (25 per cent of the men) who did not check this response initially, it was a difference affecting 8/25 or 32 per cent of those who could change. This difficulty—that only those who do not initially give the desired response can be changed in the desired direction—is a recurrent problem. The procedure illustrated, of expressing the obtained amount of change as a proportion of the amount of possible change, was frequently used to take account of the difficulty, particularly where items or groups of men, with differing initial frequency of responses, were compared. This ratio will be referred to as the "Effectiveness Index." For further discussion of the logic of this measure see Appendix A.

In addition to this purely statistical restriction, it would also be expected that a selection process would have been operative so that those who could still change their opinions in the desired direction would be more resistant to change. If a great majority of the total audience had been convinced of a particular point of view that is well publicized it is likely that the remaining proportion of the population, which still does not accept the view of the majority, contains the "die-hards" who are particularly resistant to (or incapable of) having their opinion changed.

These factors of ceiling and selection undoubtedly did operate in some cases of questions designed to test for effects on orientation objectives. In general such questions showed the majority opinion to be in the desired direction. This can be seen, for example, in the questions aimed at general attitude toward England in the study of "The Battle of Britain." Over half the men gave pro-British answers to each of these questions. It is of interest to compare this finding with the average initial level of only 44 per cent checking the key response to opinion items that were significantly affected by "The Battle of Britain" as shown in Table 2, and the initial level of only 29 per cent for the fact-quiz items used with this film, as shown in Table 1.

It should be noted that wherever the ceiling and selection factors do apply, one of the assumptions of the orientation program—namely that a sizable proportion of the Army held misinformed opinions—did not apply. Wherever the civilian sources had already done the maximum orientation job, further material was not needed except on the possibility of influencing the remaining "die-hards."

It should also be noted, however, that these factors do not apply in all cases. This is particularly true in the area of willingness to serve—the main target of the orientation program. Here the usual result was that less than half of the men checked the desired response, which left considerable room for changes due to the films. This was also true of other of the general questions dealing with subobjectives of the orientation program. Thus other factors must also be involved.

2. CONFLICTING MOTIVATION

Another hypothetical factor that might have applied in the case of some of the orientation objectives is the possibility of resistance to change because of motivations running counter to the implications of the orientation content. This would be particularly expected in such areas as willingness to go overseas or serve in combat, where the audience might have a large number of reasons for not wanting to fight to offset anything presented in the "Why We Fight" films. Fear of injury, pressure from a wife or mother, and so forth, would be strong motivations to compete with the motivating effects of the film. Or, as another example, the audience might have considerable resistance to accepting the idea that the war will be long and difficult. If they wanted to be out of the Army soon, if they hoped they would not be needed for combat, or if they hoped that even in combat they would not run many risks, they would have strong motivation to resist evidences for a long and difficult war.

By contrast, the audience might have little or no motivation to reject, for example, the idea that the British blocked an invasion attempt. Some ethnocentric or anti-British individuals might be unwilling to give the British credit for a victory, but most individuals would see in this interpretation no conflict with their own interests and would accept the film's interpretation if it were convincingly presented. Thus strong motivation to resist acceptance of certain of the orientation objectives may have accounted in part for the lack of motivating effects of the films.

3. INEFFECTUALITY OF A SINGLE 50-MINUTE PRESENTATION

It might be argued that sizable changes in motivation as a result of a single 50-minute film are very unlikely simply because the film is such a small influence relative to perhaps years of exposure to points of view contrary to material presented in the film. For example, exposure to various patriotic communications over a period of years might convince a man that America is unbeatable; the interpretations in a film that real peril existed would be relatively too small a portion of the total indoctrinational influences to change his mind to the point of view that America was in real danger.

This suggests the possibility that while a single orientation film might not produce effects large enough to be statistically reliable, the entire series of seven "Why We Fight" films might have produced definite changes in motivation. A study along these lines was contemplated but never carried out, largely because of a number of practical considerations, among which were delays in the production of later films in the series combined with a transfer of responsibility for the films from the Information and Education Division to the Signal Corps.

The nearest approach to such a study was the experiment testing the cumulative effects of Films 2 and 3. As has been shown, these cumulative effects were not at all impressive, although the joint exposure to these two films produced the only reliable change obtained on an item dealing with resentment of the enemy. Unfortunately, this same item was not used with other films and it was an item in which sensitivity to change was increased through a comparison of the relative resentment for Nazis versus the Japanese. It is significant that other resentment items, which had been used in the other film studies, showed no reliable cumulative effects of the two successive presentations.

4. LACK OF SPECIFIC COVERAGE

Another possible factor which might account for lack of effects on general questions designed to measure attitudes related to orientation objectives is lack of specific coverage in the material presented by the film. There are some lines of suggestive evidence pointing in this direction. For example, fact-quiz items, all of which dealt with material specifically covered in the film, were nearly always reliably affected by the film. Moreover, in nearly all cases opinion changes were found on questions related to main themes of the films. Nearly all of the opinion changes found were on questions that had been prepared on the basis of film-content analysis. On the other hand almost no changes were found on opinion items prepared independently of film content. It is interesting that the largest opinion change obtained on an independently prepared "scale" area question was the 12 per cent difference between control and film groups in rating the German air forces as first or second strongest in the study of "Prelude to War." In the film the Luftwaffe had been shown in action and was specifically described as "the world's largest air force."

Another line of evidence that specific coverage is important was found in a study of several radio transcriptions. Sizable effects were obtained with specific coverage of an orientation topic which none of the films had significantly influenced. This study is reported in detail in Chapters 5 and 9, but a summary statement is relevant here. The orientation objective in this study was the difficulty of the job of winning the war; the main question used was the men's estimates of the probable length of the war. This question is not subject to ceiling effects because answers along a time continuum can be dichotomized at any point and individual changes of any size determined. In this study single radio transcriptions (15 to 20 minutes in length) devoted to discussion of enemy strength *as related to* the probable length of the war were found to cause about 40 per cent of the men to revise their estimates upward by at least six months. By contrast the show of Nazi strength in "Prelude to War" and succeeding films had no reliable effects on such estimates. Precise comparison of the results of the transcriptions (which had specific coverage) and the films (which did not have specific coverage) cannot be made because of differences in the two media and because the above-mentioned figure of 40 per cent effect was obtained under conditions of immediate measurement whereas film effects were measured four to seven days after presentation. Nevertheless, the result definitely suggests that, for this orientation objective at least, the lack of film effects was due to lack of specific coverage.

In the preparation of the radio transcriptions the script writers and the producers were in on the experiment almost from the beginning. They drew their material from an outline of relevant factual information prepared by Research Branch personnel and they knew at the outset the actual wording of the main question to be used in testing the effectiveness of the programs. The success of these programs in changing opinions on an independently prepared question aimed at one of the orientation objectives suggests not only the importance of specific coverage, but also the possible importance of the production personnel's having in mind at the outset of production the criteria they are striving to influence.

The whole question of "specific coverage" raises the interesting research problem of whether or not effects are generally possible in a communication that carries an implied rather than a stated "message." To expect that the orientation film would cause changes in certain of the criterion questions involves the assumption that opinions will change as a result of the *implications* of factual material even though the inference is not explicitly drawn and stated in the communication. In these terms the expectation that a show of Nazi strength would increase estimates of length of war rests on the assumption that the audience would make the inferential step involved. It may be that only a limited number actually do this without help.

Another interesting problem for future research is the relationship between changes in specific opinions and changes in general opinions (or attitudes). It would appear that changes in specific opinion can occur without being accompanied by changes in general orientation toward an issue.

Presumably opinions reflect a person's outlook on a more general topic with which a particular opinion item is concerned. If he has little specific, relevant information his opinion is likely to be determined by his general outlook and can be used as an index of his bias on the more general topic. As a consequence, if a series of specific questions on the same general topic are asked, on each of which he has no very well-informed opinion, he would be expected to reveal his bias by a consistent trend in the nature of his answers; this is presumably what is sought in attitude scales. Under these circumstances if one presents relevant arguments, covering specifically the topics of the opinion items used in measuring a communication's effects, the specific opinions may be altered without basically altering the outlook or "attitude" toward the more general subject.

Thus, opinions may be influenced by attitudes, and they may also be influenced by specific coverage of relevant arguments and factual information. But a change in specific opinions does not necessarily lead to any change in the presumed attitude that the opinion item was designed to measure. And it may be that concentration on specific coverage, even though it produces large changes in opinion, leaves attitudes untouched. If such changes in attitude or underlying bias are the real objective of a film, they might be overlooked in a preoccupation with large-scale changes in response to specific opinion items which were specifically covered by the content of the film.

5. NEED FOR A "SINKING IN" PERIOD

In all of the orientation film findings discussed thus far the experimental measurements were made from four to seven days after the film showings. It was thought that this would select a point on the forgetting curve at which the relatively lasting effects of the films could be determined. However, it is possible that this was not a long enough period for some of the films' effects to be felt. Perhaps, for example, the influence of factual information is not in the immediate changes in opinion produced but in its effect—as a store of knowledge—in affecting the interpretations of subsequently learned facts. Or perhaps the implications of facts are not seen immediately but instead require a period to think them over or see their relevance in subsequent discussions. The main point being made is that films may have delayed or "sleeper" effects that require a lapse of time to become evident, and this may be particularly true of opinion changes of a more general nature such as were involved in the orientation objectives.

Findings bearing directly on this problem are taken up in Chapter 7, in which is reported a study of the time factor after presentation as a variable influencing the effects of a film in changing opinion and factual knowledge. Some fairly clear-cut cases of "sleeper" effects were obtained in this study, and several possible mechanisms that could bring about such effects are discussed. These findings definitely open the possibility that the "Why We Fight" films may have had effects on some of the orientation objectives that were not discovered in the main studies simply because the effects were delayed.

IMPLICATIONS CONCERNING THE ASSUMPTIONS OF THE ORIENTATION PROGRAM

The foregoing hypotheses have not explicitly questioned the general rationale behind the orientation program that motivation can be increased as a result of an information program by "letting the facts speak for themselves." It may be worth while to examine the assumptions involved, since it is possible that the lack of effects may be due simply to the fact that the attitudes and motivations investigated in these studies cannot be appreciably affected by a program which relies primarily upon communicating factual information. Such a program may be effective with only a small percentage of individuals whose attitudes are primarily determined by rational analysis of the relevant facts. For the majority of individuals it may be true that motivations and attitudes are generally acquired without regard to rational considerations and are practically impregnable to new rational considerations.

The operation of the Army orientation program—of which the orientation films were a part—rested primarily upon two basic assumptions concerning mechanisms for affecting motivation by means of "orientation." The first assumption was that giving men more information about the war and its background would give them more favorable opinions and attitudes toward our participation in the war. The second, related assumption was that improvement of opinions, attitudes, or interpretations about the war would lead in some measure to higher motivation in terms of greater willingness to accept the transformation from civilian to Army life and to serve in the role of soldier.

The results presented earlier in the chapter cast considerable doubt on the first assumption. The films produced sizable increments in information, but produced almost no reliable increments on the general opinion items designed to measure changes in the orientation program's objectives. This negative conclusion was also supported by data from other studies of the orientation program which showed that scores on information tests were only slightly correlated with orientation opinions and increases in information were only slightly correlated with improvement in the opinions concerning the war and our allies.

With respect to the second assumption—concerning the relationship between the improvement of opinions and change in motivation —no evidence was provided by the experimental studies of films since the films produced almost no increments in relevant opinions. However, establishment of this relationship poses a difficult methodological problem. Even if there had been changes in opinion and motivation it would be difficult to know whether to attribute the change in motivation to the change in opinion. This difficulty cannot be overcome by controlled experimentation since it is difficult to see how the relevant experiment could be performed. The methodological difficulty is created by the problem of varying independently the variables in the hypothetical causal relationship. In this situation the independent variables are themselves *reactions* of the individual and as such require a stimulus; by consequence it is difficult or impossible to know whether the dependent variable was affected by this reaction or whether it was directly affected by the stimuli used to bring about the reaction. For example, if a movie altered attitude toward the justice of America's cause in the war and it is found that the altered attitudes are accompanied by increased motivation, how does one know the movie did not affect the motivation directly rather than that the change in motivation was caused by the improvement in conviction that our cause is just? By phrasing the problem in terms of a causal relation with a *reaction* as the "independent" variable we are forced into a correlational analysis, with its attendant limitations, rather than an experiment.

Data for a correlational analysis were obtained in the study of "Prelude to War." The questionnaire contained five items concerning motivation which formed a "scale" measuring eagerness to get into active service overseas. For simplicity of presentation, the results below are shown in terms of just one of the questions, which asked the men whether they would like it better, worse, or about the same if they "got into the real fighting soon." The results for this question were consistent with the scale as a whole. In the following charts illustrating the relation between various beliefs and desire for combat, the degree of belief is divided into three categories, labeled "least," "intermediate," and "most," based on the number of items in the opinion scale answered in a manner "favorable" from the standpoint of the orientation objectives.

1. *Belief that war was a military necessity.* Men with stronger conviction that war was unavoidable also expressed stronger desire to get into active service as measured by the willingness-to-fight items. This relation is illustrated below for the scale of three items

used to measure strength of belief that the war was a military necessity:

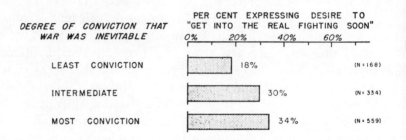

2. *Belief in an internationalistic policy.* Four questions formed a scale of strength of belief that we should follow a policy of intervention in support of oppressed countries. Men with stronger belief that we seek freedom for all countries were found to express a stronger desire to get into action overseas. This relation is illustrated below:

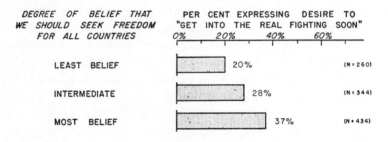

3. *Expressed resentment toward the enemy.* Degree of resentment, as indicated by expressions of aggressive feeling toward the enemy, was ascertained by a scale of four questions. The comparatively slight relationship illustrated below suggests that contrary to expectations resentment or hatred of the enemy may be of comparatively little importance in determining a man's desire for combat:

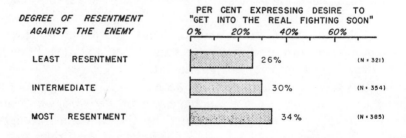

4. *Respect for the enemy's strength.* Men's appraisal of the strength of the enemy was measured in terms of the way they ranked the principal allied and enemy nations with respect to the strength of their air forces, strength of their ground forces, and the fighting ability of their individual soldiers. Men rating enemy strength high relative to ours were found to express somewhat *less* desire for combat than those giving a low rating to the strength of the enemy:

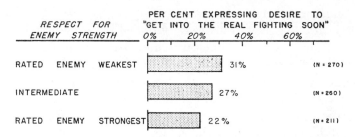

The positive correlations obtained, while not very impressive, were regarded as encouraging for the possibility of increasing motivation through orientation programs aimed at the significant opinion areas. It is interesting, however, that the largest opinion change produced by "Prelude to War" was an increase in men's estimate of enemy strength, which was a factor *negatively* correlated with motivation for active service. This suggests that the effect to be expected from the film would be *decrease* in motivation. This particular orientation objective may, therefore, have run counter to other objectives.

A more extensive correlational analysis was made in conjunction with an experimental study made of a "model" regimental orientation program carried out as part of a larger study of orientation programs in Infantry divisions and replacement training centers. This study was designed as an experiment to determine the effects of a closely supervised orientation program with, as control, an unsupervised program judged to be poor by orientation personnel. The experimental variable in this case was supposed to be a well-organized barrage of all the orientation materials and methods available. It was hoped that in this study sizable changes in both information and opinions would be achieved, providing a basis for a better check on the orientation assumptions than had previously been possible. Unfortunately, the "model" orientation program in this experiment was not as closely supervised as had been anticipated, and the experiment actually turned out in the main to be a comparison of the effectiveness of one set of orientation personnel with that of another. In any case, the large changes in information and opinion which had been expected from the "model" program did not materialize. Thus the attempt to intercorrelate changes in information, opinions, and motivation did not have much significance. However, the opportunity was provided to get extensive correlational data on the relation between initial responses on these three kinds of items. Data for these correlations were based on questionnaire responses of approximately 13,000 men in training.

Fairly sizable correlations were obtained between opinion scores and questions designed to measure motivation to serve. Not only were positive correlations found for each of a number of different motivation items, but they were also found to hold at each educational level. The relationship is illustrated in the figure below for one of the motivation areas used in the studies of the orientation films (willingness to accept the soldier role). The wording of this question was as follows:

> If it were up to you to choose, do you think you could do more for your country as a soldier or as a worker in a war job? (Check one)
>
> _____ As a soldier
> _____ As a war worker
> _____ Undecided

Opinion scores were based upon a series of ten items concerning U.S. participation in the war, the integrity of the allies, etc., selected as being representative of the areas which the Orientation Branch of the Information and Education Division believed essential.

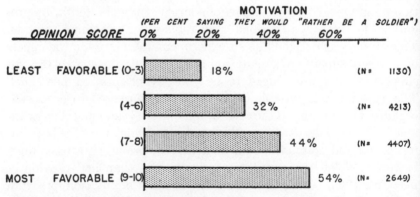

Figure 1. Relationship between opinion scores on orientation objectives and responses on an item concerning motivation.

The preceding results shown have been based on the "before" measurements and show the correlations among responses given by the men at that one point in time. Another relevant manner of phrasing the problem is in terms of whether *improvement* of one variable is associated with *improvement* in the other. The question therefore arises as to whether any different results would be obtained if *changes* from "before" to "after" were correlated. It is conceivable that where zero correlation is found between two variables there would nevertheless be positive correlations between their increments. This would be more likely where increments were produced experimentally; it would be much less frequent if the increments were merely observed, in which case it would often happen that the same factors would operate from "before" to "after" as operated in causing the correlation initially. Correlations of changes may be called "dynamic" to distinguish them from the "static" correlation just shown.

Results concerning the correlation between changes in opinion and changes in motivation are shown in the figure below, based on data from the same study of orientation quoted above. The changes in opinion scores are the differences between the individual's "before" and "after" scores on the series of ten opinion items referred to above. The associated changes in motivation show the per cent of individuals for a given category of opinion change who changed their responses to "would rather be a soldier" on the question concerning their willingness to accept the soldier role.

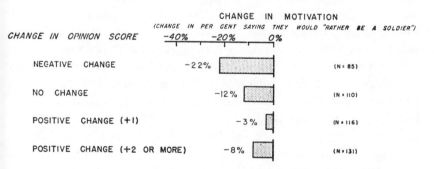

Figure 2. Relationship between change in opinion scores on orientation objectives and change in response on an item concerning motivation.

A tendency is shown for "improved" opinion to be correlated with increased motivation. It is to be noted, however, that in each category of opinion change the changes in motivation are negative—i.e., more of the men shifted *away* from the alternative "would rather be a soldier" than shifted *toward* it. Nevertheless, the greater the positive change in opinion, the less the "deterioration" in motivation. Presumably an overall tendency existed for men to become less highly motivated with increased service, but this "deterioration" is less for men whose opinion changes are in a positive direction.

Correlational data such as these obviously cannot provide conclusive evidence concerning causal relationships. "Static" correlations can exist between two factors which are not directly causally connected, due to the operation of some third factor. For example, incomes may be highly correlated with years of education, but an individual's income may not be the result of education—rather, the individual's income *and* education may both have been determined by the socio-economic status of his parents, and thus a positive correlation between education and income is indirectly produced. On the other hand, correlation between two variables may be absent even though a true causal relationship exists between them. For example, it might be true that "liberalism" is increased by education, but that no correlation is obtained between education and liberalism. This could occur if those with higher economic status tend to be more conservative due to family influences but also furnish a higher proportion of the better educated individuals.

Similarly, "dynamic" correlations are subject to the same kinds of limitations. Thus, an observed positive correlation of increments in two variables may be produced by increments in a third variable. And the correlation between increments may be zero, even though changes in one variable actually cause changes in the other. For example: the Army's indoctrination program may have a favorable effect on "morale," but amount of indoctrination may show a zero correlation with morale due to the fact that the amount of indoctrination a man has been exposed to depends primarily on how long he has been in the Army. But the longer the individual is in the Army, the more his morale may be adversely affected through disillusionment about Army life. Hence in the correlation of increments a real causal relationship between indoctrination and "morale" may be obscured by a third factor.

On the average, "dynamic" correlations will tend to be smaller than "static" ones for corresponding variables, due to the fact that correlation is affected by the reliability of measurement; in the case of "dynamic" correlations the unreliability of both the "before" and the "after" measurements are compounded. In the extreme case, even with a causal relationship actually existing between two variables unreliability may produce chance increments and decrements which are therefore uncorrelated.

While correlations (whether "static" or "dynamic") are not crucial evidence concerning the presence or absence of causal relationships, it seems likely that on an actuarial basis, correlation is more apt to be found where a real causal relationship exists and conversely that causal relationship is more apt to exist where correlation is obtained. In any case the data contribute to the empirical evidence respecting the implications which follow from a particular formulation of the relationship between variables.

On the basis of these considerations it can only be said that the foregoing correlational analyses incline the balance in the direction of indicating that motivation is directly related to the opinions stressed by the orientation program. Thus it seems likely that if a more effective method of changing opinion had been available, improvement in motivation might have been produced, despite the fact that with the type of information program actually employed little overall effect was observed on either opinion or motivation.

CHAPTER 4

THE AUDIENCE'S EVALUATION
OF FILMS

CHAPTERS 2 and 3 dealt entirely with the experimental determination of the effects of orientation films. This was done by making a comparison of questionnaire results of an experimental and a control group without the awareness of either group that the film was being tested. These experimental findings constituted the chief basis for evaluating the films; they revealed the extent to which the films actually accomplished their objectives of changing the men's motivation, opinions, and factual knowledge. However, it was also of interest to know how the *audience* evaluated a film—that is, what they thought of the film from the standpoint of interest, authenticity, and so forth. As was suggested in the introductory chapter of the book, the audience's criticisms are often useful in the overall evaluation of the effectiveness of educational films and in getting ideas for product improvement.

The function of getting the audience's "reactions" to an educational film has frequently been misconstrued. Perhaps because the "reaction" at sneak previews of a new feature picture may provide useful evidence about the ultimate box-office success of a movie, there is a tendency to think that the critical test of any film is what the audience thinks of it. In the case of most educational films, however, the best criterion of success is not whether the audience *approves* of a film but rather whether the audience *learns* from it. This cannot be determined from the audience's approval or disapproval, nor can it be determined by asking the audience how much they learned. It can be determined only from an experiment utilizing a test of performance on whatever is to be learned.

Even though audience "reactions" do not serve directly as criteria of effectiveness, they may often be relevant factors in a film's educational value. A likely hypothesis is that an interesting film that captures the audience's attention will teach better than a dull film, which may tend to put the audience to sleep or start them daydreaming. On the other hand, it is conceivable that the interest value of a film may detract from its educational effects. For example, an animated cartoon might be much more interesting and entertaining as a film vehicle than a serious documentary presentation, but the cartoon might have little educational effects because it was *too entertaining*—the audience might be "set" to be amused rather than to learn and the message of the animated cartoon might be lost completely. Thus interest and the various ways of arousing interest may be important factors to relate to educational effects even though interest is not an adequate criterion of effectiveness.

Another likely hypothesis is that if the members of the audience doubt the authenticity or honesty of the film, or believe the film has an ulterior motive in its efforts to teach them, they will be more resistant to its influence. A documentary film that is regarded as "propaganda" by the audience would be expected to have less effect than one not so regarded, and the effect of a given film might be increased if the parts of it that stimulate the audience members to label it "propaganda" are cut or altered. On the other hand it may be that under certain conditions an audience can be affected just as much when it feels it is being propagandized as when it feels that an honest presentation without ulterior motives is being given. At least it has been shown that people can be influenced by material they know to be propaganda.[1] Again it is not justifiable to use the audience's evaluation as an index of effectiveness of the film as an educational device but the evaluations may be an important variable to relate to effectiveness.

To the extent that audience evaluations are related to effects they are of particular value because they are fairly specifically tied to film content. The audience members can frequently specify what things in the film they liked and disliked, or what made them think it was propaganda. This information can be used as a basis for "cleaning up" a particular film, and, over a series of films, can be used as a basis for arriving at inductive generalizations about factors that affect audiences in a particular way.

Research on audience evaluations can take two main forms: an attempt to find out what kinds of comments by the audience are

---

[1] Collier, R. M. "The Effect of Propaganda Upon Attitude Following a Critical Examination of the Propaganda Itself." *J. Soc. Psychol.*, 1944, *20*, 3–17.

related to effects of the films and an attempt to arrive at generalizations about what kinds of film contents elicit desirable and undesirable comments by the audience.

ANALYSIS OF AUDIENCE EVALUATIONS OF THE ORIENTATION FILMS

In each of the orientation film studies, evaluations by the audience were obtained by questionnaire responses or by group interviews of men who had seen the film. The main purpose of obtaining these audience-evaluation data was to provide the film-makers with information which would assist them in producing films better calculated to win the *approval* of their soldier audience. For this purpose, part of the research took the very simple form of getting the significant approval and disapproval responses of the men for a given film, classifying them according to the content of the criticisms and origin in the film, and preparing a report composed mainly of quotations of typical comments, with a rough indication of frequency. In addition, an attempt was made to keep track of any categories of criticisms that recurred with successive films, in which case there would be a presumptive basis for making generalizations applying to future production of all such films.

Similar audience-evaluation studies were also made of a series of "general interest" films in which the interest and approval of the audience were the main criteria of the success of the films and where there was, consequently, no experimental measurement of effects.

The other phase of the research was an attempt to relate audience evaluations to orientation film effects. For this purpose audience evaluations were obtained at the end of the same questionnaires used for the experimental evaluation of the orientation films. In this way individuals' comments about the films could be related to experimentally determined effects of the films in changing their information and opinions.

In the present chapter, material from both phases of audience-evaluation research on orientation films will be presented. A description will also be given of the evaluation procedure and results for the study of a series of "general interest" films.

Procedures Used to Study Audience Evaluations of Orientation Films

1. *Questionnaires.* Always included in the questionnaires used for the experimental study were several items permitting the mem-

bers of the group who had seen the picture to record their reactions to it. These items were introduced by the question: "During the last two weeks did you see any of the movies on the history of the war that were shown to men here in camp?" This was followed by a question asking the men to designate what the film was about. This insured that they actually were talking about the film being studied rather than one of a number of training films or commercial features they might have seen. (As part of the experimental design, other orientation films were not shown to any of the men involved during the period of the experiment.) To avoid having the mention of the film affect the men's answers to other questions, these items about the film were put at the very end of the questionnaire. Particularly useful were the men's statements as to whether they liked the film, what they thought its purpose to be, and whether they believed it gave a true picture of the facts. Inclusion of items on these topics in the experimental schedule not only was economical (in that film evaluations and experimental results were obtained from the same samples of men) but also permitted analysis of the relationship between the men's evaluation of the film and its effect upon them.

Another type of questionnaire, used in obtaining audience evaluations in the study of Film 2, was a short questionnaire made up primarily of questions about the film. In this case, of course, the men involved were not used as experimental subjects. They were shown the film and then told that the film-makers wanted to know in some detail what they thought of it. This procedure permitted detailed questioning on many aspects of the film and had the practical advantage of getting extensive comments economically from a large sample, an advantage lacking in the interview procedure to be described next.

2. *Procedure with group interviews.* To supplement written comments by the men, personal interviews were also employed. It was found that for the purpose of getting ideas for improvement of the films and for discovery of some of the detailed reactions to the film, group interviews were fairly successful. In addition to the economy of time involved in using group interviews instead of individual ones, the group interviews provided social stimulation in getting men to express their opinions.

For this purpose a sample of about 150 men was selected so as to be a roughly representative cross section with respect to age, education, etc. These men were not a part of the experimental group who saw the film but were given a separate film showing. After the film showing, these men were assembled in groups of 10 to 12 men each and questioned about their reactions to the films. It appeared to work out well to have the groups composed of about this size although no comparisons with larger or smaller groups were made. Each interview group was fairly homogeneous with respect to intelligence as indicated by the men's educational level and by their scores on the Army General Classification Test. Experience indicated that in more heterogeneous groups the tendency was for the better educated and more articulate members of the group to do all of the talking, leaving little indication of the reaction of less intelligent and less articulate men.

The setting for the interviews was usually a camp recreation hall, with the men and the interviewers seated informally around in a circle. Considerable effort was made to keep the situation as informal as possible by encouraging the men to smoke, providing comfortable chairs, etc. The groups were interviewed successively by the same personnel rather than concurrently by different interviewers. Thus it was possible to accumulate experience as the interviews progressed and follow up leads obtained with early groups. The first group was generally started immediately after the film and successive groups were scheduled on the hour. Thus the time after seeing the film was variable from group to group but was brief relative to the time interval used in the experimental investigation. It was felt that the function of the interviews was best served if the details of the picture were still fairly fresh in the minds of the men.

As soon as a group had assembled for an interview, a brief introduction designed to gain as much rapport as possible was given by one of the interviewers, who explained that the purpose of the interview was to get men's criticisms and ideas about the film in order to assist the film producers in making better films in the future. It was found advisable to assure the men that the interviewers were not themselves the producers of the films, and to use other devices to encourage the men to be as uninhibited and critical as possible.

Before the beginning of the interview proper, the men filled out a short questionnaire. This permitted obtaining an independent appraisal by each man before he had heard the evaluation of the other men in the group, and also permitted correlating biographical data asked for on the questionnaire with the statements made in the interview. Once the interviewing was started, all questions and answers were recorded by a stenographic team seated unobtrusively in the background. In order to get responses that were as unbiased as possible by the type of questions asked, the interviews were opened with extremely general questions to which men's responses were obtained before proceeding to more specific points. These general questions inquired as to whether the men had liked or disliked the film and why; what had impressed them the most about it; what they felt they had learned from the film; how they thought the film could be improved; what particular things about the film they had liked or disliked, and so forth. Answers to these general questions usually led into more specific questions. The framework for asking the latter was provided by making an advance outline of the points which the interviewer wanted to get at (including probes to get at men's possible negative reactions to specific sequences in the film). Additional questions were asked to get at more details concerning revealing remarks, sometimes of an unexpected character, that men made during the course of the interview, or to get the reaction of the other men in the group to a comment made by one of the men.

Results of Audience Evaluations of the Films

The findings presented here are from the questionnaire items dealing with the film and the comments of the men in the group interviews. Data for all four of the orientation films studied are included wherever available. In general, the results are presented topically rather than by source, so that data bearing on a particular question, such as interest or skepticism of the films, are presented together rather than being taken up separately for different films and different interview or questionnaire sources.

1. *Liking for the film.* At the end of the experimental questionnaires, following the previously mentioned questions about whether the men saw a film on the history of the war and what the film was about, was this question: "If you saw one of the camp movies mentioned above, did you like it?" Of those indicating they saw the film, the proportions checking each of the answer categories are shown below for Film 4 and for Films 2 and 3 combined.[2]

---

[2] Results for "Prelude to War" are omitted because different answer categories— that did not discriminate sufficiently—were used. On the basis of the "Prelude to War" results it was found necessary to break the "like" category into "very much" and "fairly well" in order to make the question more discriminating by reducing the proportion choosing the superlative category.

DISTRIBUTION OF RESPONSES

Answer categories	Film 4: "The Battle of Britain"	Films 2, 3: "The Nazis Strike" and "Divide and Conquer"
Yes, very much	77%	64%
Yes, fairly well	16	25
No, not very much	4	5
No, not at all	2	5
No answer	1	1
	100%	100%

Favorable results of this sort are always reassuring to the producers, but difficult to interpret. The frequencies are meaningful only if the same question is asked of comparable audiences for a series of films. Then variations may indicate real differences in preference. However, in the present instance only an approximation of the desired conditions was possible. Audiences of the different films were not strictly comparable. Furthermore, it is possible that the interest of men shown a series of films might have increased (or decreased) progressively, although their interest in any one of the films (had they not seen the series) might not have been noticeably different from the others. Given the present conditions, we can only say that the results suggest that "The Battle of Britain" was better liked than "The Nazis Strike" and "Divide and Conquer," but the results must be considered in the light of the limitations mentioned.

Since the great majority of the men liked the films, a special analysis was made of the minority who said they did *not* like them. As compared to men who said they liked the films, those who did *not* like them tended on the whole to be less well educated, to have foreign-born parents (particularly from Axis countries), to come from smaller cities and towns, and to have isolationist attitudes. In the case of "The Battle of Britain" the men in the "dislike" group were also more likely to feel that they ought to be civilians rather than in the Army and to blame Britain for our entering the war.

In response to a further question "What did you like about the film?" a great many interesting comments were obtained. Most of these merely expressed principal content themes of the picture in the men's own words. The comments were classified and turned over to the makers of the films to give them the men's own ways of expressing ideas and their detailed reactions to various parts of the film, as a guide to possible changes in later films in the series.

2. *Fairness of presentation.* To get information as to men's evaluation of the truthfulness of one of the films ("The Battle of Britain"), the following question was asked: "If you saw one of these movies [referred to in a previous question], did you think it gave a fair and accurate picture of events?" The distribution of answers to the three check-list categories among men who reported seeing the film is shown below:

65% checked "Yes, it gave a true picture of what was happening."

33 checked "It was true in most respects but it seemed to give a one-sided point of view at times."

2 checked "No, it did not give a really true and honest picture of the facts."

_____

100% total

This question has some of the same difficulties of interpretation as the question about how well the men liked the film. However, if taken at face value it indicates that the great majority of the men accepted the film as either mostly or completely fair and accurate in its presentation of the events. The same general tendency was shown in answers given in supplementary film-evaluation questionnaires concerning Film 2, "The Nazis Strike." The men were asked the question, "Do you feel that the film . . . shown here gives a true picture of the facts about the war, or do you think it gives an untrue and one-sided picture?" Of those answering, 81 per cent checked "a true picture of the facts," 18 per cent checked "mostly facts, but a little untrue or one-sided in places," and less than 1 per cent checked "mostly untrue or one-sided."

3. *Manipulative purpose.* In the study of "The Battle of Britain," an item was also included asking men: "What do you think was the reason for showing this movie to you and the other men?" This question was accompanied by space to write in an answer rather than having a check list of answer categories, and its purpose was to permit those men who suspected the film of being propaganda, or who suspected they were being "guinea pigged," to write in an appropriate comment. It was expected that this question would raise no suspicions in the minds of those men who had none but would be used as a vehicle for expressing suspicions among men who already had them.

The majority of answers were classifiable simply as statements that the reason was to teach them the facts of the war. A code category was established which classified all answers that implied a manipulative motive to the film showing exclusive of the attempt to teach historical facts. Such answers as "to raise our morale," "to improve the fighting spirit," "to make us want to kill those sons of bitches," "just for propaganda," etc., were included in this category. With this classification, 27 per cent of the answers suggested that the film had as its purpose some aim of manipulating the attitudes and motives of the men. Only a negligible proportion of these answers used the word "propaganda" in their statement of what they thought were the reasons for showing them the film. Evidence of this sort is useful in indicating whether or not a substantial proportion of an audience believes that the film was propagandistic. The evidence in this study indicates that in terms of either the falsification connotation or the manipulative aspect of "propaganda" the film was not regarded as propagandistic by the great majority of the men.

4. *Interview comments on propagandistic aspects.* Although only a minority of the men criticized the films as partly or wholly propagandistic, this minority might be regarded as a particularly important segment of the total audience. These men were for the most part in the better educated group who are more articulate and perhaps more likely to influence the reactions of their fellows to the film. For this reason, it appeared useful to investigate in the group interviews the particular types of content or aspects of presentation which tended to evoke the reaction that the films were propagandistic in their method or intent. It was felt that to the extent that criticism tends to cluster around particular procedures which may recur from film to film, the already small proportion of individuals making this criticism might be further reduced to a significant degree by correcting the types of things that appear likely to lead to a "propaganda" reaction.

In the interviews, as in the questionnaires, the great majority of opinion was favorable to the films and few of the men volunteered statements that the films were propagandistic. But when such a comment was volunteered, it was fairly intensively followed up with questions directed to all members of the group. If the subject was not brought up by one of the men, the question was raised and followed up by the interviewer before the end of a session.

It was observed that the term "propaganda" had several meanings for the men. In general, the two principal interpretations were these: first, *untruthful or biased presentation*—distortion of facts;

and, second, a *manipulative purpose* or motive in showing the films, regardless of whether the attempted manipulation is accomplished by presenting only factually accurate material or also uses false or misleading material. In interview and questionnaire comments, in fact, the word "propaganda" appears to be used relatively infrequently; more often, comments that indicated questioning of either the authenticity or the purpose of the film were made without use of this term. The quotations that follow are representative examples of the kinds of comments made. The reader should be reminded that these comments are not typical of most comments about the films but restricted to those few comments elicited about the propaganda aspects. The majority of the quotations shown are from the stenographic records of the men's spoken comments during the interviews rather than from the preliminary questionnaires filled out by the interview groups. Some of these remarks were spontaneous, some were in response to another man's comments on propaganda aspects of the film, and some were made after a deliberate attempt by the interviewers to lead the discussion around to the subject of propaganda by direct or indirect questions.

(a) *"One-sidedness"*: A fairly frequent criticism of the films, related to men suspecting them of propagandistic or manipulative intent, was that the films were "one-sided." Films 2 and 3 which showed the Nazi conquest of Western Europe were occasionally criticized as showing "only part of the picture." Some men objected that the film showed only the strength of the enemy, and that *our* military strength should have been portrayed also. Similar criticisms were made of the first film, "Prelude to War":

This picture shows the enemy as being pretty strong, but we have as much or more power than they have.

The fact of our enemy's strength instead of showing theirs—show a little of what we have.

Comment suggesting "one-sidedness" in a more general sense appeared less frequently. The following quotation is illustrative:

If all circumstances were laid bare . . . would the picture still convey your meaning?

The criticism of one-sidedness came up quite frequently with respect to the fourth film, "The Battle of Britain," where it took the form that British losses were deliberately underplayed.

It was one-sided.   It never showed any English planes being shot down.

I think that it is too much like fiction when it is too one-sided.   It does not seem
possible . . . because it was so lopsided.   A few planes go up to destroy a large
number of planes and the small number return whereas the large number is de-
feated.

There was only one English plane that fell during the picture and mostly German
planes went down.   I believe they should show more of the British losses.

   (b) *Repetitious shots:* Consistently criticized from film to film in
indicating what parts of the film seemed "fake" or "untrue" was
repeated use of identical or nearly identical scenes in the visual
material.   For example, some of the men felt that the action shots
of planes in combat, both in "The Battle of Britain" and other
films, were padded by using the same shot over and over.

There was too much repetition of scenes that were first filled in to make a picture.
It was too noticeable, such as the shattering of a wing section of a plane shown
over and over.

Where the British pilots shot down the German planes it looked in the picture
like the same picture was used.

The picture itself had too much repetition like a propaganda picture.   Those
parts that were filled in like the four shots just the same of a wing section on the
plane being torn away.

   (c) *"Exaggeration," "unrealistic" or "overdramatic" presentation:*
The theme of the calm, courageous spirit with which the British
met the Nazi attack was generally highly effective throughout "The
Battle of Britain."   But certain of the sequences came in for criticism as being overdone.

Was the spirit of the British people really as light as the picture indicated?

Did the people of England take everything as calm as the movie shows?

   In this connection the scenes showing the fortitude of the people
as a whole were not questioned.   Scenes of the British people in
large groups seemed real, but shots involving individual reactions
were suspected of having "the Hollywood touch."

The scenes were more like they were acted.   The whole groups of English people
seemed real, but the old man and woman and a couple of others seemed just a
little bit too dramatized.

It looked faked. You'd think they had a camera all set up to take it. [Referring to a humorous shot of two men repairing a cable during a London air raid—a shot which was otherwise generally approved.]

Such comments also appeared, less frequently, with respect to the other films of the series.

(d) *Source of film materials:* A consistent and relatively frequent basis for expressed suspicion of the films arose from men's apparent inability to understand where certain pictorial sequences had been obtained. This basis for suspicion appeared with appreciable frequency for every film on which group interviews were conducted. To counteract this reaction some of the later orientation films carried an explicit introductory statement indicating that the source of many of the pictures was "captured enemy film." The effectiveness of such an initial explanation is a matter for speculation, since no tests were made of parallel presentations of any film with and without this description of the source of the material.

Questions as to the source of film material occurred with greatest frequency concerning pictures taken in enemy territory. Some men concluded that any pictures showing the enemy in enemy territory must have been faked. To such men all captured footage was regarded as unauthentic. Many who did not think of the pictures as actually faked were curious as to how they could have been obtained, and often skeptical.

Those pictures of Hitler and Goering mapping out plans . . . how did they get them?

Are the scenes depicting the German Air Force authentic or are they of the Hollywood style?

I do not believe some of these were really pictures of Hitler—just men made to look like Hitler.

I don't think they were real . . . because if anyone would get that close to him [Hitler] they would shoot him.

(e) *Close-up shots in combat:* A related form of criticism occurring in the case of "The Battle of Britain" was that when the film portrayed action close-ups some men wondered how a cameraman could get such pictures. Often they concluded these must have been Hollywood production shots. In some cases this conclusion was correct since occasionally the story was tied together with production footage as in a scene showing the reaction of German fliers to the British attack.

Most people know that those planes are so fast that it would be impossible to get those close-up shots of enemy pilots.

How could they film the actual men in a German bomber?

In other instances, however, the men criticized shots merely because they did not know that most fighter planes carried cameras that were synchronized with the machine guns to verify enemy losses and to instruct fighter pilots.

I heard several fellows say they wondered how those pictures were taken when it showed the RAF and the Nazis in dogfights.

(f) *Favorable reactions to "propaganda":* Not infrequently when the question of propaganda was raised a favorable reaction to propaganda in the film was obtained. Some men felt the film contained propaganda but thought this was necessary or desirable.

I think the picture is well presented with the touch of propaganda that every war film needs to keep morale up. Too much propaganda is out, though.

I think there is some propaganda mixed in every now and then to help bolster morale. It had just enough.

5. *Men's suggestions for improving the film.* In the preliminary questionnaire of the interview groups, questions were asked concerning the men's suggestions as to what should be taken out or added to the films to improve them. These items were found to have very limited usefulness. The men did not view the picture as critics and asking them afterwards to assume such a role led to sterile replies. Most frequently they merely said the film was "O.K." and that nothing should be taken out or added to it.

Product-improvement suggestions dealt mainly with film content, although occasionally comments on the technical aspects of the film were made. These two categories of comments are illustrated by material from the group interviews in the study of "Prelude to War."

I would like to have understood more clearly why the Allied nations did not prepare for war too.

Some might be added on the rise of the different dictators to power. How they achieved such great power.

Hard to hear. Speaker voice too mild. A poor movie, from a professional standpoint. Good subject matter tho.

Of the comments made, many were contradictory: for example, some men suggested in the study of "The Battle of Britain" that more be shown on British planes and equipment and less on civilian participation; others said exactly the opposite.

6. *Attempts to infer effects from audience-evaluation responses.* The interest in interview comments was sometimes so great that the producer tended to infer from the comments the nature of the effects of films on attitudes, opinions, and factual information. Obviously, however, such interview data constitute an inadequate method for determining these effects of a film. Group interviews could possibly be used as an alternative to questionnaires as a means of measuring responses, but it would be necessary to have control interview groups that had not seen the film as a baseline against which to determine the film's effects, and direct mention of the film would have to be omitted in both the control and the experimental interviews. This is quite a different situation from the present one in which the film is the topic of discussion and there is no control group.

In some instances, effects suspected on the basis of group interviews were actually found when the results for the experimental measurements were analyzed, but in other cases suspected effects, which some of the interviewers fully expected to materialize on the basis of what men said at interviews, were completely absent in the experimental data.

For example, the frequent comments of the men about the effect of the film on their "fighting spirit" led some interviewers to expect sizable effects of the film on men's willingness to fight. Comments of the following type were very often obtained:

The film was very stirring. I was fighting mad at the brutality of the Nazis.

It made me feel like killing a bunch of those sons-of-bitches.

But experimental measurement with questions about combat service showed that no real change had occurred in the percentage expressing willingness to get into combat. It is, of course, possible that the films sometimes had the effect of intensifying already existing attitudes such as the desire to retaliate against the Nazis, without increasing the number of men holding such attitudes. This could not be proved or disproved by the present studies, due to the absence of adequate measures of intensity of feeling.

As another example, interview comments suggested that many of the men interviewed after seeing "The Battle of Britain" had an exaggerated idea of the extent of American aid to Britain, and that one or two scenes in the film created or bolstered a conviction that the United States had won the Battle of Britain by providing the material used to defeat the Nazis.   Such comments as the following were not infrequent:

I think they can thank the good old States that they are alive.   Everything in the fight came from this country.

The point was brought out in the picture that all these countries that are fighting Germany are fighting with U.S. equipment.

Tomahawks and Spitfires are both made in this country.   In other words we are sending the goods to England to keep them in the war.

The inference from interviews that an effect on this belief had been produced by the film was checked experimentally when the study was conducted at the second camp.   The question used was:

As you remember it, how much lend-lease aid was England getting from the United States when the Nazis started bombing England after the fall of France?   (Check one)

	Control	Film	Difference
_____ a great deal	44%	38%	−6%
_____ a little	36	40	4
_____ none at all	3	4	1
_____ haven't any idea	17	18	1

The film produced no increase on this question in estimates of the actual amount of aid we had sent to the British.   As in various other instances, the impression gained from the interviews as to the men's ideas about the amount of aid sent by the United States was probably based on expressions of opinion by men who already held this point of view before seeing the film, rather than on effects of the film.   The incorrect notion that we were giving much aid to Britain at the time of the German attacks was common before the film showing; its high frequency during the interviews was mistakenly interpreted as an effect of the film.

Relation of Audience Evaluation to Effects of Films

The foregoing results show degree of liking and disliking of the films, skepticism and lack of it, and indicate some of the contents that are singled out by the men as reasons for suspicion of the authenticity of the presentation. Such data help relate audience evaluations to film contents. However, as mentioned earlier, there is the additional problem of relating audience evaluations to the teaching effectiveness of the films.

On a priori grounds, we would of course expect these factors to be of influence. Interest would be expected to bear a relation to effects, whether the purpose of the film was to produce attitude changes or to transmit factual information. An extreme example of the relevance of interest to attention was the situation obtaining with certain Army training subjects which were compulsory and were not "sold" as being important. It was observed that typically a significant number of the soldier trainee audience would sleep through an entire session of training films.

The additional factors of confidence in the integrity of the presentation (as opposed to skepticism of the film's authenticity and purpose) might be expected to be particularly significant where the film had the purpose of obtaining acceptance of interpretation of facts, i.e., of modifying opinion.

The analysis which follows is based on an orientation-film study in which effects were related to audience evaluations. Since there was no external motivation the film's effectiveness should be maximally affected by interest, and since a major concern was with changes in *opinion*, acceptance or skepticism would be expected to be important.

1. METHODOLOGICAL CONSIDERATIONS

The analysis requires the use of an experimental design in which questionnaires are given both before and after the showing of the film. This design is required because men with different evaluations of the film generally have different opinions on the subject presented by the film. The experience in the orientation-film studies was that initial responses on the significant opinions (related to the content of the film) generally differed among men who differed in their evaluations on such topics as whether they liked the film, whether they thought it truthful, whether they thought it was for propaganda purposes, and so forth. Thus it would be necessary to compare the various subgroups with their *counterparts* in the control group rather than with the control group as a whole, and it was not possible to identify in the control group those men who *would have* liked or disliked the film, thought it truthful, etc., if they had seen it. With the before-after procedure the initial attitudes of the members of each group are known so the men can serve as their own controls.

It should be pointed out, however, that even with the before-after design, the control is always partly incomplete in comparing two groups who have different evaluations of the film. While each man serves as his own control, there is no control on possible *differential effects due to other causes than the film* among the different evaluation subgroups. If it is found, for example, that men who thought the film was propaganda were less changed than other men in the period between the "before" and "after" measurements, it is nevertheless possible that this difference might reflect the differential effect of some outside cause that operates selectively on these two kinds of men. Complete control on outside causes is not possible for the reason already mentioned, namely, that it is not possible to identify in a control group, which did not see the film, those men who would give the designated evaluations if they had seen the film.

A further possible difficulty with using each man as his own control is that obtained shifts in response due to transient mood changes may be correlated with the evaluations of the film, giving rise to a spurious factor in the analysis. Suppose, for example, a respondent filling out the "after" questionnaire in the study of the "Battle of Britain" feels in a generous mood. As a result he gives more pro-British answers than before, and at the same time gives a favorable evaluation of the film. Another respondent with an opposite mood may swell the ranks of those who changed to more anti-British responses and at the same time give the film an unfavorable evaluation. The spurious factor is this correlation of errors in responses to the two kinds of questions, those measuring effects and those measuring evaluations. It seems probable that this spurious factor is small or absent—i.e., that absence of correlation in errors of measurement would be the general rule. To the extent that such a factor is present, however, it cannot be separated from correlation of true evaluations and true changes in opinion if one merely uses each man as his own control. This is one of the weaknesses inherent in correlational as contrasted with experimental analysis.

2. EFFECTS FOR SUBGROUPS WHO "LIKED" AND "DISLIKED" THE FILM

All of the data here presented come from the before-after study (one camp) of the effects of "The Battle of Britain." As already noted, the question used in determining overall approval was the simple one as to whether the individual "liked" the film or not, with the answer categories, "very much," "fairly well," "not very much," or "not at all." For the purposes of analysis, men in the film group who had indicated in answer to a preceding question on the questionnaire that they remembered having seen the film, "The Battle of Britain," were sorted into these four response categories. Changes from before to after for a selection of eleven opinion items were determined for each of these groups. These items were selected on the basis of being judged by the analysts to be definite expressions of pro-British or anti-British attitudes. The effect of the film was measured simply in terms of after-minus-before differences for each subgroup because of the aforementioned lack of control subgroups. On the basis of preliminary examination of the data, the "very much" and "fairly well" groups were combined as being essentially alike in the effect of the film. The "not very much" and "not at all" groups were also combined because of the very small numbers of cases (26 men in all!). The two combined groups thus formed are referred to below as "like" and "dislike" groups. The data for effect of the film in terms of after-minus-before differences for the film subgroups are shown in the tabulation below:

TABLE 1

EFFECT OF FILM ON GROUPS WHO LIKED AND DID NOT LIKE THE FILM

	PER CENT DIFFERENCE, AFTER-MINUS-BEFORE IN FILM GROUP	
Content of opinion item	"Like" Subgroup (N = 288)	"Dislike" Subgroup (N = 26)
1. Best fighting job was done by RAF	15	7
2. British did well at Singapore	0	−20
3. British not taking it easy	4	−4
4. British had done much more fighting than we	−3	−4
5. British kept us from bombing	11	−4
6. British saved U.S. from fighting on home soil	6	−15
7. British doing all they can	9	−4
8. British will make just peace	7	4
9. British fighting for freedom for all	7	−4
10. Britain deserves most credit for holding off the Axis	9	4
11. RAF gave Nazis their first defeat	23	23
Mean difference:	8.0%	−1.5%
		P Diff. <.02
Mean index of effect*	17%	−3%

* Average difference expressed as a proportion of the maximum change that could have occurred in the direction indicated by the difference.

Giving each person a difference score in number of pro-British responses before and after the film, the mean difference for the "dislike" group ($-.16$) is reliably smaller (beyond the 1 per cent confidence level) than the mean difference for the "like" group (.88). Also, the result was consistently obtained from item to item, the "dislike" group showing less positive effect for 10 of the 11 items. Thus the expected relation between approval and effect was obtained. It should be remembered, however, that the analysis is subject to the methodological difficulties previously mentioned—a genuine control is not possible.

The significance of the findings hinges in part on the extent to which approval or disapproval depends on agreement with, or disagreement with, the interpretations presented in the film versus the extent to which approval can be obtained without altering the basic interpretations. Thus, can pro-British arguments be presented to anti-British individuals without arousing disapproval for the presentation? If this is possible, then it may be possible to improve the effects of a presentation by procedures that increase the amount of approval it obtains. From the present finding we can only say that effects and approval were positively correlated, which may only mean that those strongly opposed to the interpretations were not influenced to change their opinions because of their opposition and did not like the film for the same reason. The present analysis does not untangle the causal relations between the material presented, the approval or disapproval obtained, and the opinion changes produced. The kind of experimental analysis required will be discussed after the presentation of the relation between opinion changes and evaluations by the audience as to the authenticity or the "propagandistic" nature of the film presentation.

3. EFFECTS AS A FUNCTION OF SKEPTICISM OF THE FILM

The extent to which interpretations such as would be represented by changes in men's opinions are influenced by a film obviously depends not only on *learning* of the material—but also on the *acceptance* of the material presented. Men might have learned what the film *said*, but if the film presentation were viewed with skepticism or suspicion they might not accept the interpretation as the correct one.

In orientation material of the type studied in the "Why We Fight" films, suspicion of the material would be related to men's ideas of *propaganda*. As indicated earlier, this term might mean to them either falsity of the material presented, or the intent to manipulate or influence their beliefs in a particular direction, or both. Disapproval and suspicion related to a conception of the film as propaganda in the manipulative sense might detract from the acceptance of interpretative material based on facts presented, even though the facts themselves were not questioned.

Two questions were included to tap "propaganda" reactions: a check-list question to get at the falsification aspect, and an open-ended question to get at the manipulative aspect of men's possible reactions to the film as propaganda.

a. *Relation of effects to evaluations concerning falsification.* The question aimed at the falsification aspect came at the end of the questionnaire and was worded as follows:

> If you saw one of these movies, did you think it gave a fair and accurate picture of events?
>
> _____ Yes, it gave a true picture of what was happening.
>
> _____ It was true in most respects but seemed to give a one-sided point of view at times.
>
> _____ No, it did not give a really true and honest picture of the facts.

This question was used in only half of the questionnaires as a precautionary measure in case it caused some of the men to divine the real purpose of the questionnaires and go back over their questionnaire and change their answers. It was omitted in half the cases to keep at least half the sample free of this possibility. Thus only a relatively small number of cases was available for analysis. Moreover, the distribution of answers was very unfavorable for analysis. The majority picked the first category, only 50 men (27 per cent) picked the second category and only half a dozen picked the third category. Thus the number of cases for this last group was too small to warrant analysis. The mean effect on the 50 men who said the picture's presentation was "true in most respects" did not differ significantly from the effect on the larger number who indicated that the facts presented were entirely true.

It may be that the choice of categories in the question used was unfortunate, preventing the separation of a large enough number of the more extremely suspicious men to detect a correlation between evaluations of the film's authenticity and changes in opinion. Or it may be that this aspect of the men's evaluations was unrelated to effects. At least no evidence for a relation was obtained even though the men were divided by the question into about the upper three fourths and the lowest one fourth in their confidence in the truth and fairness of the film's presentation.

b. *Relation of effects to evaluations concerning manipulative purpose.* The question asked to get at men's conception of the film as propagandistic in the sense of their conceiving its purpose to be a manipulative one was simply the open-ended question described earlier: "What did you think was the reason for showing this movie to you and the other men?" It was anticipated that an appreciable number of men would characterize the purpose of the film as "propaganda." As it turned out, however, only a very small percentage (around 4 per cent) of the men used the term "propaganda" in their comment. However, a considerably larger proportion gave answers that were classifiable as indicating a *manipulative intent* as the purpose of the film. These men were classified as regarding the film's purpose as "propagandistic," and the film's effects on this group were compared with effects on two other groups: those whose answers either indicated a purely informational or educational function, and those who gave ambiguous answers not so clearly falling in the "propaganda" or "informational" categories.[3]

For convenience, the three major subgroups will be referred to as the "manipulative," "ambiguous," and "informational" subgroups, in terms of the classification assigned to the answers they gave concerning the purpose of the film. The numbers of cases falling in the three major categories above were 103, 147, and 121, respectively.

Effects for these subgroups ascribing different purposes to the film were determined for five opinion items appearing in the before and after questionnaires which showed significant over-all effects of the film. The results are shown below.

Comparison of the effects shown in the next table indicates *less effect* for those who imputed a "propagandistic" or "manipulative" purpose to the film than for those who characterized the reason for showing the film in terms of an "informational" purpose or gave

---

[3] Illustrative answers classed as *manipulative*: "make us work harder," "build up morale," "make us hate the enemy." Illustrative *informational or educational* answers: "give us information about the cause of the war," "show what was happening," "show us what to expect in the war." Answers classed as *ambiguous*: "show us the nature of the enemy," "show us why we fight."

TABLE 2

MEANS OF RESPONSES TO FIVE OPINION ITEMS FOR SUBGROUPS DIFFERENTIATED BY
ANSWERS ON QUESTION CONCERNING "PURPOSE" OF FILM

	"Manipulative" Subgroup N = 103	"Ambiguous" Subgroup N = 147	"Informational" Subgroup N = 121
Final level (% after)	56.9%	63.5%	62.5%
Initial level (% before)	42.9	45.7	42.5
(% After minus % before)	14.0	17.8	20.0
Effectiveness index	24%	33%	35%

answers classified as "ambiguous"; the measured effects for the last
two groups did not differ greatly. The pattern of effects seen for
the overall results is also obtained when the data are tabulated separately for men of high and low educational levels. However, the
difference in "effects" between those ascribing a propaganda purpose and those ascribing other purposes to the film was especially
marked for the men with less than a complete high school education.
The data for separate education groups are shown below:

TABLE 3

MEAN EFFECTS ON FIVE OPINION ITEMS BROKEN DOWN BY EDUCATIONAL
STATUS

	"Manipulative" Subgroup	"Ambiguous" Subgroup	"Informational" Subgroup
Low education men (grade school, some high school)			
Final level (% after)	50.1%	65.8%	64.0%
Initial level (% before)	45.3	53.1	49.0
(% After minus % before)	4.8	12.7	15.0
Effectiveness index	11%	24%	29%
High education men (high school graduate, college)			
Final level (% after)	63.8%	75.0%	73.6%
Initial level (% before)	48.9	55.2	52.9
(% After minus % before)	14.9	19.8	20.7
Effectiveness index	34%	32%	44%

The foregoing results appear to indicate that men who like films
learn more from them than those who do not and that men who are
skeptical of the film are less influenced than others. The results

do not, however, show that the specific material which is best liked or most accepted is that which is best learned. Such a result could not be analyzed, partly because acceptability is related to demographic variables and partly because the acceptance was not analyzed separately for the specific contents in this study of a single film.

In absence of alternative presentations which can be compared, the process of sorting men on the basis of answers to the questions as to whether they liked or disliked the film cannot be said to furnish an answer to the question, "Is material that is liked learned better than material that is not liked?" Rather, it furnishes only an answer to the question, "Did those men who liked the material learn it better?"

The best analysis to answer the question of whether greater effectiveness will result from making film material in such a way that it will be "liked" or regarded as "authentic" would appear to demand the preparation of alternative versions of film material in which the effectiveness of alternative presentations of the same material, found to differ in terms of these audience evaluation factors, is studied. However, manipulation of the extent to which men express interest or approval in the material necessarily involves making specific changes in the presentation—one cannot manipulate interest or approval directly and as such. Hence there is still a logical difficulty involved in making a clear-cut analysis of the "effect of interest" on material learned. If the problem of the relationship between audience evaluation and effect is conceived to refer to evaluation differences which are created by the manner of presentation of the specific material which it is desired to test, this logical difficulty is apparently insurmountable: whatever device or devices are introduced to manipulate degree of interest may also affect directly the effectiveness of the presentation in ways other than through the mediation of increased interest in the material.

It would appear that a rigorous answer to the question of the relation between interest and effectiveness can be obtained only when the question is asked with respect to differences in effectiveness resulting from interest-arousing contextual material that is not in itself a part of the presentation of the material to be tested. Thus, one might measure the effect of a humorous introduction to a film in arousing interest and thus facilitating the learning of factual material subsequently presented. But there would be difficulty in obtaining a rigorous measure of the influence of interest aroused by presenting a fact dramatically, since dramatic presentation of the fact would involve other changes potentially producing differential effectiveness as well as the concomitant change in interest value.

AUDIENCE EVALUATION STUDIES OF FILMS WITH A GENERAL INTEREST PURPOSE

A number of film studies were undertaken by the Experimental Section in which no experimental evaluations were made, the only measurements being the quantification of the opinions of sample audiences about the film. Some of these studies had very specialized purposes—for example, one was carried out to determine if a film explaining the Army educational program was "too Hollywood"—and are of little interest here. One series of such studies, however, is of particular interest from the standpoint of audience evaluations because the purpose of the film was stated as being simply to satisfy interests of the soldiers, and therefore for the present purposes audience evaluations were the only criteria used in determining the success of the films. With this purpose there was no problem of relating audience evaluations to effects—the audience's "reaction" itself revealed how successfully the films achieved their objectives.

The studies referred to dealt with a series of films called "The War." This was a short feature issued twice a month designed to be shown along with entertainment movies in camp theaters. Attendance at these films was voluntary, and the men were free to leave the theater at any point. Each issue was made up of five episodes. Usually four of the episodes were much like newsreel feature stories, each one being accompanied by a running narration and dealing with wartime topics of presumed general interest such as the training of a particular military branch, a well-known naval or military battle, a famous personality in the war, and so forth. Some of these episodes were of a similar kind from issue to issue and had the same title in each successive issue. For example, "Back Home" and "I Was There" were repeated titles, dealing respectively with the contribution of civilians and with individuals who had personally participated in some important action in the war. The fifth episode was generally of a humorous nature, most of these being animated cartoon comedies of the "Silly Symphony" variety, involving a character named "Snafu." These "Snafu" cartoons related the exploits of the Army's worst soldier, and each contained an implied moral in that the undesirable outcome of Snafu's behavior was portrayed.

PROCEDURES USED

For obtaining men's reactions in terms of immediate interest, it was found useful to supplement the techniques of interviews and questionnaires by use of a polygraphic recording of audience judgments of like and dislike.[4] The technique, long used in radio program testing, involves providing members of the audience, during the showing, with a pair of push-buttons, and having them indicate parts of the film they "like" by pressing one push-button and parts they "dislike" by pushing the other as they view the film.[5] The responses of the audience are electrically recorded and can be cumulated and analyzed. Since the continuous record can be related to specific portions of the film, this technique is also used, as described below, in conjunction with subsequent interviews.

The main function of the procedure is to get an appraisal of reaction to specific film content. Hence it is mainly useful when interest or enjoyment is the sole or principal criterion of a film's success. A unique advantage of the method is that it affords a continuous indication of *immediate* response to the film, rather than a retrospective reaction such as is obtained through the use of questionnaires or interviews conducted after the film showing.

1. METHODS AND PROBLEMS IN POLYGRAPH RECORDING
   OF "LIKE" AND "DISLIKE" RESPONSES

a. *General arrangements and apparatus.* Because it is believed by some motion picture producers and critics that the reaction of an audience depends to a considerable extent on its size and that reactions from small groups might differ materially from those where a large audience is present, it was felt advisable to have a fairly large group present while the reactions were being recorded. The equipment used was sufficient to record responses for 20 men at one time. These men were seated at the back of the theater. The remainder of the audience viewed the showing without push-buttons, but filled out a questionnaire about the film afterward.

---

[4] The equipment used was the Esterline-Angus, model A.W. portable operation recorder, with 20 ink-writing polygraph units.

[5] Cf. Hallonquist, T., and E. A. Suchman. "Listening to the Listener," pp. 265–334 in *Radio Research, 1943–1945* (Lazarsfeld, P. F., and F. N. Stanton, editors), New York: Duell, Sloan, and Pearce, 1944.

Each pair of push-buttons had a number corresponding to the number of its recording pen. The numbers were later used as a basis for referring to the various members of the audience in the group interviews; the "likes" and "dislikes" of individual men could be used as a basis for focusing questions on specific reasons for an individual's liking or disliking various portions of the film.

b. *Synchronization of records.* One of the procedural problems in this use of the "program-analyzer" was that of synchronizing each program-analyzer record with the script of the film. This required using a motion picture projector which ran at a constant speed.

In order to correlate program-analyzer reactions with film contents a timed "script" was prepared for each film. Ordinarily, film scripts do not include the detailed scene sequences, and last-minute improvisations are often introduced in production and cutting, so that for using the program-analyzer a final script must be made from the completed product. For this purpose the films were viewed and a detailed list of all sequences and sound effects, together with a word-for-word transcription of the narration, was prepared. This list was then timed and used as a reference in analysis of responses and in questioning the men about their reasons for pressing one or the other button at a particular time.

A specimen excerpt from such a timed list is shown below. (The sequences outlined are those from a film subject entitled "Finishing School," which showed the training of Ranger amphibious troops in invasion tactics.)

Excerpts from timed script	*Time*
Starting cue: first two notes of "Artillery Song"	0'-00"
End of Marine Hymn	0'-20"
Title: "Finishing School"	0'-25"
Men climbing on net	0'-30"
Men jumping from platform	0'-37"
Commentator: "They're toughening up for a little job ahead"	0'-47"

c. *Standardization of responses and instructions.* It is to be noted that the program-analyzer technique as described here affords no gradation of "likes" or "dislikes" of individual members of the audience, since the "like," "dislike," and "neutral" are recorded in all-or-none fashion for any one subject. It was found that there was considerable variability from subject to subject in the way in which the like and dislike buttons were employed, and that the instructions given in advance of the showing were an important feature in attempting to standardize this pattern of response. The pattern sought was for the subjects to push the right-hand button when they liked what was being shown, to hold it down as long as they liked it, and release it when they did not especially like the material; similarly, they were to press the dislike button when they disliked what was being shown and to continue to hold it down as long as they disliked the material. They were instructed to depress neither button when they had no particular feeling of liking or disliking the material, but felt neutral or indifferent towards it.

Variation in instructions was found to have marked effects both on the general level of response (frequency of pressing either like or dislike button versus neither) and on the type of evaluation made the basis for the "like" or "dislike" response. In the first film studied, in which there were a number of scenes of Japanese soldiers and other shots of the enemy, it was found that the men showed a strong tendency to press the "dislike" button (as it turned out later in interviewing these men) as an expression of disapproval of the enemy and not because they necessarily disliked *seeing the pictures* about the enemy. This necessitated emphasizing in the instructions the meaning of "like" and "dislike," and examples were given of what was *not* meant by disliking. Even with these precautions, there were occasional instances where men were found to have pressed the "dislike" button because of disapproval of the referent even though they were greatly interested in observing the film.

Another difficulty that was never completely solved was the tendency for the subjects to become so engrossed in the film when it was particularly interesting that they forgot about their push buttons. Still another problem was the tendency always to push one or the other of the two push buttons, the "neutral" category in such cases losing its meaning. No completely satisfactory instructions were worked out in the course of the studies, although it was felt that these tendencies were reduced by including in the instructions humorous examples of what not to do, thereby motivating the subjects to be superior to some of the "horrible examples" the film-testers had found in previous experience.

d. *Use of program-analyzer records as a basis for group interviews.* As mentioned previously, the program-analyzer records were sometimes used immediately after the showing as a basis for inquiring as to the reason for likes and dislikes of individual men. In doing this it was found convenient to transfer, during the showing, parts of the individual like and dislike records to a sheet which contained an outline of the timed script, together with columns for recording the responses of each individual. The overall procedure in studying the film was usually to show the film, obtaining the program-analyzer record, and to follow this immediately by a short period in which the men who had used the push buttons filled out questionnaires concerning the film. The interval while the men were filling out the questionnaires afforded time to complete the transferring of the records of individual responses from the polygraph paper to an outline such as that mentioned above. This provided the interviewer with a convenient record for use in asking questions during the group interviews which followed the filling out of the questionnaires.

2. USE OF QUESTIONNAIRES

The questionnaire filled out by men who were tested with the program-analyzer was also filled out by the rest of the audience. The purpose of this questionnaire was three-fold: (1) to get the reactions of the men who had used the program-analyzer before they heard the comments of others in the group interview, (2) to get reactions in retrospect at the end of the film as contrasted with the immediate reactions shown by the program-analyzer, and (3) to get a larger number of cases for quantitative report than was practicable with the push-button equipped groups of only 20 men per showing that was the maximum possible with the available equipment.

The questionnaire was presented as having the purpose of improving the film shown and future films by finding out for the film-makers what the soldiers themselves thought of the films. The film testers emphasized that they did not make the films and their feelings would not be hurt if the men were critical. All questionnaires were anonymous, but the men who had used the push buttons were asked to write their push-button number on their questionnaire.

The questionnaire started with an overall question about whether or not the men liked the movie and then went on to more detailed questions asking them to rank the successive episodes from most interesting to least interesting, and to tell what impressed them most, what they disliked if anything, what they thought should be taken out, how they thought the film could be improved, and so forth.

3. CONDUCT OF THE GROUP INTERVIEWS

All of the audience members filled out the questionnaire after a film showing, but only the 20 men who had used push-buttons were interviewed. All 20 were interviewed as a group, with as informal a setting as it was possible to achieve. The usual practice was to begin with nondirective questions such as "What did you think of this movie?" Unsolicited comments generally determined the direction of the questioning at the outset. Where relevant, the polygraph record was referred to and either the group was questioned about sequences that were liked or disliked by the majority, or individuals were questioned about their own responses. In addition, certain planned topics for interviewing were prepared, and if these were not spontaneously mentioned by the men, questions about them were specifically raised by the interviewer.

During the course of the studies it was found convenient to prepare still pictures of distinctive portions of the films. These could be used to make sure the interviewer knew what portion of the film a man was commenting on and similarly to identify for the men the portion the interviewer had in mind when he raised questions about specific contents. It was felt these "stills" also helped to reinstate the film content where the men's memories would otherwise be vague.

All questions asked by the interviewer and the answers and comments by the men were recorded stenographically.

REPRESENTATIVE RESULTS

Some detailed results of one of the studies of these films will be presented, followed by a summary of the inductive generalizations about the men's reactions that appear to have possible significance for the series as a whole. Actually not a large enough number of studies were carried out for these generalizations to have a great deal of validity as inductive generalizations.[6] The "conclusions" that were stressed in the reports to the film-makers were ones that had considerable plausibility in addition to having been revealed as potential generalizations by the audience's evaluations. In other words, the reasonableness of a finding carried considerable weight in determining whether it was incorporated as a guiding principle in future productions. However, the procedure, if carried out over a

---

[6] Four studies were carried out, one on each of the odd-numbered issues of the first eight films produced in the series.

large enough number of films, appears to be a highly efficient one for arriving at useful generalizations and is well adapted to product improvement of a series of fairly homogeneous films. Each production principle tentatively adopted and used in succeeding films is automatically checked and modified or discarded depending on its actual degree of generality.

1. RESULTS OF THE STUDY OF ISSUE 5 OF "THE WAR"

Issue 5 serves as a fairly typical example of the series tested. The contents were the following:

Episode a: *"Finishing School."* This showed training of amphibious (Ranger) troops in invasion tactics such as embarking and disembarking and advancing under live ammunition.

Episode b: *"Back Home."* This showed machine tools being produced by a small family shop in Connecticut which was awarded the Navy "E" for its contribution to war production.

Episode c: *"I Was There."* This featured an Army Nurse's eye-witness account of the bombing of Manila and the fall of Corregidor, with action shots to illustrate part of her commentary. The whole story was told in the nurse's voice and was introduced and concluded by shots of the nurse telling her story.

Episode d: *"First Birthday."* This documentary reviewed the founding and first year's activities of the Women's Army Corps and depicted the training and duties of Wacs.

Episode e: *"Snafu."* This was an animated cartoon showing the adventures of a comic character called "Private Snafu," whose complaints about Army routine and duties led to his magically being put in charge of the camp, with disastrous consequences.

Figure 1 on page 110 shows the overall questionnaire ratings given by the men in ranking the five episodes as units. Figure 2 on page 111 shows the moment-by-moment record of instantaneous "like" and "dislike" reactions as cumulated from the polygraphic records. In cumulating the data, a "like" reaction was scored if a given individual "like" button was depressed at any time during the recording interval (6 seconds), regardless of whether the pressure was continuous or intermittent.

Some of the results that can be seen in these two charts represent findings that were verified with other issues and therefore have at least some status as inductive generalizations. These are described below.

If Figures 1 and 2 are compared, one of the most notable observations is the discrepancy between the program-analyzer record of the interest shown in the "Snafu" cartoon and the interest in retrospect as revealed by the questionnaire. The cartoon was highest in interest in terms of the immediate reactions but ranked only third in terms of the questionnaire responses of the same men. An equivalent result was obtained in the one other film tested which had a "Snafu" cartoon. This was not due to any obvious difference in the frame of reference for the questionnaire ratings as compared with the like-dislike responses recorded during the showing, although the wording of instructions was necessarily not the same in the two cases and may actually have stressed different kinds of judgments. The questionnaire item explaining how the rating was to be done was phrased entirely in terms of which episode they thought was "most interesting," "next most interesting," and so forth, whereas the instructions for using the push-buttons, while partly phrased in terms of interest, tended more to use "like" and "dislike" as the key expressions. Perhaps the word "interesting" connotes some measure of utility of the material whereas the "like-dislike" emphasis in the case of the push-buttons suggested enjoyment without regard to utility. Some suggestive comments written in by the men

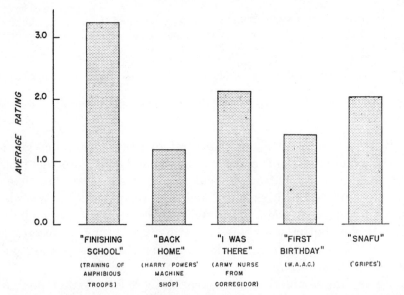

Figure 1.   Questionnaire ratings of the five episodes in Issue 5 of "The War."   The men were asked to rank the five episodes in the film as "best," "2d best," etc.   Ratings for each episode were then scored as follows: "best," 4 points; "2d best," 3 points; "3d best," 2 points; "4th best," 1 point; "worst," 0 points. The values plotted are the average scores for the men whose polygraph records are averaged in Figure 2.

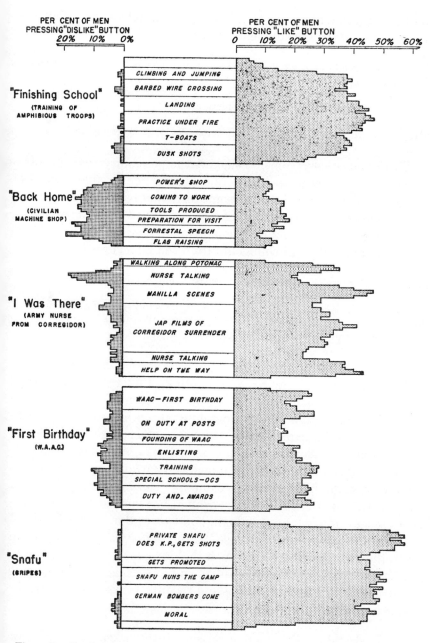

Figure 2. Continuous polygraph records of the group "likes" and "dislikes" during showing of issue 5 of "The War."

indicate a different frame of reference in the retrospective evaluations given on the questionnaire items.

The comedy should be cut out because we should have our minds on the job we have to do.

Snafu does not go with the rest of the picture.

Parts of Snafu too much on the comedy side.   Not realistic enough.

These and other comments suggest the possibility that, in retrospect on the film as a whole, a serious instructional value to most of the material was sensed, and to some men Snafu seemed out of place by comparison even though it had been enjoyed while it was being viewed.   That this reaction was not unanimous, however, is illustrated by the following comments from the interviews:

A cartoon to amuse one with a very necessary Army moral to it.

A thing like that is comedy and is a very good lesson and keeps a fellow interested, too.   You learn something and it's a little different than what he usually sees in training films, and it is also a very good lesson.

Further examination of Figure 2 reveals another finding that was typical of results obtained in the other studies—disapproval of close-ups of a person speaking.   It can be seen in the figure that the lowest "like" point in the program-analyzer record and the highest "dislike" point came during a sequence of a speech by the Secretary of the Navy, and the low points in the "I Was There" episode came during shots in which the nurse who narrated the episode was merely speaking in front of the camera.   During other portions of the episode she was not shown speaking, but instead her voice narrated scenes from Manila, Bataan, and Corregidor.   This low level of "like" responses during close-ups of a person speaking—even when the verbal content was much the same as during narration of action—was found in the other films and was revealed in comments by the men in the questionnaires and the interviews as well as in the program-analyzer record.

[There should be] a little bit less of close-up of their talking and more action pictures.

. . . these two Army nurses were sitting there and their conversation had no point to it.   Mentally I was fidgeting around waiting to see some action.

I think we had a majority of speeches since we are in the Army.   We don't like
to hear speeches.   [In reference to the shots of Forrestal's talk.]

By contrast with the reaction to the close-ups of the nurse telling
her story, the portions of "I Was There" where the narration was
illustrated with action shots reached relatively high points on the
program-analyzer record, and the episode as a whole was ranked
second in retrospect on the questionnaires.

The other outstanding results shown in Figure 2 are the popularity
of the first episode, especially in retrospect, and the unpopularity of
the second episode, which ranked worst both in immediate judgments on the program-analyzer and in retrospect on the questionnaires.

The first episode, while it dealt with training, was concerned with
simulated combat, including live ammunition.   In all instances the
men liked action shots from real combat, especially with reference
to the instructive value of seeing the "real thing."   The realistic
training sequence apparently capitalized on this reaction.

It's exciting.   It gave me a sense of what was coming.

We may be doing that ourselves.   Know what it is all about, get a view of it now,
and when the time comes, we will know what to do.

The negative reaction to the "Back Home" episode was not one
for which opportunity was provided for replication in other films.
The consensus of the men's comments seemed to be that there was
too much emphasis on what they thought to be pseudo-patriotism
in a group—the civilians—which was not exposed to the hardships
of Army life and at the same time was being well paid for its "patriotic" efforts.   While no opportunity to check the generality of this
interpretation was possible, it appeared to have considerable probability from other sources of information about soldiers' opinions.
Illustrative comments on the episode were:

That rubs a soldier the wrong way.   They don't like to see civilians getting credit.
I feel a little prejudiced, as every soldier does.

Everybody has a brother that is working in a plant that has an Army "E" flag.
It is just done for publicity purposes, and it's purely propaganda.

I think that is Army "hokum."   We are at war, and everybody should do his
duty, whether in the Army or not.   They are getting $90 and $100 (per week) for
the work they are doing.   They are getting well paid for it.

2. ATTEMPTED GENERALIZATIONS FROM PARALLEL STUDIES OF SEVERAL ISSUES

The fact that each issue of "The War" was constructed according to a fairly consistent pattern afforded a basis for comparing different presentations of similar types of material, thus providing an opportunity to check on the generality of the conclusions from single studies. As already mentioned, four issues were studied, including the one just described. In each issue, one of the five episodes was always an eye-witness report of actual action with a commentator who had "been there"; another was an additional account of military action; another was concerned with the construction, testing, or repair of equipment; and another was a humorous episode, involving either a comic dialogue or an animated cartoon. This similarity in the pattern of episodes was not specific to the four issues studied but was the projected plan of all future issues. Further, the recurrence of various types of action, commentary, visual material, and subject matter *within* various episodes provided somewhat more than the four replications of content obtained from testing four parallel issues.

The following aspects of men's reactions were found to obtain in every episode or issue which was available for analysis. The first two points noted below are illustrated by the program-analyzer records in Figure 3.

"On-the-spot" narrator: Audiences of the type studied—enlisted men in training—showed considerable interest in accounts of action as narrated by a commentator who had actually "been there." However, there appeared to be considerable differences, in terms both of the program-analyzer data and of men's retrospective judgments, in the interest shown in eye-witness accounts, depending on whether the narration was accompanied by action scenes or whether it was simply a close-up of the eye-witness telling his story.

Scenes of action vs. scenes of talking: Where the pictures on the screen showed only the narrator speaking, interest tended to be relatively low; when real shots of action were used to illustrate what the commentary was describing, interest tended to be high. This was suggested in the study of the first issues by comparison of reactions to episodes in which the only pictures were those of the commentator, as against episodes in which a considerable number of action shots were used to illustrate the story. The preference for action shots was even more clearly seen in subsequent issues where com-

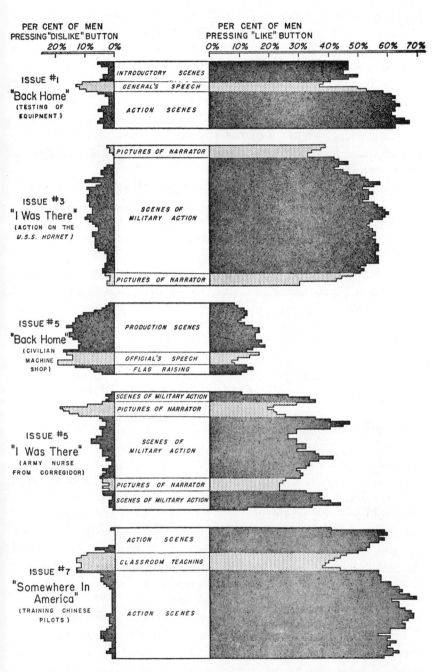

PER CENT OF MEN
PRESSING "DISLIKE" BUTTON
20% 10% 0%

PER CENT OF MEN
PRESSING "LIKE" BUTTON
0% 10% 20% 30% 40% 50% 60% 70%

ISSUE #1
"Back Home"
(TESTING OF
EQUIPMENT)

INTRODUCTORY SCENES
GENERAL'S SPEECH
ACTION SCENES

ISSUE #3
"I Was There"
(ACTION ON THE
U.S.S. HORNET)

PICTURES OF NARRATOR
SCENES OF
MILITARY ACTION
PICTURES OF NARRATOR

ISSUE #5
"Back Home"
(CIVILIAN
MACHINE
SHOP)

PRODUCTION SCENES
OFFICIAL'S SPEECH
FLAG RAISING

ISSUE #5
"I Was There"
(ARMY NURSE
FROM CORREGIDOR)

SCENES OF MILITARY ACTION
PICTURES OF NARRATOR
SCENES OF
MILITARY ACTION
PICTURES OF NARRATOR
SCENES OF MILITARY ACTION

ISSUE #7
"Somewhere In
America"
(TRAINING CHINESE
PILOTS)

ACTION SCENES
CLASSROOM TEACHING
ACTION SCENES

Figure 3. Polygraph records of group "likes" and "dislikes" for five episodes in which comparisons of action and talking scenes could be made within the same episode.

parisons could be made *within* episodes which included both shots of the narrator speaking and illustrative action shots described by the narrator. A related and also recurrent characteristic of men's likes and dislikes found in the studies was the unpopularity of official speakers and of speechmaking generally on the screen. This also was reflected both in the program-analyzer records and in the comments and ratings men gave in their interviews and questionnaire answers. Figure 3 shows the program-analyzer records for five episodes in which internal comparisons of action and talking scenes can be made.

The results with respect to speeches and close-ups of the narrator talking may well have applicability for teaching films in general. A not infrequent practice of Army training films was to devote portions of the film to showing an instructor in close-up while he proceeded to explain the points in lecture fashion. This might be an effective method if the speaker is a very well-known and prestigeful or relevant personage who could not be presented in person and would be generally available only through the medium of motion picture. But if the speaker is simply an unknown instructor or an actor playing the role of instructor, this device of showing him lecturing in close-up—while it is a very simple and inexpensive expedient in production—probably does not at all capitalize on any of the special characteristics of film presentation.

Other points: Several other characteristics of men's likes and dislikes appeared to be fairly general, at least to the extent that they recurred in different film episodes. One of these was narration by the commentator purporting to parallel what was shown in the film without actually doing so, or otherwise not appearing in keeping with the film. For example, in a picture showing activities of Japanese soldiers, the commentator's remarks noted the "cruelty" of the Japs, while actually the action of the Japanese soldiers as shown did not appear to the men to be more cruel than the behavior of American soldiers under comparable circumstances. Also tending to evoke unfavorable criticism from soldier audiences, both in the studies of "The War" and in evaluations of the "Why We Fight" series of orientation films, were scenes which the men regarded as "old stuff." Thus, newsreel shots which they had seen previously, even if relevant to the material currently being shown, were criticized by some men as being a repetition of what they had seen before. (At the same time, other men felt newsreels helped to give the film an air of authenticity.) Any scenes depicting Army life which the soldiers felt were unrealistic in terms of their own experience were quite consistently disliked by soldier audiences.

The most consistently *liked* type of material was that involving action shots either of training or military operations, especially action which appeared to be highly realistic. This popularity seemed to stem from a motivation on the part of the men to find out what to expect their own future experiences to be like.

3. COMPARISON OF AUDIENCE-EVALUATION RESULTS OBTAINED BY PROGRAM-ANALYZER AND QUESTIONNAIRE

It is of methodological interest to compare the results of evaluations as given by the men's immediate reactions on the polygraph record with their retrospective judgment in terms of questionnaire answers or interview comments. This was done for evaluation of complete episodes, which were rated as units in retrospect in addition to the continuous judgments recorded throughout on the program-analyzer. Differences in the relative evaluation accorded different episodes by the two methods does not, of course, necessarily mean inconsistency in men's judgments, since the two techniques may measure somewhat different things. In addition to the fact that in one case evaluation is immediate and in the other case retrospective, it is possible that there was a difference in the type of evaluation which men were making. As noted earlier, in giving their reactions with the program-analyzer, emphasis was placed on judgments of "like" or "dislike," whereas in the questionnaire evaluations, the wording of the ranking question was in terms of how "interesting" each episode was. It appeared from men's comments that they often considered such factors as how appropriate or valuable they thought the material was for soldier audiences in general (in spite of the attempt, in giving the instructions, to avoid this type of evaluation). This may account for the fact that in the two film issues containing animated cartoons, the cartoon episodes were rated appreciably lower in terms of questionnaire ratings than in terms of reactions shown by the program-analyzer. The correlation between average program-analyzer rating and questionnaire ratings for the five episodes of each of the four films studied is shown diagrammatically in Figure 4.

EXPLANATION OF FIGURE 4

The percentages plotted for the program-analyzer evaluations are the average net percentages of favorable reactions for each episode,

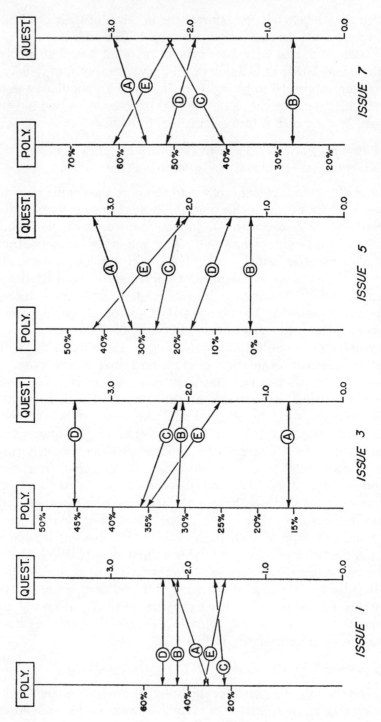

Figure 4.   Comparison of "Program-Analyzer" Data and Questionnaire Ratings of various episodes (A-E) in Issues 1, 3, 5, 7 of "The War."

obtained by subtracting "dislike" from "like" averaged over the total time interval for the episode.   The questionnaire ratings were those obtained in answer to the question asking the men to rank the five episodes of each issue from best to worst.   Ratings for each episode were then scored with four points for first place, three points for second place, two for third, one for fourth, and none for worst. The values plotted are the average scores for the total audience of each film.   Exactly comparable results for program-analyzer and questionnaire evaluation would give lines that connected the corresponding measures for the various episodes without crossing.

CHAPTER 5

EXPERIMENTAL COMPARISON OF ALTERNATIVE PRESENTATIONS

I N THE experience of the Experimental Section, one of the most frequent and insistent requests was for research to answer questions as to the relative advantage of one class of products as compared with another. "Which is more effective in presenting orientation materials on the radio, a 'documentary' (dramatic) or a commentator?" "How does a film-strip compare with a sound-scored motion picture?" "Isn't a film always superior to a lecture?" These were the kinds of questions on which film and radio producers wanted research information.

Such questions could have immediate practical significance, as when the best of two or more existing products must be chosen because only one can be used. Here only an empirical answer is needed; there is no problem of generality other than the adequacy of the sample of men studied and the representativeness of the conditions in presenting the products experimentally. Such research can serve a very useful function of guiding an organization as to the best of available means for carrying out its program.

However, the questions were rarely asked in the form of an empirical comparison of alternative *existing* products, one of which was to be selected. Rather, as can be seen in the examples above, they were phrased in general terms applying to a whole class of products. When thus stated, the questions inherently involve many serious problems concerning the generalizability of specific comparisons of two existing products (no matter how well the comparisons may be conducted in respect to sampling and experimental control). For example, the question, "Which is the better teaching medium, a film or a lecture?" immediately raises further questions such as: *"What* film?" "Who will be giving the lectures—an expert speaker or a novice?" "For what kind of audiences?" "For what kinds of subject matter?" Many other relevant questions could

also be raised, and the research problem—to be properly answered
—would have to be expanded into an experimental analysis of many
interacting factors involved in lecture presentations and in film
presentations.   It is unlikely that a definitive answer could be given
to the original question in its unqualified form.

Nevertheless, several studies aimed at questions taking this relatively unqualified form were carried out, partly because of the insistence of the requests and partly to get leads that would provide a
beginning for an analysis of the factors underlying the effectiveness
of various media.   Of the studies that were carried out, three seem
to have general interest from the standpoint of providing such leads.
The first to be reported is a comparison of a motion picture versus a
film-strip presentation of the same subject; the second is a comparison of a "commentator" radio program versus a "documentary"
or dramatic radio program as a means of changing opinions on an
orientation subject; and the third is a comparison of introductory
discussion versus review as a means of increasing what is learned
from a film.

The scientific status of these studies should be clearly delineated.
They are carefully controlled experimental studies of two particular
alternative products, but as far as generality is concerned, the results
are generally restricted to providing a basis for *hypotheses* about the
factors that distinguish the two.   Many instances can be found in
the literature of teaching-film research in which two different presentations are compared and where, from the results of this comparison, sweeping generalizations are made about the two classes of
communications represented or about the factor alleged by the experimenter to be the distinguishing feature of the two.   The risks
involved in such overgeneralizations are obvious, and the studies
reported in this chapter should be regarded as experimental comparisons of the effectiveness of specific alternative presentations
rather than as experiments with controlled variation of the factors
that appear to distinguish two alternative classes of presentation.

The Comparative Effectiveness of a Sound Motion Picture and a Film-Strip Presentation

1. GENERAL DESCRIPTION OF THE STUDY

This study was designed to determine the relative effectiveness of
a sound motion picture as compared with a "film-strip" presentation
as educational devices in a basic training subject.   (A "film strip"

is comparable to slides, except that successive "stills" are developed as positives on a strip of film; these are used either in conjunction with a synchronized recording or with explanations by an instructor.)   The purpose of the study, as conceived by those responsible for the request from the military Training Division, ASF, was to compare the teaching effectiveness of training movies, which are expensive and time-consuming to produce, with that of film strips, which can be quickly produced with a minimum of equipment and cost.   Their belief was that film strips were close enough in effectiveness to movies that the time and expense factors were the more important ones to consider.   On the other hand, the general feeling in training circles at the time of the study was that sound movies are far superior to film strips.

The instructional topic used in the study was the elementary principles of map reading.   This choice of subject was dictated in part by the availability of a standard, widely used Army training film and of a film strip presenting the same topic.[1]   The film used is quite typical of a large number of films on technical and semitechnical subjects and was, according to distribution figures, one of the most widely used Army training films.

The choice also involved considerations of feasibility in measuring the effects of instruction for large groups of men.   A "paper and pencil" test was considered to afford a sufficiently practical and realistic test of the abilities involved in a subject such as elementary map reading.   (In contrast, a practical test of the effects of film instruction on many other subjects, such as rifle marksmanship, would of course have to include shooting records or similar measures of actual performance in the use of equipment.)

The basic plan of the experiment was to show the map-reading film to one group, while at the same time another group was taught the same subject by film-strip presentation.   About half a day after seeing the film or film strip, each group was given a pencil and paper test designed to measure knowledge of the subject matter that had been presented.   The same test was also given to a control group that had received no instruction.   The test approximated the types of response involved in utilizing the instruction in actual performance in map reading.

The film was tested on a group of trainees at a Quartermaster Replacement Training Center.   The men were slightly higher in in-

---

[1] The sound-film used was the U.S. Army subject TF 5-12; the film strip was the Army film strip FS 5-1.

telligence and in amount of formal education than the Army as a whole. None of them had received any previous Army instruction on the subject of map reading.

2. EXPERIMENTAL PROCEDURE AND DESIGN

Selection and balancing of the groups to be given each form of instruction. As indicated above, the essential method of comparison was to select groups that were as closely identical as possible with respect to all relevant factors except the type of instruction they had received, and then to compare the scores of these groups on a test of the material covered. The effect of each form of instruction is indicated by the differences between the mean score for each instructional group and the mean scores made by the "control group" which received no instruction on the subject. None of the men in the experimental groups were told in advance that they would be tested on the material covered.

As in studies of orientation films, the sample was selected in company units rather than on an individual basis. From company rosters giving the AGCT classification and educational level of each man, two companies to be given each form of instruction were chosen in such a way that the different forms of instruction would be applied to groups of similar composition. The final samples used in analysis were exactly equated for AGCT class and educational level achieved.

The schedule of instruction was arranged so that the groups receiving the two different kinds of instruction would be balanced as closely as possible with respect to average length of time in training, time at which instruction was carried out, and kind of activity preceding and following instruction. Similarly, these factors were balanced as closely as possible between the control group and each of the two instruction groups.

Details of Procedure for the Two Forms of Instruction

Motion picture. The men who received sound-film instruction were shown the standard Army training film on map reading during the course of an hour's session of training-film showings in a post theater. One company of men saw the film in the early afternoon, the other group early in the morning. The map-reading film required 43 minutes showing time. In accordance with usual practice at this and other replacement training centers, two additional short films (on a different subject) were also shown to complete the hour's session of films. These two short films preceded the map-reading film in the morning session and followed it in the afternoon session.

Film-strip. The four platoons of one company received instruction in the morning; the platoons of the other company met in the afternoon. Thus half of the men both in the film-strip and movie groups received morning instruction, and half received afternoon instruction. The film-strip instruction was given in recreation buildings to only one platoon at a time, each platoon being taught by a different instructor. This was desirable in order to keep the size of groups below the maximum generally considered to be feasible for film-strip instruction, and to simulate as closely as possible the actual conditions of use in field installations. The film-strip instruction for each platoon covered a period of approximately 50 minutes, or just slightly more than the time required to show the training film to the other groups.

In order to control the way the instruction was given and to obtain greater comparability of the material covered by various instructors, each instructor was given a schedule of the procedure to be followed and an outline of the major points that the film-strip instruction was to cover. Each instructor also previewed the film strip, and received copies of the "Notes on Map Reading," issued in connection with the film strip. Since the film and film strip differed somewhat in the emphasis given to various topics, these notes were edited slightly in order to make the film-strip presentation more nearly parallel to that of the motion picture.

These arrangements were desirable to insure some degree of uniformity in the use of the materials by various instructors. They also served to approximate roughly, in the opinions of training officers, the amount of supervision and assistance that instructors would normally be expected to receive in a Replacement Training Center operating on the basis of a centralized training program. All instructors were, however, requested to prepare their instruction independently. The instructors used were selected from a large pool of available officers in such a way as to approximate "average" teaching ability as indicated by ratings made by their immediate superiors.

The instructors were aware of the purpose of the experiment and were assured in good faith that the results of tests would not be used to reflect credit or discredit on the instructors as individuals, but were designed only to test the *method* of instruction. It was made clear to them that, accordingly, they should prepare and carry out their instruction with the same amount of effort and care—no more and no less—as they would normally apply to regularly scheduled instruction. Finally, the instructors and all other relevant personnel involved in the study were cautioned against revealing the purpose of the experiment to any of the men serving as subjects and they were shown the necessity of treating all of the instruction exactly as if it were part of the regularly scheduled training program.

"Fairness" of the comparison between sound-film and film-strip. It is apparent that various alterations in details of procedure noted above might have altered the relative effectiveness of the two types of presentation. The film-strip presentation could, for example, have been held to exactly the same time limit (43 minutes) as was required to show the film; or the showing of the two additional short subjects to the film group, which might introduce some interference effects, could have been omitted; or more expert instructors could have been used for the film-strip presentations. Choice of the particular conditions used was, however, based not on an attempt to provide ideal or optimal presentations for each medium, but only on an attempt to approximate prevailing conditions under which each type of instruction was likely to be used in typical Army training programs.

3. CONTENT AND ADMINISTRATION OF THE TEST USED

The test used consisted of 39 multiple-choice items, each requiring the men to select the correct answer out of four answers printed on the blank. For example:

The direction in which a compass points is called . . . (check one)

☐ true north
☐ grid north
☐ azimuth north
☐ magnetic north

Since the film instruction was expected to impart, in the main, only the essentials of the subject, the test was composed almost entirely of questions designed to find out how well these *essentials* had been learned. The questions did not therefore, test the extent to which men had learned to make relatively complex applications of the material shown, such as, for instance, the construction of profiles from a contour map. Half of the questions involved verbal knowledge of facts, terms, or principles; the other half required the men to refer to simple maps and diagrams printed on the test blanks.

Since the test covered only factual material, it was not necessary to camouflage the purpose of the test as in the studies of orientation films, in which opinions as well as facts were involved. In the present case it was administered *as a test,* the men being told it was to find out how well they had learned how to read maps and being asked to sign their names to their test paper. This tended to maximize test motivation. Having the papers signed also permitted the experimenters to obtain AGCT scores from company rosters as an additional item of background information.

As mentioned earlier, no prior announcement of the test had been made. Officers were trained to administer the tests in a standardized manner. The testing was conducted in recreation buildings, each test group consisting of two platoons of men. If instruction had been received by a particular pair of platoons in the morning, the testing of that pair of platoons was performed the same afternoon; if instruction was given in the afternoon, the men were tested the following morning.

4. OVERALL EFFECTIVENESS OF THE TWO INSTRUCTIONAL METHODS

Figure 1 summarizes the overall relative effectiveness of the sound-film and film-strip instruction studied by showing the average test score received by the men in each group. The test scores are expressed as the *average percentage* of correct answers.

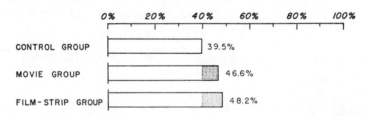

Figure 1.   Average test scores received by men in each group (N = 253 in each group).

The data show reliable evidence of learning from both forms of instruction, but there is no reliable evidence that either form was superior to the other.[2]

The comparison shown in Figure 2 indicates that the same results are also obtained when more intelligent men (AGCT Classes I and

[2] The critical ratios of the mean difference between control group and either experimental group are larger than 4.0, indicating less than one chance in a thousand that such differences would be obtained by chance. The difference between the film-strip and movie groups, however, is only about 1.3 times its standard error, and differences this large in one direction or the other would be expected to occur by chance about one time in five if the two presentations were actually equally effective.

II) and the less intelligent (AGCT Classes III and IV) are considered separately.[3]

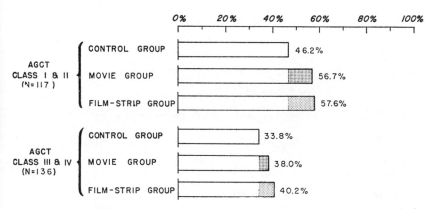

Figure 2. Average test scores received by men in each group (shown separately for men with "higher" and "lower" intelligence scores).

5. COMPARING EFFECTIVENESS FOR DIFFERENT TOPICS

The relative effectiveness of the two presentations in conveying material was compared for each of the main topics covered in the instruction. The bulk of the subject matter fell into three main categories: (1) distance and direction, (2) "azimuths," and (3) contour maps and elevation. Table 1 shows the average test scores on these main subdivisions of the subject matter for men in each instructional group. The test score here is the average percentage answered correctly of those items dealing with each main topic.

TABLE 1

AVERAGE TEST SCORES ON MAIN SUBDIVISIONS OF SUBJECT MATTER

	SUBDIVISION OF SUBJECT MATTER		
	Distance and direction (11 test items)	Azimuths (11 test items)	Contours and elevation (11 test items)
Control group	46.5%	37.2%	33.5%
Movie group	49.5	41.1	48.5
Film-strip group	53.9	42.5	46.9

[3] The critical ratios of the differences between control group and either experimental group for the high and low intelligence subgroups compared are in all cases larger than 3.0. The critical ratios of the differences between film-strip and movie groups, however, are only about 1.4 for AGCT Class III and IV men and 0.7 for AGCT Class I and II men.

These data show no statistically reliable superiority for either experimental group over the other for the second and third of the three main topics considered. The mean difference of 4.4 per cent in favor of the film-strip group on the first topic ("distance and direction") is reliable at about the .01 probability level. Essentially the same picture, as far as direction of differences between film strip and film for various topics is concerned, was found for the low AGCT men as for the Class I and II men.

6. COMPARATIVE EFFECTIVENESS FOR SPECIFIC POINTS

A comparison of the effectiveness of the two presentations in getting across *specific points* covered by both presentations revealed few suggestions as to educational advantages or disadvantages inherent in either of the two media.   For some specific points in which one presentation or the other was superior in effectiveness, the differential effectiveness appeared to be the result of differences in the particular device that happened to be used to present the point, rather than being a function of any inherent difference in the two media as such.   For example, in attempting to teach men to use a graphic scale to measure distances on a map, the movie used the rather unrealistic device of showing the distance scale being lifted up out of the corner of the map and applied to the map distance to be measured.   The film strip, more realistically, illustrated the use of a strip of paper to transfer map distance to the scale for measuring.   It was interesting to observe that the film-strip presentation appeared to be the more effective in increasing the already high proportion of men who were able to measure correctly the distance between two points on a map.   This result is shown in Figure 3. (The high initial level of performance shown for this particular point is doubtless due to familiarity with the scaling procedure already gained by many individuals in the course of their schooling.)

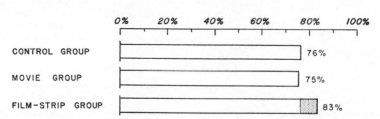

Figure 3. Proportion of men who knew how to use a distance scale to measure distances (average of 2 test items).

This finding suggests that, in either medium, reliance should not be placed on the audience members to make for themselves the transfer from a general explanation to the specific details of performance. Thus in this instance the presentation which showed precisely what to do to measure distance was the more effective one. (The data also suggest that in this instance the superiority of the more explicit method was greater for the less intelligent men, although the second order difference between AGCT groups is not large enough to be reliable.)

Most of the differences found in effectiveness on other specific points appeared, similarly, to be a function of particular presentation devices which could be used in either medium. However, there was one outstanding case of a differential effect which probably illustrates a real difference between the media, and an advantage for motion pictures over projected stills in teaching certain kinds of material.

In showing the measuring of contour interval, the motion picture used a moving viewpoint (from horizontal to vertical) to show how differences in elevation of terrain are projected onto a map in the form of contour lines. Here the movie was more effective than the film strip, which could not use a comparable device. The comparative data are shown in Figure 4.

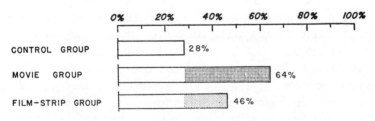

Figure 4.   Proportion of men who knew what the space between contour lines represents on a map.

Here the large effect of the motion picture appears to be due to the fact that in a movie the object being photographed can remain still while the angle from which it is viewed is progressively altered. Thus we have the hypothesis that where familiarity with three-dimensional spatial relationships is important in learning the material, movies have an inherent advantage that cannot easily be equalled by film strips.

Perhaps the most interesting aspect of the results of this study is the fact that on the whole the two presentations were about equally effective. But, as has already been stressed, this finding tells us little about the inherent potentialities of the media of still versus moving pictures as components in presenting instruction. Since the study did not employ controlled variation of the factor of motion with other factors held constant, the results merely show that this particular film strip was on the average about as effective as this particular movie. However, this finding does have a practical bearing on the assumption sometimes made that motion pictures *always* provide better instruction than that attainable with the less costly film strip. Obviously, a single exception such as that provided by the present study suffices to disprove such a generalization.

The Comparative Effectiveness of "Documentary" and "Commentator" Radio Presentations

The study reported in this section furnishes an additional example of the kind of research in which specific examples of two media are compared. As in the study just described, the results are strictly applicable only to the specific presentations studied although the data may suggest some hypotheses as to inherent advantages or disadvantages of the media represented by these presentations.

At the time this study was conducted, a topic of debate among technicians and producers of informational radio programs concerned the relative effectiveness of the dramatic "documentary" and the commentator type of program. In the documentary, use is made of actors, sound effects, and background music to present factual material by "acting out" the underlying events. In the commentator type of program an "expert" in a position to know and interpret the facts discusses the topic.

The preponderance of opinion among radio personnel appeared to be that the documentary was far superior to the commentator program, but a few believed the latter would be equally or more effective at changing men's opinions. In this controversy the main argument on the side of the documentary program concerned the factor of interest. It was alleged that the audience would pay closer attention to a dramatic show because of its greater interest and would therefore learn more from it, whereas they would be likely to pay less attention to a commentator. The argument on the other side of the case was that a dramatic program would not be taken seriously—it would be reacted to much as a "soap opera" or a dramatic show for entertainment purposes. Moreover, it was alleged that such programs would be regarded as propagandistic, the musical effects being perceived as a means of influencing emotions and the use of actors being treated as evidence of the fictional and unauthentic nature of the material used. A further consideration was that a commentator program could be written and transcribed in one day, with a minimum of expense, whereas a documentary usually took longer to write, rehearse, and produce and involved an expensive cast of actors, some "live" music, technicians to "dub in" recorded music and sound effects, and so forth.

An experimental comparison of the two types of programs was carried out in conjunction with a study using controlled variation of content that is reported in Chapter 8.   Four programs were prepared, two each of the commentator and documentary type.[4]   The two forms of each type of program differed with respect to a content variable that is not the concern of the present treatment (presentation of arguments on "both sides" vs. just on "one side" of a controversial issue).   Only those aspects of the study relevant to the comparison of the commentator and documentary types of presentation will be reported in the present chapter.

1. NATURE OF THE RADIO PROGRAMS

The radio transcriptions used were prepared specifically for experimental purposes by the Armed Forces Radio Service in consultation with Experimental Section personnel.   The subject of both the "commentator" and "documentary" programs was the same— the difficulty of the job ahead against the Japanese.   The "message" of the programs was that there still remained a difficult job against Japan that would probably take at least two years after VE Day to accomplish, a message that turned out to be grossly incorrect but which in absence of knowledge of the atomic bomb appeared reasonable at the time of the study.   The factual material in the program was obtained from official War Department and Office of War Information releases, and the message was in line with the informational policy of both agencies at the time of the study.

The degree of comparability in the content of the two programs is perhaps best indicated by describing how the content was determined.   An outline of the factual documentation was prepared by Experimental Section personnel.   The two script writers, one for the commentator programs and one for the documentaries, used

---

[4] The writer for the commentator programs was Lloyd Shearer; the writer for the dramatic programs was Robert Lee.

this outline as the source of their material. Because the commentator programs were also being used as part of the material for the controlled-variation study referred to earlier, the writer of these programs adhered closely to the sequence of topics in the outline and was more restricted in his range of improvisation. The writer and producer of the documentary shows had a freer hand in the preparation of his programs; consequently the content of these programs differed from that of the commentator programs in various details. However, these differential factors did not greatly influence the preparation of the programs. Both writers took on the job without any advance preparation of their own material, and they both followed fairly closely the outline provided for them.

2. EXPERIMENTAL DESIGN AND ADMINISTRATION

The experiment used the before-after design. One week before the presentation of the radio programs a "survey" was made in the outfits used in the study. This "survey" was ostensibly on the topic of redeployment from the European to the Pacific Theater of Operations and the point system for discharging veterans, but it permitted the introduction of questions about the probable length and difficulty of the war with Japan after VE Day in a very logical context of questions. Men's answers to these questions constituted a "before" measure to be used in ascertaining the effects of the transcriptions. One week after this "before" survey, the transcriptions were presented in orientation meetings as introductory material to be used as a basis for discussion of the topic, "How Long Will the War with Japan Last?" The orientation meetings, held in platoon-size groups, were conducted by second lieutenants selected from the available local personnel on the basis of previous teaching experience and trained as "orientation officers" for the experiment. At the outset of each meeting the officer explained that before the meeting was thrown open for discussion he would play a transcription of a radio program giving some of the facts on the Pacific War. These were the projected conditions for using such programs. A significant feature of these conditions was that the radio programs could not be tuned in or out by the men; rather, attendance was required as with orientation films.

After the transcription had been played, the men were given a short questionnaire which constituted the "after" measurement in the experiment. The conditions of administering the "after" survey were made as different as possible from those obtaining in the "before" survey; they were administered by different personnel, in different buildings, with different groupings of men, and with formally different questionnaire blanks.   The officer told the men that the people who made the program wanted to find out the soldier's "own honest opinions" of the transcription and had prepared a brief anonymous questionnaire for the men to fill out.   In addition to getting the men's opinion of the program, the questionnaire contained some "incidental" questions concerning opinions about the content of the programs—e.g., opinion concerning whether the program seemed overoptimistic or overpessimistic, and what the men personally thought would be the probable length of the war.   These responses were designed to provide information on the effectiveness of the material; obtaining this "additional" information was actually, of course, the main purpose of the study.   Men in control platoons who heard no program filled out a similar questionnaire about what they thought of the Army orientation programs in general, a questionnaire which also contained the "incidental" questions significant to the study.

The study was carried out among the personnel of eight Quartermaster Training Companies during the first two weeks of April 1945.   Sixteen of the 32 platoons attended orientation meetings at which one or the other of two *commentator* programs was played; eight platoons heard one or the other of two *dramatic* shows; the remaining eight platoons served as a *control* and heard neither of the programs.   This allocation of subjects, giving more cases to the commentator program, was in line with the primary purpose of the study reported in Chapter 8, which was the comparison of the controlled content differences between the two commentator programs.   The platoons were utilized in a manner so that any inter-company differences were controlled.   In each of the eight companies one platoon served as control, two platoons heard one each of the two commentator programs, and one platoon heard one or the other of the two dramatic programs.

About half of the men surveyed were new recruits receiving their first military training, and about half were veterans who had been in the Army for some time and who were being trained for reassignment.

As has been noted in the foregoing description of the experimental procedures, two kinds of data were obtained for comparing the programs: the audience's evaluation of the programs and the before-after measures of opinion for determining experimentally the programs' effects. The former will be presented first.

3. AUDIENCE EVALUATIONS OF THE TWO KINDS OF PROGRAMS

Level of general interest. One direct and two indirect measures of general interest were contained in the questionnaire. On the direct measure the vast majority (over 90 per cent) of both groups of men —those who heard the commentator program and those who heard the dramatic program—found the program either *very* or *fairly* interesting. The question and results are shown below for the two types of programs.

Question: "Was this radio program interesting to you, or was it dull and uninteresting?"

	PROPORTION OF MEN CHECKING EACH ANSWER	
	Commentator programs (N = 524)	*Dramatic programs* (N = 245)
"Very interesting"	69%	71%
"Fairly interesting"	26	25
"Not very interesting"	3	3
"Very dull and uninteresting"	2	1
Total	100%	100%

It is apparent that no significant differences between programs were obtained with respect to this point.

One indirect measure of interest was also obtained by asking the men whether in future orientation meetings they would like to hear other radio transcriptions of the same sort.

Question: "In future orientation-hour meetings would you like to hear recordings of radio programs like this one on other subjects connected with the war?"

	PROPORTION OF MEN CHECKING EACH ANSWER	
	Commentator programs	*Dramatic programs*
"Would like to hear them"	83%	88%
"Would not like to" or "Would not care one way or the other"	15	11
No answer	2	1
Total	100%	100%

As before, the slight difference in favor of the dramatic programs was not statistically significant.

Another indirect measure of interest was obtained by asking the men who heard a program whether they thought it was too long, too short, or about the right length. Very few of the men thought any of the programs were too long, a finding which may be interpreted as indicating a high degree of interest. The results are shown below, subdivided according to the actual length of the programs.

Question: "How about the length of the program you heard today—was the program too long, too short, or about the right length?"

PROPORTION OF MEN CHECKING
EACH ANSWER

	Commentator programs		*Dramatic programs*	
	1	*2*	*3*	*4*
Approximate time in minutes	*15*	*19*	*16½*	*20½*
	(*N = 261*)	(*N = 263*)	(*N = 104*)	(*N = 141*)
"Too long"	2%	1%	2%	3%
"About the right length"	66	76	52	67
"Too short"	31	21	45	28
No answer	1	2	1	2
Total	100%	100%	100%	100%

If the category "too short" implies a high level of interest, these results indicate that both the shorter (3) and the longer (4) versions of the dramatic program were more interesting than the corresponding commentator forms (1 and 2, respectively). On this question the difference between programs 1 and 3 is statistically reliable (at the 1 per cent level of confidence). It can also be seen that "too long" was a very infrequent response to any of the programs, indicating that neither program was boring. (This may be partly due to the fact that the use of radio transcriptions in orientation meetings was a novel experience to the men; under other circumstances the degree of interest expressed in the same programs might have been lower.)

Belief in authenticity of the programs. With any type of information program there were always some of the men who regarded the materials as "misleading" or as "propaganda" despite great care in factual documentation. An important possibility mentioned earlier in connection with the authenticity of radio transcriptions is that a dramatic presentation, with its background music, sound effects, actors' voices, and dramatizations, might be considered by the men as trying to work on their emotions and as "fictional" rather than "based on facts."   However, the findings for these programs show no important differences between the commentator and dramatic shows as far as the men's evaluation of the authenticity of the transcriptions is concerned.

Three questions were asked dealing with the authenticity of the programs: one concerning the accuracy of the facts, a second on the fairness of the selection of material, and the third about the presence or absence of "propaganda."   The results are shown in Table 2.

TABLE 2

THREE MEASURES OF AUDIENCE EVALUATION OF PROGRAM AUTHENTICITY: PROPORTION OF MEN CHECKING THE VARIOUS ANSWERS TO EACH QUESTION

	Commentator programs	Dramatic programs
1. *Question:* "Did you feel that the information about the Pacific War given in this radio program was true and accurate?"		
"It all seemed accurate"	65%	68%
"Mostly accurate, but partly inaccurate"	20	18
"Often inaccurate"	2	3
"Don't know"	11	10
No answer	2	1
Total	100%	100%
2. *Question:* "Do you feel that the radio program gave a fair and honest picture of the job ahead of us in the Pacific, or did the facts given seem too one-sided?"		
"It gave a fair and honest picture"	72%	75%
"It seemed too one-sided"	26	23
No answer	2	2
Total	100%	100%
3. *Question:* "Was there anything about the radio program that seemed like propaganda?"		
"None of it seemed like propaganda"	65%	62%
"Some of it seemed like propaganda"	29	29
"All of it seemed like propaganda"	4	6
No answer	2	3
Total	100%	100%

On each of the three questions above, the differences between the two types of programs are too small to be outside the range of sampling error.   The frequent allegation that documentaries would seem propagandistic certainly received no support from these data.

For both types of program the results seem to indicate a relatively high degree of confidence in the authenticity of the material, especially in view of the fact that the majority of the men were initially opposed to the "message" (over 70 per cent believed at the outset that the Pacific War would end in less than 2 years after VE Day).

4. EXPERIMENTAL EVALUATION OF TRANSCRIPTIONS

Effectiveness of the transcriptions in getting across the main orientation "message."   The main question used to evaluate the effectiveness of the transcriptions in getting across the "message" of the programs was one asking the men for their best guess as to the probable length of the war with Japan after Germany's defeat.   As mentioned earlier, the content of the programs aimed directly at counteracting "overoptimism" about a quick end of the Pacific war.

The effects of the programs in this area were obtained by determining the net proportion of men who revised their estimate *upward* as a result of hearing the transcription.   The "net proportion" is the proportion who revised their estimates upward by at least one-half year minus the proportion who revised their estimates downward by one-half a year or more.[5]   The results are shown below:[6]

TABLE 3

PROPORTION OF MEN WHO REVISED ESTIMATE OF PROBABLE LENGTH OF WAR WITH JAPAN AFTER GERMANY'S DEFEAT (REVISION = AT LEAST ONE-HALF YEAR)

	No program (control group) ($N = 181$)	Commentator programs ($N = 401$)	Dramatic programs ($N = 179$)
No change	63%	45%	42%
Revised estimate *upward*	18	47	50
Revised estimate *downward*	19	8	8
Net per cent revising upward: (Per cent revising upward minus per cent revising downward)	−1%	39%	42%

It can be seen in the above table that there was virtually no overall change in the control group during the period of about a week that intervened between the two surveys.   Among those men who

---

[5] A discussion of this statistic is presented in Appendix B.

[6] The numbers of cases given in this table are smaller than those for preceding tabulations because individuals who failed to give an estimate in either of the questionnaires could not, obviously, be used in this analysis of change in response.

heard no program, about as many made a shorter estimate as made a longer estimate.   However, among the men who heard either kind of transcription there was a marked change during the same period in the direction of revising estimates upward.   The overall effect for the two programs is seen to be about the same; the slight difference favoring the dramatic program is not reliable statistically. Analysis of the data for high and low educational groups separately also showed no reliable differences between the two programs.

In addition to the general question as to the probable time required to defeat the Japanese, three other questions bearing on the difficulty of the job of finishing the war were included in the schedule given before and after the playing of the transcriptions.   These related to Japanese resources, the possibility of Japanese surrender, and the extent of damage to Japanese industry by American air forces.

Effectiveness of the transcriptions in modifying men's estimation of Japanese resources.   Past opinion surveys showed that one of the common beliefs of men who expected Japan to be a "pushover" was that Japan had insufficient resources and supplies to stay in the war for more than a short time.   One of the points made in the radio programs was that Japan was estimated to have sufficient quantities of most war materials for at least two years of fighting.   The natural resources in Japan's conquered empire and the stockpiles built up in the home islands since Pearl Harbor were both stressed.

The effectiveness of the two types of programs in getting across this idea was tested by a question asking the men whether or not they thought the Japanese had sufficient supplies of oil, steel, and other raw materials to last them through a long war.   The results are shown below:

Question: "Do you think the Japs will have enough oil, steel, and other war materials to last them through a long war?   (Check one)"

PROPORTION OF MEN CHECKING KEY ANSWER; I.E., "THE JAPS WILL SOON RUN OUT OF MATERIALS."

	No program (control group) (N = 197)	*Commentator* programs (N = 428)	*Dramatic* programs (N = 188)
Earlier survey	60%	56%	53%
Later survey	54	35	32
Difference	6%	21%	21%

The results show no difference in the effects of the two kinds of programs. Both program groups showed about 21 per cent decrease in the number of men expecting that Japan would soon run out of supplies. This change was considerably greater than the 6 per cent change in the control platoons that heard no program.

Effectiveness of transcriptions on men's expectations of Japanese surrender. Another point made in the transcriptions was that Japan would not give up. According to the programs, the Japanese were expected to fight on to the very end in the hope that our casualties would become so large that we would seek a compromise.

Neither of the two kinds of programs effected a very great change in opinion on this subject, and no significant differences were obtained between the commentator and the dramatic program. The results are shown below:

Question: "Do you think Japan will give up and surrender on our terms before they lose everything, or do you think they will keep right on fighting to the very end?   (Check one)"

PER CENT SAYING THE JAPANESE WOULD
GIVE UP AND SURRENDER BEFORE THEY
LOSE EVERYTHING

	No program (control group) (N = 197)	Commentator programs (N = 428)	Dramatic programs (N = 188)
Earlier survey	40%	48%	44%
Later survey	43	40	33
Difference	−3%	8%	11%

Effectiveness of transcriptions on men's evaluation of the damage done by our Air Force. Another argument for a short war with Japan frequently encountered in earlier opinion surveys was the belief that our bombing of Japan was doing so much damage to the Japanese war effort that they would soon be out of the war. Both types of programs attempted to counteract overoptimism about the damage that had been done by our air raids up to that time (April 1945). Each kind of program produced a fairly strong effect in reducing the men's estimation of the damage that had already been done to the Japanese war effort by our bombings, but the dramatic programs produced a significantly greater effect than the commentator programs. The results are as follows:

Question: "What is your idea of how much damage our air raids in Japan are doing to the Jap war effort?   (Check one)"

| | PER CENT SAYING OUR AIR RAIDS HAD ALREADY GREATLY DAMAGED JAPANESE WAR EFFORT | | |
	No program (control group) (N = 197)	Commentator programs (N = 428)	Dramatic programs (N = 188)
Earlier survey	46%	45%	50%
Later survey	49	29	20
Difference	−3%	16%	30%

It should be pointed out that the programs did not all devote equal time to this subject.   The two commentator programs used about 3/4 minute and 1-1/2 minutes respectively on America's air war, and the two dramatic programs used about 1-1/2 minutes and 1-3/4 minutes respectively on this topic.   However, almost identical results were obtained when only the two programs devoting about 1-1/2 minutes each are compared.   It seems likely, therefore, that the greater effectiveness of the documentary on this point was due to a superior procedure used by the dramatic programs.   The tonnage of bombs dropped on Germany was compared with that dropped on Japan by means of a bombing sound-effect; the noise was maintained for about 15 seconds to represent the tonnage that had been dropped on Germany up to that time, and for about a second to represent the tonnage dropped on Japan.   This device, which was termed "sound graphing" by the writer of the documentaries, appears to be an advantage of this type of program that is not as applicable to (or at least not characteristic of) the commentator program.

CONCLUSIONS

As far as the initial question is concerned, the outstanding findings of this comparison of alternative presentations lie in the slightness of the difference found between the two kinds of programs.   Contrary to some expectations, the commentator programs were just about as interesting as the dramatic programs, and the latter were considered just about as authentic and nonpropagandistic as the commentator programs.   Both were about equally effective at changing estimates of the length of the war.   The one outstanding difference between the two programs—effects on evaluation of the damage done by our Air Force—suggests that the variety of methods available to the documentary provides such programs with some more effective procedures of presentation of material.

COMPARISON OF INTRODUCING SUPPLEMENTARY MATERIAL AT THE BEGINNING AND THE END OF A TRAINING FILM

A frequently recognized consideration among users of instructional films is that the teaching value of a film may very likely be increased by some form of supplementary material that either focuses attention in advance on the important points to be presented in the film or consolidates after the film showing the material that has been presented. Thus one may either prepare the audience for the most effective reception of the film or one may assist the audience after the film to get the most out of what has been shown.

The locus in time of these two alternative procedures for supplementing the material presented in the film determines to a certain extent the character of the supplementary material used. Supplementary material *before* the film will generally take the form either of motivating the members of the audience or of focusing their attention on the salient points to be presented. On the other hand, after the film showing it is too late either to motivate the learning or to get the audience to pay maximum attention during the parts of the film judged important. Thus supplementation after the film usually concentrates on a review of what has just been seen. In this case the audience members may be motivated to retain selectively what has been shown by focusing attention on important points so that these will be rehearsed.

The present experiment was one in which these two alternative ways of supplementing a film were compared. The general question on which the study was based was more or less as follows: "If we have extra time to use in supplementing the showing of a training film, is it best to use this time before the film to focus attention on significant points or is it better to use the time for a review exercise after the film?" As in the two media comparisons just reported, this question in unqualified form probably cannot be given a definitive answer. The generality of the present findings is thus subject to restrictions of the kind noted earlier as characteristic of such comparisons of alternative procedures.

The experiment was carried out with the same 43-minute film on map-reading and the same test that has previously been described.

The introductory and review procedures used with the film are described below.

1. NATURE OF THE INTRODUCTORY MATERIAL

The introductory exercises consisted of a preliminary description by an instructor of what was to be presented in the training film. It stressed the importance of learning how to read maps and called attention to important points that should be learned from the film. This introductory session was conducted in groups of two platoons each, four platoons in the morning and four in the afternoon. At each session one pair of platoons was given the introductory explanation inside the camp theater where the film was to be shown, while at the same time the other two platoons were receiving the instructions outside the theater. The length of the introductory exercises was from 15 to 20 minutes; showing of the 43-minute film immediately following thus made the total time spent in instruction just slightly over one hour.

2. NATURE OF THE REVIEW EXERCISE

As in the case of the introductory exercise, this was conducted in four groups of two platoons each, one company in the morning and one in the afternoon. The film was shown without introduction. For the review exercise, conducted immediately after each showing, half of the men filed outside to an area in back of the theater, the other half remained seated in the theater. The basis of the review exercise was a quiz composed of 15 true-false questions designed to cover each of the major topics in the film, and was given orally by the instructor. After the men had marked answers to the questions on cards provided for the purpose, the instructor gave the correct answer to each question and explained briefly *why* the given answer was correct, thus reviewing the points to which the questions related. The entire exercise took up a little over 20 minutes.

3. SELECTION AND BRIEFING OF THE INSTRUCTORS

The instructors who gave the supplementary exercises were selected from a group of available officers and assigned on the basis of systematic ratings of their ability as classroom instructors made by a number of their superior officers. The assignments were made in such a way that each form of instruction would be represented by four officers as typical as possible in the range and average level of their rated abilities as instructors.

Each instructor was provided with a schedule of procedure and an outline of the major points to be covered by the film. References to manuals were furnished, arrangements were made for previewing the film, and, in the case of the follow-up exercise, a set of quiz questions was provided. In order to preserve a normal range of diversity in the quality and style of presentation, however, each instructor was asked to prepare his presentation independently. As in the case of the film-strip study previously described, the amount of assistance and supervision thus furnished was in the opinions of training officers roughly comparable with what would normally be the case in regularly scheduled instruction under a centralized training program in a Replacement Training Center.

All instructors and other personnel involved were cautioned against telling the trainees about the purpose of instruction and testing, which were carried out in all essential respects as if they were part of the regular training program. None of the trainees were informed in advance that they would be tested on the material covered by the instruction.

4. AVERAGE AMOUNT LEARNED FROM EACH TYPE OF FILM INSTRUCTION

The effectiveness of each type of instruction is shown in the chart below. It can be seen that the control men who had not seen the

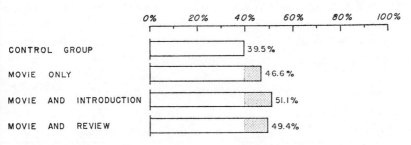

Figure 5. Average test scores for each group (N = 253 in each group).

training film averaged 39.5 per cent correct answers on the multiple-choice questions, whereas men who had seen the training film averaged higher and men who had one or the other of the supplementary exercises averaged still higher. The advantage shown for the film plus a supplementary exercise over the film by itself is statistically significant; however, the apparent slight advantage of the introductory over the review exercise is not reliable.[7]

5. AMOUNTS LEARNED BY MEN OF DIFFERENT INTELLIGENCE LEVELS

A comparison was made of the amount learned when the men were dichotomized into higher and lower intelligence groups. This dichotomy was based on scores on the AGCT; "higher" was defined as Classes I and II on this test and "lower" was defined as Classes III and IV. No Class V men were included in the sample.

In comparing the results for men of different intelligence levels, account must be taken of the differing initial levels of knowledge of the two groups. Since the more intelligent men already knew more of the correct answers, fewer of the correct answers could be learned by them from the film. The proper comparison, therefore, must be based on the *decrease in the proportion of initially incorrect* answers—that is, the comparison should be based on the change obtained relative to the maximum change possible. (See also Chapter 3, pages 65–66).

The percentages obtained in the four groups of lower-intelligence men and in the four groups of higher-intelligence men are shown in the top part of Table 4 below. The lower part of this table is a tabulation of the average "effectiveness-index" or magnitude of the effects relative to the magnitude of the effects possible.

The last two lines of Table 4 indicate the gains from the addition of a supplementary exercise to the film showing. It can be seen that the gains were not greatly different for either type of supplementary exercise or for either intelligence group.

6. POSSIBLE MOTIVATING EFFECTS OF THE INTRODUCTORY EXERCISE

An introduction preceding a film may increase the amount men learn about the film's subject matter in at least two ways:

a. By explaining and clarifying in advance some of the more difficult points to be presented in the film.

---

[7] There were 253 cases in each group. A difference as large as that obtained between the introductory and review exercises would occur by chance 28 times in a hundred in one direction or the other. The chances of obtaining differences as large as those between a supplementary exercise and film alone are about 3 in a hundred for review and less than one in a hundred either for introduction or for combined results on introduction and review.

b. Simply by stimulating men's interest, motivating them to attend more closely to the showing and remember what they are shown.

Data indicate that the introduction operated in *both* of these ways in the case of the film studied. These data are derived from an accidental feature of the administration of the experiment. None of the instructors got all the way through their outlines of their talk in the time allowed for the introduction. Thus certain topics in the films were covered in the talks and others were omitted. This

TABLE 4

A. AVERAGE PERCENTAGE OF CORRECT ANSWERS

	Less intelligent men (AGCT Classes III, IV)	More intelligent men (AGCT Classes I, II)
Control group	33.8%	46.2%
Movie only	38.0	56.7
Movie and introduction	43.0	60.4
Movie and review	41.4	58.6

B. AVERAGE EFFECTIVENESS INDEX

(*Difference from control group, divided by per cent wrong in control group*)

	Less intelligent men (AGCT Classes III, IV)	More intelligent men (AGCT Classes I, II)
Movie only	6.3%	19.5%
Movie and introduction	13.9	26.4
Movie and review	11.5	23.0
Differences from movie only		
Movie and introduction	7.6	5.2
Movie and review	6.7	3.5

accidental "experimental variable" provided the interesting finding that effects of the introductory talk were obtained on topics not covered in the introduction, as well as on topics covered. In the table below, the values at the left show the average effect of the introduction on a series of questions covering topics which instructors outlined and explained in some detail just before the film was shown. The figures at the right show the corresponding average effect on questions concerning film topics which were *not* given attention in the introduction.

Average effectiveness indices on two sets of material

	Topics covered in introduction	Topics not covered in introduction
Movie and introduction	16.0%	29.5%
Movie only	5.8	22.7
Difference	10.2%	6.8%

As seen by the difference at the right, inclusion of the introductory exercise produced an appreciable gain in the amount subsequently learned about topics which were not given attention in the introduction itself. It is unlikely that this result is due to interaction with effects on the material that was covered; the two topics were sufficiently distinct in content so that better understanding of the material covered would have contributed little to the understanding of parts not covered. A likely interpretation is that the introduction had a motivating effect that made all parts of the material better learned.

Aside from the foregoing hypothesis, which forms an interesting by-product of the study, the principal result of the present experiment was that supplementing the film by either a short introduction or a short review increased the effect of the film presentation but that, with the introduction and review procedures used, neither had a significant advantage over the other. It is evident that the relative effectiveness of the two supplementation methods compared is a function of the particular procedures used in each. This restriction on generality well illustrates the limitations of the kind of research represented by the three studies reported in the present chapter, in which alternative procedures "representative" of different media or instructional methods are compared but without controlled variation of specified factors governing the effectiveness of the alternatives.

EFFECTS OF FILMS ON MEN OF DIFFERENT INTELLECTUAL ABILITY

THE primary function of evaluative studies described in the preceding chapters was to determine the effectiveness of particular completed film products. Data thus obtained, however, can also be of value in formulating and testing general hypotheses concerning the effects of the films on subgroups of the total audience differentiated in terms of various demographic characteristics. As a basis for such differentiation, the questionnaires used in evaluating orientation films usually contained a number of items concerning such characteristics as age, education, religious affiliation, and marital status. In studies of training films, the characteristics usually obtained were years of schooling completed and scores on the Army General Classification Test (AGCT).

At the outset of the orientation film studies, analyses of the possible influence of a number of demographic factors were routinely made. These analyses were undertaken in the expectation that men's knowledge and opinions would be significantly related to characteristics of their personal history. But the studies showed the surprising result that region of birth, religious affiliation, marital status, Army rank or grade, length of Army service, age (within the adult range represented by the Army population), and several other personal-history items introduced in special studies showed few consistent or significant relationships to initial knowledge and opinion, and were almost uniformly unrelated to the effects of the films.

The one relationship which emerged clearly and consistently was the relationship of both information and opinion to intellectual ability, as indicated by AGCT score or years of schooling completed. Accordingly, this relationship will be our primary interest in the present chapter.

Special interest attaches to the analysis of the effects of films as a function of intellectual ability because of theoretical considerations.

The effects of a film presumably depend on the *learning* of material presented to members of the audience, and intelligence is intimately related to learning proficiency. Not only is intelligence related to ability to learn, but also it is related to other factors determining the effects of a film. For example, the more intelligent would be expected to be better able to see the general implications of the material presented even where conclusions are not explicitly drawn by the film. Similarly, intellectual ability would be expected to affect individuals' ability to evaluate critically the validity of implications and generalizations made in the film.

In order to relate intelligence to the effects of the films, it was necessary to adopt a suitable *index* of intellectual ability. Intelligence test scores would have had many advantages as such an index. However, it was not feasible to administer comprehensive tests of intelligence to the men who served in the present experiments. In the case of studies of training films it was possible to utilize the already available scores on the Army's standard test of general intellectual ability (Army General Classification Test or "AGCT").[1] But in studying orientation films, men did not put their names on their questionnaires because it was considered important to preserve anonymity, and it was therefore not possible to ascertain the AGCT scores of individual respondents. However, in these latter studies, respondents were always asked to indicate the number of years of schooling they had completed; and it was found that in the Army population there was a high correlation between years of schooling and AGCT scores. Accordingly, in the orientation film studies, educational level (years of schooling completed) was used as the index of intellectual ability. The use of this index was further supported by the finding in training film studies, when both educational level and AGCT score were available, that the two showed a closely similar relationship to the effects of the films.

Data supporting the use of level of schooling attained as an index of intelligence are furnished in a study by Lorge,[2] which reports a correlation of .66 between Otis intelligence test scores and highest grade completed. Correcting for the unreliability of the test and for the restriction of range of his subjects would of course be ex-

---

[1] For a general account of the development and characteristics of the AGCT, see "The Army General Classification Test," reported by the Staff of the Personnel Research Section, Classification and Replacement Branch, AGO, in the December 1945 issue of the *Psychological Bulletin* (Vol. 42, No. 10, pp. 760–68).

[2] Lorge, I "The 'Last School Grade Completed' as an Index of Intellectual Level." *Sch. and Soc.*, 1942, *56*, 529–32.

pected to increase this value materially. Results obtained in the present studies and in more extensive tabulations made by the Personnel Research Section, AGO,[3] confirm the existence of a substantial degree of relationship between level of schooling attained and scores on mental ability tests. In Figure 1, distributions of test scores on the Army General Classification Test for individuals with differing amounts of schooling are presented for a sample of 644 men used in one of the training film studies. The distributions are plotted in percentage measures, so that the area of each distribution totals 100 per cent.

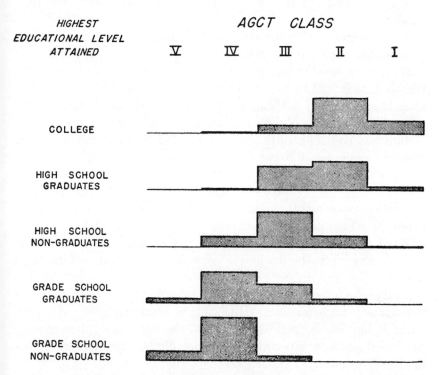

Figure 1. Relation between AGCT Class and educational level attained, for a sample of inductees (N = 644).

A correlation coefficient of slightly over .7 is indicated for the relationship shown when the AGCT classes and educational categories available are treated as equally spaced units. For other samples used in connection with the film research studies, the correlations ranged from about .50 to .80. The AGO studies report a correlation

[3] *Op. cit.*, p. 765.

of .73 between AGCT score and highest grade of school completed, for a sample of 4,330 soldiers.

The relatively high degree of relationship obtained is attributable in part to the fact that an adult population is involved, members of which have stopped their schooling at various points. The factors which cause individuals to drop out or continue in the educational system are closely correlated with intelligence. It is only because of this selective process that years of schooling may be used as an index of intellectual ability in an adult population. In a population still attending school, on the other hand, the correlation between intelligence and current grade level would undoubtedly be quite small.

The research design for studies of differential effects on various educational subgroups is relatively simple. Since the population characteristic used in analysis is not affected by the showing of the film, it is sufficient to have a control and experimental group tested after the showing of the film and to determine the differential effects of the film on groups of different intellectual ability by a comparison of film and control results among these different subgroups. This research design establishes only the nature of the correlation between intellectual ability and effects of the film. It obviously cannot establish the definitive causal relationships obtainable from controlled experiments. The correlational analysis can reveal the extent to which people of different levels of intellectual ability are affected by seeing a film, but it will not establish to what extent the relationship is due to native capacity per se and how much is due to other factors which vary concomitantly with intellectual capacity—for example, such factors as socio-economic status, and opportunity for schooling. However, in studying the effects of a variable like intellectual ability use of the experimental method is precluded since an experimenter cannot directly manipulate an individual's intellectual capacity.

Factual Information Learned by Groups
of Differing Ability

1. Information Learned Prior to the Film Presentation

Even before the film showings, there existed wide differences in the amount of factual knowledge possessed by men of different educational attainments. Many of the points of factual information tested could be answered on the basis of sources other than the film.

The superior initial performance of men of greater ability would reflect not only greater exposure to opportunities to acquire general information, but also greater ability to *learn and retain* the material to which they had been exposed. The relationship between information and intellectual ability (as inferred from educational attainment) is presented below for men in control groups who did not see the orientation films.

TABLE 1

PERCENTAGES OF MEN IN DIFFERENT EDUCATIONAL GROUPS KNOWING
ANSWERS TO INFORMATION ITEMS BEFORE FILM SHOWINGS

	Grade school men	High school men	College men
Average for all items significantly affected by orientation films studied	21.1%	28.6%	41.8%
Examples on specific items:			
Identity of Quisling: "Norwegian Traitor"	23	52	69
German Tactic for Blocking Allied Advance: "herding refugees into the roads"	18	31	52
Reason Hitler wanted Norway: "bases for bombers and U-boats"	31	51	60

For material covered in *training films* a similar relationship was found between education and initial level of knowledge expressed on information tests.

TABLE 2

AVERAGE PROPORTION OF MEN AT THREE EDUCATION LEVELS KNOWING
ANSWERS TO ITEMS OF INFORMATION

	Grade school men	Men with some high school education	High school graduates and college men
Map reading film	26.1%	28.9%	37.1%
Two first aid films (Av.)	50.7	57.9	64.8

The pattern of responses for the majority of individual items asked of the men is fairly consistent with the average results shown above. A similar picture was found for the relation of AGCT score to knowledge of material covered in training films. Mean scores for men in three AGCT categories for the same film subjects are shown below.

TABLE 3

AVERAGE PROPORTIONS OF MEN IN EACH AGCT CATEGORY CHECKING
CORRECT ANSWERS TO FACT-QUIZ ITEMS IN TRAINING FILM STUDIES

| | | AGCT Class | |
	IV and V	III	I and II
Map reading film	25.1%	30.5%	38.4%
Two first aid films (Av.)	50.2	57.9	65.7

2. AMOUNT LEARNED FROM FILMS

As would be expected, men of superior ability not only had better information at the outset but also acquired more from the film presentation. Illustrative of the general results on this point are those for the following item from the study used to evaluate the film "Prelude to War."

TABLE 4

PROPORTION OF MEN AT EACH EDUCATIONAL LEVEL WHOSE ANSWERS TO A
FACT-QUIZ QUESTION INDICATED THEY KNEW THE EXCUSE THE JAPS
GAVE FOR INVADING MANCHURIA

	Control group	Film group	Difference
Grade school men	13%	35%	+22%
High school men	18	60	+42
College men	25	73	+48

The positive correlation between educational attainment and film effects on information items was a consistent phenomenon throughout the studies. The illustrative item also shows the previously noted relation of educational attainment and initial amount of information. To take account of the differential room for improvement occasioned by differing initial levels, the correction introduced by the "Effectiveness Index," referred to in Chapter 3, is employed.

Average results for all orientation films combined are expressed in these units in the table below:[4]

AVERAGE EFFECTIVENESS INDEX FOR FACTUAL INFORMATION IMPARTED BY ORIENTATION FILMS (AVERAGE FOR 29 INFORMATION ITEMS SIGNIFICANTLY AFFECTED OVERALL BY ORIENTATION FILMS STUDIED).

Grade school men	16.3%
High school men	36.6
College men	54.2

Closely parallel results were obtained in studies of training films, in which AGCT scores were available for analysis.

Probably the most significant factor accounting for the obtained results is the superior proficiency in learning which is associated with greater intellectual ability.   But it is also well to bear in mind that the effects of superior intelligence will also be manifest in a number of indirect ways.   More intelligent men, as a function of both selection and training, probably have a *higher degree of interest* in the material presented and *more motivation* to learn it.   For another thing, individuals with more intelligence and more schooling will have acquired a *better context of related information* which would facilitate the acquisition of new facts.   Also, the more intelligent and better educated men will probably have learned *better techniques of learning and remembering* facts presented to them.

3. DIFFERENCES IN THE LEARNING OF EASY AND
   DIFFICULT MATERIAL

The results just presented show that on the average the men of greater intellectual ability show more proficient learning of the correct answers to fact-quiz items covered by a film than do those of less ability.   A factor that would be expected to affect this relationship is the difficulty of the material to be learned.   Variation in difficulty would certainly be expected to raise or lower the overall level of amount learned.   Thus the curve relating amount learned to intellectual level would be raised or lowered as a whole depending on the difficulty of the material.   In addition, however, it might be expected that difficulty would change the shape of the curve.   This would be expected on the presumption that the most proficient

---

[4] Values for "average effectiveness index" given in this chapter are computed individually for each item and then averaged for the series of items.

learners would tend to learn virtually *all* of the material, whether easy or difficult, whereas the amount of learning by the least proficient learners, regardless of difficulty of the material, would always be close to zero. At any intermediate level of learning proficiency, men would tend to show the greatest amount of learning for easy material, an average amount for average material, and the smallest amount for the most difficult material. Consequently, if separate curves are plotted to show the amount of learning of easy, average, and difficult material—with units of learning proficiency arbitrarily selected so as to give a linear relationship for "average" material— the curve for easy material would be expected to be negatively accelerated and the curve for difficult material positively accelerated, as illustrated in the hypothetical curves below.

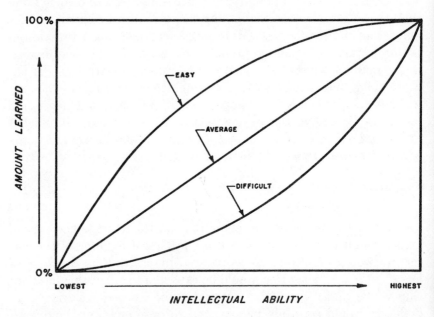

Figure 2.   Hypothetical relationship between intellectual ability and amount learned, for easy, "average," and difficult items.

The question arises as to how important a factor difficulty of material is as a determiner of the form of the relation between amount learned and intellectual ability. In investigating data with reference to these relationships it becomes necessary to specify first how "difficulty of material" and "amount of material learned" are to be measured. In many situations involving tests, where one is dealing with a test as a general measure of aptitude or proficiency, the "difficulty" of a test item is ordinarily thought of as inversely related to the proportion of men who can answer the question correctly. That is, the higher the proportion of initially correct responses, the "easier" the item would be considered. But in the present situation, where we are concerned with *changes* in information, or amount of learning, the more appropriate measure of "difficulty" is not *initial level* of correct response but difficulty of *learning* the material.

In order to determine the effect of difficulty on the shape of the relation between intellectual ability and amount learned, the effects of the orientation films on fact-quiz items of varying difficulty were analyzed separately for each educational level. A total of 42 fact-items were used to measure information changes for the four films studied. Of these, twelve were discarded because they showed no significant effects of the film. The remaining thirty items then were divided according to level of difficulty, as defined in terms of *overall effectiveness index* for all education groups combined. The total set of thirty items was subdivided into three groups: an "easiest" group (7 items), a "middle" group (16 items), and a "hardest" group (7 items). The composition of these groups of items in terms of overall level of difficulty is shown below.

RANGE OF EFFECTIVENESS INDEX FOR ITEMS OF VARYING DIFFICULTY

	Range of effectiveness indices (for all men tested)
7 "easiest" items	51% to 72%
16 "medium difficulty" items	17 to 45
7 "hardest" items	4 to 16

The amount of material learned by each of three education groups is shown in the table below for the easiest, middle, and hardest groups of items. The first three lines of figures show the amount learned by each education group, in terms of the average effectiveness index for each level of difficulty. The second three lines of the table show the differences between successive education groups obtained from the three preceding lines of figures.

A slight degree of curvilinearity in the relationship is indicated by the fact that the difference between the lower and middle educational categories is larger than that between the middle and upper categories in the case of the *easiest* material, whereas the larger difference is between the two higher educational categories in the case of the *most difficult* material. (In the lower part of the table it is seen that the difference in learning between the grade school and high school groups is 26 per cent for the *easiest* material and only 12 per cent for the hardest material, whereas the difference between high school and college men is about 17 per cent for the *hardest* material and 15 per cent for the easiest material.) This pattern of differences is in line with the expectation that positively and negatively accelerated curves, respectively, would be found for easy and difficult material. However, the degree of curvilinearity obtained is very slight—the three curves relating amount learned to intellectual ability are nearly linear despite the fairly large differences in overall level of difficulty of learning the material. Apparently diffi-

TABLE 5

RELATION BETWEEN EDUCATIONAL LEVEL AND LEARNING OF FACT-ITEMS
FROM ORIENTATION FILMS, AS A FUNCTION OF DIFFICULTY OF ITEMS
(AMOUNTS LEARNED BY EACH EDUCATION GROUP, IN TERMS OF
AVERAGE EFFECTIVENESS INDEX)

| | EFFECTIVENESS INDICES | | |
	Grade school men	*High school men*	*College men*
Material:			
Easiest	35.1%	60.7%	75.3%
Middle	11.6	30.3	49.9
Hardest	2.6	14.3	31.7
Differences:			
Easiest		25.6%	14.6%
Middle		18.7	19.6
Hardest		11.7	17.4

culty of material does not greatly alter the shape of the relation of amount learned to intellectual ability, even though the range of intellectual ability is fairly large in the present results. It seems likely that if the range of intellectual ability could be extended the curves would converge at both ends. However such convergence as might be obtained would represent effects on only the very small proportions making up the most intelligent and the most unintelligent members of the population as a whole. For the great majority of the population it would appear from the present results that the relation between intellectual ability and amount learned is essentially linear regardless of difficulty.

Similar results were obtained in studies of training films where both educational level and AGCT scores were available. Analysis by both indices of intelligence showed the same relationship as the results previously presented for the orientation films. These results based on all the significantly affected items from tests covering the effects of two training films on first aid are shown in the accompanying figure.

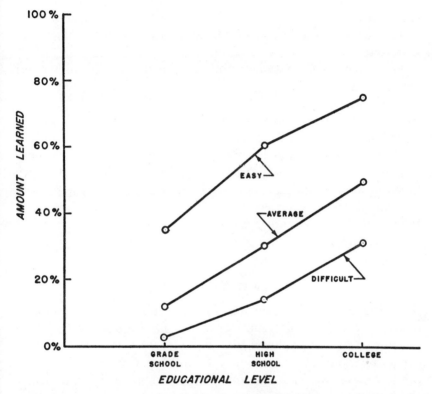

Figure 3. Obtained relationship between educational level and average per cent of fact-quiz items learned.

In the foregoing discussion of the shapes of the "curves" relating intellectual ability to amount learned, it should be borne in mind that the problem of equivalence of units along either the vertical or the horizontal axis is critical to the shape of the curve obtained. In plotting results in the present studies, AGCT classes (I through V) were treated as if equally far apart. Presumably they are separated by equal distances in standard deviation units, since this was the basis used for designating the five classes. Also the educational categories of grade school, high school nongraduate, high school graduate, and college have been dealt with as if equally spaced.

The latter is obviously an inexact and arbitrary treatment.   Using the number of years of schooling attained would have provided at least a superficially more equivalent set of units, but in the present studies the exact number of years of schooling was generally not recorded.   However, while the effect of nonequivalence of units of intellectual ability is to make the absolute shape of a particular curve an arbitrary matter, it does not affect the direction of trends in the shape of the family of curves as a function of difficulty of material.

The same considerations apply to the units used to measure amount learned.   In the present studies the effect of difficulty of material was investigated by using "effectiveness index" units— that is, amount learned was measured as the per cent change obtained divided by maximum change possible.   Use of these units at least compensated for nonequivalence due to differing initial levels of knowledge (and consequent statistical ceiling effects) among the different intellectual groups, but the units used cannot be regarded as equivalent on other counts.   However, the nonequivalence of these units (as in the case of units of intellectual ability) presumably does not prevent appropriate description of the *direction of changes* in shape as a function of the difficulty of the material.

"A LITTLE KNOWLEDGE"

An interesting exception was found to the otherwise uniformly obtained positive correlation between intellectual level and the amount of change produced by a film on fact-quiz items.   A *negative* correlation between effect and intellectual level was found in the few cases in which the film produced appreciable increases in the percentage choosing an *incorrect* answer.

An example illustrating this kind of result was observed in studying the cumulative effects of the second and third orientation films, "The Nazis Strike" and "Divide and Conquer."   The films had shown that by the terms of the Munich Pact, Britain and France agreed to let Hitler take over part of Czechoslovakia, and also presented repeated instances in which the Nazis proceeded to occupy territory to which they had earlier disclaimed any interest.   A question designed to get at the former point—terms of the Munich Pact—was worded as follows:

By the terms of the Munich Pact in 1938:

_____ The Nazis promised to stay out of Austria

_____ Britain and France allowed Hitler to take over part of
     Czechoslovakia

_____ The Nazis were permitted to remilitarize the Rhineland

_____ Hitler and Mussolini agreed to support each other in case
     of war

It will be observed that the second choice is the correct answer but
that the first choice, which is incorrect, alludes to a "Nazi promise"
which was contradicted by subsequent events. The film increased
the percentage of men checking this incorrect answer, and this increase was most marked in the case of the less intelligent men (Figure 4).

On the other hand, the *correct* answer was learned by progressively
larger percentages of men as educational level increased, the low

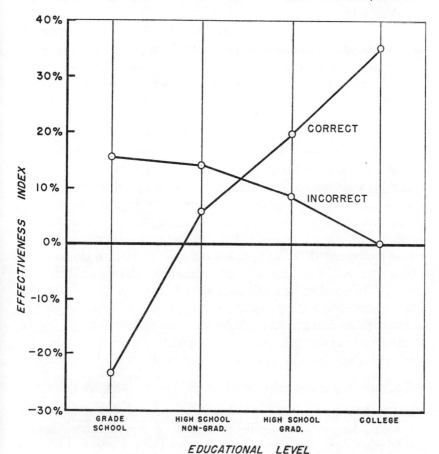

Figure 4. Effectiveness of film in changing answers to a fact-quiz item.

point in this progression being represented by the grade school men, who actually showed a decrease in the proportion giving the correct answer after seeing the film.

Apparently the men of less intellectual ability were strongly impressed by the false promises of the Nazis and did not learn the significant details of the Munich Pact. Consequently they checked the answer which seemed most reasonable in terms of what they remembered best.

Several analogous examples were found in the study of these films and of "The Battle of Britain." As already implied, an explanation for this phenomenon can be given in terms of the fact that in any film presentation some points will inevitably be more impressively presented and hence better learned and remembered than others, and some of the less impressively presented facts will be well remembered only by the more proficient learners. If a test question then presents as alternative answers one choice which is an incorrect answer to the question but which is related to a point *well remembered* by many of the men, and a correct answer which refers to a point remembered only by the better learners, it would be expected that the better learners who remember both points can choose the one which correctly answers the question, whereas the less proficient learners, remembering only one associated point (which happens to be the wrong answer), will have an increased tendency to check it because it is the answer that strikes a familiar note.

If this hypothesis is correct an implication would be the necessity of making extremely explicit distinctions in a film on points which are judged to be important, rather than relying on the men themselves to distinguish between two closely similar implications. It is also suggested that the spectacular and impressive presentation techniques should be appropriately chosen in relation to the importance of the point to be made; when used on a minor point the men may generalize in ways which are clearly incorrect. This hypothesis is closely related to one presented later in the chapter on the problem of valid and invalid generalizations made by members of the audience, which applies with particular force in the case of opinions.

Opinion Changes Among Groups of Different Ability

In the studies of orientation films it was possible to relate intellectual ability not only to the effects of films on factual knowledge but also to effects on men's opinions. Analysis of the effect of films on men's opinions raises the difficult problem of distinguishing between statements which represent "opinion" and those which represent "fact." There is often a considerable amount of arbitrariness involved in classifying statements as representing "fact" or as representing "opinion."

Perhaps the chief distinction implicit in classifying certain statements as "opinion" is that such statements are generally regarded as more difficult to verify than statements of simple fact. Thus, usually classed as opinion are statements making inferences as to intentions, motives, or reasons, or predictions as to what will happen in the future or what might have happened under certain circumstances. For example: "The Germans bombed Rotterdam [for purely sadistic reasons]," "Britain will not make a separate peace with the Germans," or "The Nazis would force us to work as slaves if they were victorious."

A related characteristic often differentiating "opinions" from "facts" is the degree of generality of the statements. Statements representing syntheses or interpretation of a number of interrelated facts are generally regarded as "opinions." Statements representing summaries, conclusions, or generalizations from sets of specific facts are difficult to substantiate fully because of the large number of facts ordinarily required to prove or disprove them. For example, an evaluative statement of opinion corresponding to the comparatively specific and simple factual point that the RAF pilots were greatly outnumbered during the Battle of Britain is the following, "The RAF has done about the best job of fighting so far in this war." In order to establish the validity of the latter statement, a large number of facts, concerning the performance of the RAF and other fighting organizations with which an implied comparison is made, would have to be established and evaluated. In addition to assembling all the relevant facts in such a case, there would be the added difficulty of determining the proper way in which these facts should be weighted or integrated so as to arrive at the "correct" interpretation.

The distinction between statements of opinion and statements of fact obviously involves a continuum between those most clearly factual and those most clearly matters of opinion. For example, the statement that "The head of the German Air Force is named Goering" would be a "fact," whereas the statement, "The British are doing their fair share in helping to win the war," is clearly a matter of "opinion." Between such fairly clear-cut extremes of facts and opinions will obviously be a number of statements which are more difficult to classify. Thus, whether the statement that "The German bombing attacks were part of a plan to invade and conquer Britain" would be regarded as "fact" or as "opinion" would depend on the amount of evidence available as to the actual plans of the German leaders.

It is to be expected, therefore, that what is regarded by one individual as a "fact" may be regarded by another as an "opinion." This factor had to be recognized in the conduct of the experimental evaluations of the film. Some items would probably be reacted to by all individuals in the audience as questions of fact; others would probably be uniformly reacted to as questions of opinion. Items that were clearly matters of opinion, or those which it was anticipated that some men would regard as "opinion" and others as "fact," were grouped together and labeled opinions to encourage a uniform set to perceive them as opinions. This was particularly important where an individual would be hesitant to express himself because he felt he lacked the necessary information or where he would be prone to give what he considered the "correct" answer (from the Army's point of view) instead of his own personal opinion.

"Fact" items were grouped together at the end of the questionnaire, and men were instructed to check the "true" answer, guessing if they did not "know" the answer. The instructions for the questions classed as "opinion," on the other hand, stressed the idea that men's "own personal opinion" was wanted—that frank opinions could be given freely because of the anonymity of the responses, that there was no "right" or "wrong" answer, etc.

ANALYSIS OF RESULTS

As in the case of factual information, an analysis was made of the magnitude of change in opinion among men in the various educational groups. Included in this analysis were data from each of the four films in the "Why We Fight" series on any opinion item which was reliably affected by the film. A total of 31 opinion items (6 for the first film in the series, 12 for the joint effects of the second and third films, and 13 for the fourth film) met this requirement. The results for these items are averaged in the table below.

A trend is seen for the effects of the films on opinion to increase with higher intellectual ability. However, inspection of the individual items shows this trend to be the result of averaging some items where the greater effects are among the men of higher intellectual ability and others where the greater effects were among those of lesser ability.   Consequently, the positive and negative correlations will partially offset each other in determining the average trend.   This is in contrast to the situation existing in the case of items of factual information where almost invariably the effects showed a positive correlation with intellectual ability.   Opinion

TABLE 6

AVERAGE INITIAL LEVEL, FINAL LEVEL AND EFFECTS OF FILM ON
OPINION ITEMS FOR MEN OF VARIOUS EDUCATIONAL LEVELS

Per cent giving favorable answers:	Grade school	Some high school	High school grad.	College
Before seeing film	45.3%	47.6%	49.4%	50.8%
After seeing film	55.2	58.1	60.3	62.8
Difference	9.9%	10.5%	10.9%	12.0%
Average effectiveness index	18.1%	20.1%	21.5%	24.4%

items illustrating both the positive and the negative pattern of relationship to intellectual ability are given below.   The first example is based on an item used in the evaluation of the second and third orientation films and concerns men's opinions that "appeasement" of Germany by Britain and France "only made things worse in the long run."   The effect of the films in this case is shown below in terms of a comparison between film and control groups in the percentages checking this answer (rather than checking an alternative answer indicating that the appeasement policy was the best thing to do at that time).

TABLE 7

PERCENTAGES INDICATING BELIEF THAT
"APPEASEMENT MADE THINGS WORSE"

	Grade school men	High school men	College men
Per cent in film group	56%	73%	82%
Per cent in control group	53	61	67
Difference	3%	12%	15%
"Effectiveness Index":	6%	31%	45%

An opposite correlation is illustrated in the effect of the same films on the number of men who thought the Germans would, if victorious, "try to control our country completely and force Americans to work as slaves." In this case a distinct negative correlation between education and effect is observed: the film materially increased the proportion of grade school men expressing this point of view, but had much less effect on men with a high school education and no significant effect on college men.

TABLE 8

PERCENTAGES INDICATING BELIEF THAT GERMANS WOULD ENSLAVE
AMERICANS IF VICTORIOUS

	Grade school men	*High school men*	*College men*
Per cent for film group	74%	66%	48%
Per cent for control group	54	61	46
Difference (change)	*20%*	*5%*	*2%*
"Effectiveness Index":	*43%*	*13%*	*4%*

The diversity among different opinion items in the relationship between effects and ability requires some exploration. In the discussion that follows several factors which may contribute to the relationship will be analyzed. Some of these factors would tend to produce a positive correlation between effects and intellectual ability; others would produce negative correlations. As a consequence the overall relationship for an item would be expected to depend on the relative weights of the various factors.

(1) *Learning ability:* As in the case of information items so also in the case of opinions we should expect that the men with higher intellectual ability should be able to learn the content of the films more readily than men of lower ability. This should be responsible in part for the positive relationship shown in Table 6. However, if learning ability were the only factor in operation this positive relation would be even more pronounced and none of the individual items would show negative correlation between effects and intellectual ability.

(2) *Acceptance of the material:* Regardless of a man's ability to learn a new interpretation, he will not adopt it as his own unless he believes in it. He may learn what the film *said* but may nevertheless consider what the film said to be incorrect. Hence his own opinion may be unchanged by what he has learned. If some of the

interpretations made by the films were not acceptable to intelligent men but were acceptable to those of lesser intelligence, the factor of learning ability might be sufficiently offset by the factor of acceptance that a negative correlation would be obtained between intellectual ability and particular opinion changes produced by the films.

Nonacceptance by more intelligent men of some of the interpretations provided by the orientation films studied would seem quite likely since the films did not always involve a purely dispassionate presentation of a series of facts but instead were often "slanted" in the direction of particular points of view and particular interpretations of the facts. These interpretations were sometimes very explicitly made by the narrator and sometimes only implied. In either case the complete documentation necessary to establish the validity of an interpretation was not always included, and anyone who recognized this fact and was conscious of the "slant" of the films would be less prone to accept the interpretations uncritically. Hence, there was a priori reason to expect that some opinion changes might be negatively correlated with intellectual ability despite the greater learning ability of the more intelligent.

In order to obtain evidence for or against the operation of the "acceptance" factor in the present data it was desired to utilize a measure of acceptance that was independent of the opinion changes produced by the films. The acceptability of an interpretation would be expected in general to be a function both of motivational factors such as emotional biases or predispositions and of rational analysis of the validity of the interpretation on the basis of available factual information. Of these two factors, the motivational and the rational, we would expect the heaviest weighting of motivational factors among the less intelligent and the heaviest weighting of the rational factors among the more intelligent. Less intelligent individuals would be more apt to accept a new interpretation because it fitted in with their own preconception and wishes regardless of any rational consideration; or they would be more apt to cling with bull-headed stubbornness to their own emotionally determined opinion despite overwhelming rational evidence that is presented against their opinion. The more intelligent on the other hand, with their superior learning ability, their superior ability to draw valid conclusions, their initial access to a greater number of relevant facts, would be more apt to accept or reject an interpretation on the basis of evidence and rational argument.

Ideally, for a complete analysis of the "acceptance factor" as it applies to the present data, one would seek separate measures both of the motivational factors and of those rational factors that determine the actual validity of a given interpretation on the basis of the available evidence. Conceivably, the motivational, irrational factors determining an opinion might be correlated with intellectual ability such that the less intelligent have an irrational bias in one direction while the more intelligent have an irrational bias in a different direction. No such independent measure of the motivational factor was available in the orientation film studies. However, it seems likely that in the typical case the motivational factors would be much the same throughout the population and the critical correlation would be that between intellectual ability and the extent to which the motivational factors affected an individual's opinion. That is, the more intelligent would be expected to have *fewer* irrational determinants of opinion rather than having *different* irrational determinants as compared with the less intelligent. Emphasis was therefore placed on getting a measure of the rational validity of an interpretation.

It should be noted that if the expected relationship between intelligence, opinion change, and rational validity can be established it would have greater generality than relationships to particular motivational factors. That is, we *always* expect those of greater intellectual ability to be more likely to accept an interpretation if it has greater rational validity, whereas to utilize any possible irrational biases that are held only by the more intelligent we must determine the nature of their bias in each case.

Probably the best way to rate statements as to soundness of opinion or acceptability of the interpretation would be to determine the extent to which adherence to the opinion is correlated with a joint measure of intelligence and amount of knowledge of the relevant facts. Opinions that are positively correlated with such a measure represent "informed" opinions. They are interpretations that are held only for chance or motivational reasons among those who cannot make proper interpretations, but they are progressively more likely to be the view adopted by those in progressively better positions to make the correct inference or the inference most likely correct on the available evidence. The validity of interpretations showing a zero correlation with the joint measure on the other hand is somewhat indeterminant. In such a case it is ambiguous whether there is insufficient evidence for even the more intelligent to make a decision, whether emotional and rational determinants are acting in combinations that cancel or supplement each other's effects, or

exactly what are the determinants of the opinion.   Opinions negatively correlated with intelligence and relevant knowledge, however,
are definitely "misinformed" opinions.   They are opinions that
are more likely to be held the less the person is in a position to make
a valid inference from factual knowledge.

In the analysis of the orientation film data it was not possible to
use a joint measure of intelligence and initial access to relevant facts
since repetition of the fact-quiz items was avoided by restricting
their inclusion to the "after" questionnaires.   In absence of a good
joint measure of intelligence and relevant knowledge, a way of
approximating this criterion for differentiating acceptable and non-
acceptable interpretations is to differentiate the interpretive statements in terms of the correlations between *educational level* and the
proportion endorsing each statement.   In doing this we assume that
the better educated men will on the average both be better informed
and be better able, in view of their higher average intelligence, to
draw correct conclusions from the information they have available.

Specifically, the assumption is that opinions expressed with increasing frequency by successively higher education groups will on
the average be more likely to be correct than interpretations showing a zero or negative correlation with education.   In line with this
assumption, opinions may be classified according to their initial
correlation with education in the control groups and the relationship
between education and effects of the film determined separately for
each class of opinions.   If the opinion is a "valid" interpretation—
i.e., if its initial correlation with education is positive—the brighter
men should show greater effects because of their superior learning
ability.   If, on the other hand, the opinion is "invalid"—negatively
correlated with education—the better educated men will be less
affected than will men with less schooling.

It is apparent that the suggested procedure does not segregate the
opinions according to their "validity" independently of motivational
factors.   Where an opinion is held in the great majority among those
of little schooling and held only infrequently among the better educated, we can be fairly sure that some motivational factor is influencing the beliefs of those of little schooling.   Similarly, if endorsement of a particular interpretation is positively correlated with
education we cannot be sure that this merely reflects the greater
validity of the opinion and the greater ability of those who get further in school to arrive at valid interpretations.   It could be that
such a correlation merely reflects a particular irrational bias among

the better educated which is not shared by the lower intelligence groups.

By itself, differences in the direction of the correlation between opinion and years of schooling achieved indicate differences in over-all predisposition—motivational and rational—to accept the interpretation represented by the opinion statement. However, the presumption is that the critical predisposing factor among those of higher education is the tendency to be guided by rational rather than by irrational factors.

In carrying out the "acceptance" analysis, only those opinion questions significantly affected by the films were used in order not to dilute the analysis with chance results. It was not feasible in this analysis to segregate the items according to whether the interpretations had been specifically made in the films or whether they had only been unstated implications of the film material (cf. p. 171f). However, it should be clear that the same factors that apply in the case of film-made interpretations also apply to interpretations not specifically mentioned in the films but which might possibly be made by the audience members as implications of the material presented. In such cases it would still be expected that the acquisition of a new interpretation would be a function of initial access to relevant facts, ability to make valid inferences, relative contribution of emotional and rational considerations, and so forth.

All opinion questions significantly affected by the "Why We Fight" films studied were sorted into three sets on the basis of their correlation between education and initial level of response in the control group. The effect of the film for each of these three sets of items, selected on the basis of *initial* correlation with education, was then computed. The *initial* correlation with education for the three sets of items is shown below in terms of the average frequency of endorsement in the control group at each of four educational levels. The opinion was considered positively correlated if there was a significantly higher endorsement among college men than among grade school men; it was considered negatively correlated if the difference was significant in the opposite direction.

OPINION ITEM SET (*Initial correlation with education*)	INITIAL RESPONSE (PER CENT "FAVORABLE" ANSWERS) AT EACH EDUCATION LEVEL			
	Grade school	Some H. S.	H. S. grad.	College
Positive (11 items)	36.3	47.4	53.5	63.3
Zero (14 items)	48.1	48.9	50.0	48.6
Negative (6 items)	55.5	45.2	40.7	34.0

When effects of the films in terms of the *effectiveness index* at each educational level were averaged separately for the opinion items in the three sets defined above according to the correlations between education and initial response, the results shown in the following table were obtained.

TABLE 9

AVERAGE EFFECTS OF FILM AT FOUR EDUCATIONAL LEVELS FOR OPINION
ITEMS WITH POSITIVE, ZERO, AND NEGATIVE CORRELATIONS BETWEEN
EDUCATION AND INITIAL LEVEL OF RESPONSE

OPINION ITEM GROUPS:	AVERAGE EFFECTS OF FILM FOR EDUCATIONAL SUBGROUPS (IN TERMS OF EFFECTIVENESS INDEX)			
(Correlation of education and initial level)	*Grade School*	*Some H. S.*	*H. S. Grad.*	*College*
	%	%	%	%
11 items with *positive correlation*	19.8	21.7	24.5	34.9
14 items with *zero correlation*	17.4	22.1	24.4	27.4
6 items with *negative correlation*	17.7	18.7	17.2	23.2

It can be seen in the table above that there is a definite trend for the effects to increase with education for those items which showed an initial positive correlation with education.   Thus, the effectiveness index rises from a value of about 20 per cent for grade school men to a value of about 35 per cent for college men in the case of the eleven positively correlated opinion items.   This relationship is similar to but less marked than that shown for information items (cf. p. 153).   On the other hand, no consistent rise is found for the six items with negative initial correlation.

More striking results on this point were obtained from the study of the delayed effects (nine weeks after the film showing) of "The Battle of Britain."   The analysis is based on items which showed significant effects at this time interval.   The results are shown in Figure 5.   (A detailed presentation of the results of this study will be found in Chapter 7.)

(3) *Audience-made interpretations from film content:* A distinction was noted earlier between interpretations provided within the film content and interpretations or generalizations made by audience members themselves on the basis of material presented.   Therefore, changes in audience opinions as a result of seeing a film involve a third factor in addition to those of learning and acceptance: namely, men's tendency to make interpretations or generalizations not made

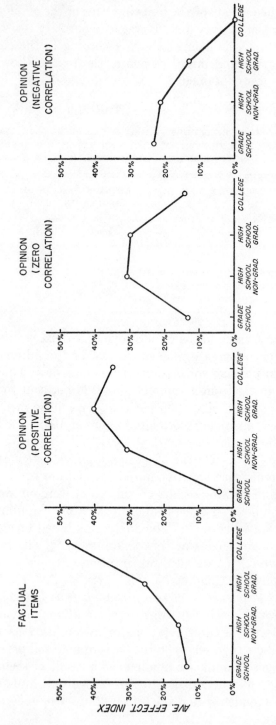

Figure 5.   Relationship between educational level and amount of change produced by film for factual items and for opinion items with positive, zero and negative initial correlation with education.

explicitly in the film but inferred by the men from material presented by the film.

The relation of intelligence to this tendency of audience members to make their own interpretation would depend on the type of interpretation specified.   The ability to make *valid* interpretations would in general be an increasing function of increasing intelligence. Thus, for valid interpretations made by the audience, the resultant of the factors of learning and acceptance would be given an additional influence in the direction of a positive correlation with intelligence.   This tendency would probably be accentuated in case of valid applications to highly dissimilar areas, where presumably it would be only the men in the higher intelligence levels who would be able to make the application.   In a purely factual presentation, the making of valid interpretations by audience members would presumably be the only way in which desired opinion changes would be produced.   If acceptance were not a factor in determining such effects, the average correlation between intellectual ability and effects would be *greater* for opinions than for information because of the added influence of greater generalizing ability for the more intelligent.   Thus, the average curves given above for opinion changes in the case of the "Why We Fight" films might not be typical of results that would be obtained from films employing a purely factual presentation of such a character that any opinion changes effected would depend entirely on interpretations made by members of the audience.

Invalid applications or generalizations from film material presented would, on the other hand, be expected to be *less* frequently made by the more intelligent men than by the unintelligent, and this tendency might also be accentuated for the areas most dissimilar to those covered by the film.   However, with a wide range of intelligence, invalid interpretations might in some cases be made more frequently by those of intermediate intelligence than by the least intelligent group, who might in some instances be unable to make any generalizations whatever, even if they assimilated the relevant facts.   For this reason, a reversal might be observed for the curve of intelligence versus effect of film on opinion statements representing invalid applications of the material presented.

It was not feasible in the present film studies to carry out a systematic investigation of the kinds of effects just hypothesized because it was found impossible to obtain consistent judgments for differentiating opinion items as to whether the interpretations they represented were made by the film or had to be inferred by the audience. Thus there was no clear-cut set of opinion items that could be used for the analysis of "audience-made" interpretations. However, one opinion item on which significant effects were obtained had been deliberately designed by the experimenters for the purpose of testing the extent to which men generalized invalidly beyond the film content in their interpretations. This was the agree-disagree statement, "The English did as good a job as possible of holding out against the Japs at Singapore," included in the questionnaires used to test effects of "The Battle of Britain." Nothing was mentioned in the film about British resistance at Singapore, and although the determined resistance of the British in defending England during the Blitz was played up, there was no direct interpretation by the film to suggest that such behavior was an invariable characteristic of the British. The effects of the film (combined results for the two camps where it was studied) are shown in the table below.

TABLE 10

PERCENTAGES AT EACH EDUCATIONAL LEVEL WHO AGREED WITH STATEMENT, "THE ENGLISH DID AS GOOD A JOB AS POSSIBLE OF HOLDING OUT AGAINST THE JAPS AT SINGAPORE."

	Grade School	Some H. S.	H. S. Grad.	College
Control group:	68%	52%	43%	28%
Film group:	68	62	48	32
Difference:	0%	10%	5%	4%
"Effectiveness index"	0%	21%	9%	6%

It is seen that the effects of the film on this audience-made interpretation are less for the higher education groups than for the "some high school" group. But the effect is also absent in the case of the *lowest* education group, suggesting the "curvilinear" type of relationship mentioned above as a possibility with a wide range of intellectual ability.

(4) *Stability of opinion:* A fourth factor to consider in analyzing the relationship between intellectual ability and magnitude of change in opinion is the relative stability of opinions in the various educational subgroups. For example, the fact that brighter men showed little superiority to the less bright in terms of opinion change but were considerably superior in learning factual material may be

due in part to a greater stability of opinion among the brighter men. Greater stability might be expected among brighter men on the assumption that they already have considered relevant facts and have a definite opinion on the subject. The less intelligent men, on the other hand, might be more likely never to have considered the subject and to have no real opinion one way or the other. Thus the film might not alter the well crystallized opinions of the brighter men, but would provide the less bright with an opinion for the first time.

The simplest method of analysis is to compare the per cent of men in each educational group who give the same answers on successive administrations of the questionnaire. Data were available from the "Battle of Britain" study to determine consistency at two time intervals—one for a period of two weeks and the other of nine weeks. To determine stability of opinion independent of the effect of the films the control groups were used in the analysis. The percentages of the men in each educational group who gave the same answer to the opinion items after a short (2 week) and a long (9 week) time interval are depicted in Figure 6.

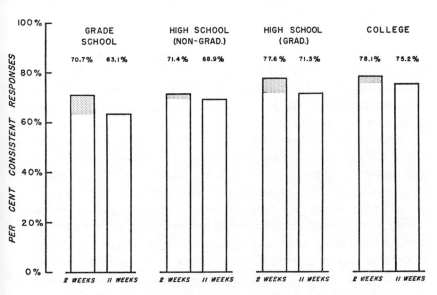

Figure 6.   Stability of opinion among men of various educational levels.

These results indicate that at both the two-week and the nine-week interval there is a slight positive correlation between educational level and amount of consistency.[5] This trend held for 16 of the 21 opinion items used in the questionnaire. The correlation is primarily noteworthy however because of the fact that it is not more marked; as compared with the consistency shown by the more intelligent men, the degree of consistency for those of lower ability is surprisingly good.

The other interesting point brought out by the chart is the comparative stability of opinion during the nine-week as compared with that during the two-week interval. Obtained changes in responses are due not only to real changes in opinion but also due to the unreliability of the measuring instrument. It seems reasonable to assume that this unreliability is the same for the two time intervals and consequently that the decrease in consistency at the long-time interval as compared with that at the short-time interval is indicative of real change in opinion. The results indicate however that these variations in consistency are small and not substantially different for the various educational groups.

The present results then show surprisingly little difference between the high and low intelligence groups in the consistency with which they hold their opinions over time intervals varying from two weeks to over two months.

Several factors have been discussed as bearing on the relationship of intellectual ability to opinion changes. The factor emerging most clearly from the present data is that of "acceptance." It is apparent from the results obtained that in the opinion areas studied some items of opinion are initially subscribed to more frequently by the brighter men than by the less intelligent, and that for these items film effects also tend to be greater among the more intelligent men. But other opinions show the reverse correlation with intellectual ability, and for such items the positive correlation between intelligence and amount of change produced by the film is not found. These findings may be interpreted by describing the initial correlation between intelligence and opinion held as a measure of "validity" of opinion and advancing the proposition that valid interpretations

[5] The amount of consistency is of course affected by initial level of opinion (i.e., opinions which are held by a high proportion of the men are more limited in the amount of change than those held by a smaller proportion of the men). In the case of the present study, however, the initial level of opinion was substantially the same for the different educational groups. Furthermore, an analysis of consistency for the high and low education groups on items of varying initial frequency showed that at each frequency level there was a constant superiority of the high education group in consistency.

will be accepted more readily by the intelligent but invalid ones more readily by the less intelligent than by the more intelligent.

Of the other two factors considered, that of the presumed greater ability of the more intelligent to draw conclusions from evidence presented does not emerge as clearly differentiable in the present data from the factor of acceptance. Analysis in terms of the third factor, stability of opinion, suggests that groups of differing ability are not sufficiently different in amount of stability exhibited to account for the tendency of some items to show a zero or negative correlation with education.

PART II

STUDIES EMPLOYING CONTROLLED VARIATION

INTRODUCTION TO PART II

$\cdots\cdots\cdots\cdots\cdots\cdots\cdots\cdots\cdots\cdots\cdots\cdots\cdots\cdots\cdots\cdots\cdots\cdots\cdots\cdots$

IN THE general introduction to this volume a distinction was made between two major classes of film research. The distinction was between purely evaluative studies on the one hand, and studies employing controlled variation on the other. The studies reported thus far in this volume were designed primarily for evaluative purposes. In such studies the generality of results is limited because they are tied to specific film content, so that statements of effects are in terms of the effect of a complex presentation in which many factors help determine the result but the contribution of any one factor is not singled out. A partial exception to this lies in the analyses, reported in Chapter 6, of the relation of intellectual ability to the effects of films.

In the studies reported in the three following chapters an attempt is made to obtain findings having a greater degree of generalizability. The method used is that of systematically varying certain specified factors while other factors are controlled. This makes it possible to determine the effectiveness of the particular factors varied. As pointed out in Chapter 1, one's confidence in the probable validity of generalized findings about the effect of a factor is increased by having selected for study factors which are critical in terms of theoretical formulation. The reason for this lies in part in the fact that the underlying theoretical basis is usually already grounded in a series of observations in varied contexts so that there is reason in advance to expect that the factor studied will be important in a variety of situations rather than specific to the particular conditions studied.

The studies to be reported in Chapters 7, 8, and 9 furnish examples of studies in which the method of controlled variation was used and where, in addition, the factors varied were selected partly in terms of theoretical considerations. They thus approach more nearly than do the evaluative studies previously described the kind of research that is required as a basis for developing a body of principles which will permit valid generalizations concerning the influence of various factors in determining film effectiveness which are more independent of specific content.

The desirable property of generalizability of findings does not, of course, follow automatically simply because the effects of varying a specific factor of theoretical interest have been carefully studied in a particular context.   As suggested in Chapter 1, it is unlikely that with the complexity of factors operating in film communication there would be many empirical generalizations which would hold without qualification for all educational films, all audiences, and all conditions of utilization.   Rather, variables would be expected to interact in such a way that the most exact and most useful empirical generalizations would emerge as a series of principles rather than a single principle.   Such a series of principles would designate how the effects of one variable are modified by other important variables operating in the situation.   For this reason in the studies reported in the following chapters several important variable factors are studied in combination instead of confining the experimental observations to the effect of a single factor.   Three studies are described:

Chapter 7 deals with the *effects of a film presentation as a function of lapse of time*.   The film used was "The Battle of Britain," which was used also in a purely evaluative study of the film's immediate effects, described in Chapter 2.   The analysis described in Chapter 7 represents an extension of the evaluation to include effects of the film after a lapse of time.   But the new data, comparing effects obtained at two time intervals, also have general scientific rather than merely evaluative implications.   Thus conclusions as to the relative magnitude of effects of a film after a long as compared with a short interval of time would be expected to have some intrinsic generalizability.   The factor of lapse of time can in a sense be considered an external variable, "manipulated" experimentally by controlling lapse of time before application of the measuring instrument.

In the experiment reported in Chapter 8, the principal variables analyzed were "content" variables.   In such studies, where the effects of *different kinds of presentations* are studied, it is usually necessary to have two or more controlled versions of the presentation with the same general objective.   In the study reported in Chapter 8, alternative ways of presenting a particular orientation "message" were compared in effectiveness.   Transcriptions instead of films were used to present the material, mainly because of the greater ease of preparing alternative versions. The experimental analysis reported in Chapter 8 deals with variations in the kind of argument presented, and studies the effect of presenting "both sides" versus presenting only "one side" in changing opinions on a controversial subject. The analysis is made in relation to the population variable of initial opinion on the topic presented by the transcription.

Chapter 9 reports a study of the effect on factual learning of variations in the content of a film strip. The difference involved the inclusion or noninclusion of a section of the film strip during which the audience rehearsed the material presented. In terms of the classification of kinds of variables as given in Chapter 1, this difference in the construction of the film strip, allowing for rehearsal, is a "content" or "film" variable from the standpoint of the film producer. However, it could also be considered as an "external" or procedural variable by the utilizer of film products. An additional aspect of this experiment was an analysis in terms of a second "external" variable—motivation in relation to the variation in the film strip's content. The motivational factor is classified as an additional "external" variable in this instance because the variation was explicitly introduced by manipulation of the procedures used.

In each of these three studies the results are analyzed as a function of the additional population variable of general intelligence, as measured either by the level of schooling that the men in the audience had attained, or by their AGCT scores. Thus in these studies the joint effects of experimentally manipulated variables and a statistically controlled variable are studied in combination.

CHAPTER 7

SHORT-TIME AND LONG-TIME EFFECTS
OF AN ORIENTATION FILM

IN CONNECTION with the use of the orientation films, the question arose as to how well the effects of the films were retained over a long period of time. The practical significance of this question lay in judging the need for later supplementary material covering the same ground as the films. In the experiments with orientation films presented earlier, the effects were determined at time intervals ranging from four to seven days after the film showings. In the present study, effects were determined at two time intervals after the film showing, one at five days and another at nine weeks. The primary objective of the study was to discover the extent to which the "short-time" (five-day) effects endure, as evidenced by the extent to which they were still present after a nine-week interval had elapsed.

The phrasing of the practical question to be answered by the study carries the implication that a decrement in effects is to be expected after a lapse of time. A more general question is to ask what is the influence of passage of time on the effects produced by the film. From this standpoint one need not anticipate only decrements with time; rather, in some cases the effect of time may be to enhance the initial effects of the film. Thus, some of the effects of the film may be "sleepers" that do not occur immediately but require a lapse of time before the full effect is evidenced. It should be realized, of course, that in making a controlled-variation study of the influence of time, it is not time per se that is the variable under study but rather the events which occur during the lapse of time.

The film used in this study was "The Battle of Britain." This film was chosen partly because its initial effects, as determined from a previous study, were relatively large, providing a better base for measuring retention than would be the case with a film having small initial effects. The sample used in this study to determine the short-term effects of the film has already been included as part of

182

the total sample in the presentation of the main effects of "The Battle of Britain" in Chapter 2.

The before-after experimental design was used. The "before" questionnaire was given to ten Infantry Replacement Training companies during the first week of the study (April 1943). During the second week, the film was shown to five of the ten companies. The other five companies were controls and did not see the film during the study. Five days after the film showings, three of the film companies and three of the control companies were given the "after" questionnaire. These six companies were used to determine the *short-time* effects of the film. The remaining four companies (two controls and two experimental) were used nine weeks after the film showings to determine the *long-time* effects of the film. A nine-week interval was used because it was the longest period during which the companies would retain the same personnel. The experimental design is outlined below:

WEEK OF STUDY	SHORT-TIME GROUPS		LONG-TIME GROUPS	
	Experimental (*3 companies*)	*Control* (*3 companies*)	*Experimental* (*2 companies*)	*Control* (*2 companies*)
First week	"Before" questionnaire	"Before" questionnaire	"Before" questionnaire	"Before" questionnaire
Second week	Film showing	————	Film showing	————
Third week	"After" questionnaire	"After" questionnaire	————	————
Eleventh week	————	————	"After" questionnaire	"After" questionnaire

It will be observed in the experimental design that the same sample of men was not used at the two different times after the film. A design involving a short-time and long-time measure on the same men was avoided on the grounds that the first "after" measure might affect the results obtained on the second. It will also be observed that more men were used in the short-time measurement of effects than the long-time measurement. The reason for this was that an incidental purpose of the study was to make a more detailed analysis of the short-time effects of the film than was possible with the after-only procedure that had been used at the first camp at which "The Battle of Britain" had been studied. To get a sizable number of cases for this analysis, the greater number of men were concentrated in the short-time measurement.

After the equating of the film and control groups, the resultant samples were 900 for the short-time effects (450 film and 450 control) and 500 for the long-time effects (250 film and 250 control).

Results with Fact-Quiz Items

The results for the ten fact-quiz items (which were included only in the "after" questionnaire) are shown in Table 1. The items in the table are arranged in descending order of magnitude of *short-time* effect.

It can be seen in Table 1 that all of the items showed a decrement with passage of time except some of the items with very small short-time effects. The long-time mean score on the fact quiz was slightly less than half as great as that obtained in the short-time measurement. Thus retention was about 50 per cent after nine weeks. If the results in Table 1 are recomputed excluding the last three items, where the obtained "effects" are of questionable reliability, the means are 29.7 per cent and 12.9 per cent for short-time and long-time effects, respectively, giving a retention value of 12.9 divided by 29.7 or 43 per cent.

Results with Opinion Items

In contrast with the foregoing findings for fact-quiz items, the results for opinion items did not show an overall decrement during the interval of nine weeks. Instead, some items showed the expected decrement while others showed reliable increments, with a mean effect that was slightly greater for the long-time measurement than for the short-time. For the entire group of opinion items used in the after questionnaire, the range was from a decrement of -17% to an increment of $+14\%$, with a mean of $+1.9\%$.[1] The variance of the differences between the short-time and the long-time "effects" was 40.3%. By contrast, when the groups were compared before the film showing, the range of the second-order differences was only from -7% to $+7\%$, with a variance of 14.6%.

Comparison of Short-Time and Long-Time Effects on Individual Opinion Items Showing a Reliable Effect at Either Time Interval

The foregoing comparisons were based upon all opinion items included in the questionnaire and therefore included many items for which no reliable effect of the film was demonstrated. Of special

---

[1] This included all opinion items except those involving ranking of enemy and allied strength and two questions about branch of service that could not be scored individually.

TABLE 1

SHORT-TIME AND LONG-TIME EFFECTS OF "THE BATTLE OF BRITAIN" ON
FACT-QUIZ QUESTIONS

FACT-QUIZ ITEM	SHORT-TIME			LONG-TIME			DIFFERENCE (*Long-time minus short-time*)
	Control	Film	Diff.	Control	Film	Diff.	
1. RAF not destroyed on ground because kept planes at edge of fields	23%	80%	*57%*	21%	53%	*32%*	−25%
2. First targets of Luftwaffe were ports and ships	13	58	*45*	13	20	*7*	−38
3. Luftwaffe ten times as large as the RAF	24	56	*32*	19	33	*14*	−18
4. Nazi plan was to destroy RAF, then invade England	30	58	*28*	26	40	*14*	−14
5. British Navy could not operate in channel because of danger of air attacks	41	60	*19*	37	44	*7*	−12
6. After fall of France British could equip only one modern division	5	21	*16*	3	8	*5*	−11
7. Famous statement, "Never . . . was so much owed by so many to so few" referred to the RAF	23	34	*11*	17	28	*11*	0
8. Goering the head of the German Air Force	58	65	*7*	51	58	*7*	0
9. "Luftwaffe" the name of the German Air Force	66	72	*6*	65	70	*5*	−1
10. Germans lost about 2000 planes in the Battle of Britain	49	54	*5*	49	58	*9*	+4
Mean	33.2%	55.8%	*22.6%*	30.1%	41.2%	*11.1%*	−11.5%

TABLE 2

SHORT-TIME AND LONG-TIME EFFECTS OF "THE BATTLE OF BRITAIN" ON
SIGNIFICANTLY AFFECTED OPINION QUESTIONS

Content of opinion item	SHORT-TIME			LONG-TIME			DIFFERENCE (*Long-time minus short-time*)
	Control	Film	Diff.	Control	Film	Diff.	
1. RAF gave Nazis first real defeat	21%	45%	*24%*	20%	27%	*7%*	—17%
2. RAF most important in preventing German conquest of England	54	78	*24*	46	69	*23*	—1
3. Nazi invasion attempt failed because of determined resistance of British	51	71	*20*	54	68	*14*	—6
4. Battle of Britain was a real invasion attempt	32	46	*14*	30	40	*10*	—4
5. England's refusal to surrender saved U.S. cities from bombing	62	74	*12*	67	74	*7*	—5
6. RAF has done about the best job of fighting in the war	49	60	*11*	42	45	*3*	—8
7. British more democratic than before Battle of Britain	55	65	*10*	59	62	*3*	—7
8. American workers in war plants should not work longer hours	48	52	*4*	42	54	*12*	8
9. America and Allies can still lose the war (disagree)	34	37	*3*	35	48	*13*	10
10. We would be fighting on American soil if Britain had not held off Nazis	52	55	*3*	50	62	*12*	9
11. British are doing their fair share of the fighting	71	73	*2*	61	77	*16*	14
12. Better just to defend U.S. rather than going overseas to fight	83	84	*1*	79	90	*11*	10

TABLE 2 (Continued)

Content of opinion item	SHORT-TIME			LONG-TIME			DIFFERENCE (*Long-time minus short-time*)
	Control	Film	Diff.	Control	Film	Diff.	
13. If England had been conquered the U.S. would have been attacked next	23%	24%	*1%*	22%	32%	*10%*	9%
14. The war will probably end in less than one year	11	10	*−1*	12	22	*10*	11
15. The British not to blame for America's having to get into the war	56	54	*−2*	44	55	*11*	13
Mean	46.8%	55.2%	*8.4%*	44.2%	55.0%	*10.8%*	2.4%

interest are the items which individually exhibited reliable effects of the film. In Table 2 the results at the two time intervals are shown for the 15 opinion items for which a reliable effect was obtained at either or both of the two time intervals.

The criterion of reliability used for the selection of items in Table 2 required a 10 per cent difference between film and control after the film showing. In terms of the empirical distributions of film-minus-control differences before the film, a difference of 10 per cent was beyond the 1 per cent level of confidence at either time interval. (The standard deviation of the distributions of "before" differences between film and control were 2.7 per cent and 3.5 per cent, respectively, for the short-time and long-time groups.) In the table the content is indicated for each of the 15 items, as well as the film and control percentages for each item at each time interval. The items are arranged in descending order of magnitude of *short-time* effect.

As can be seen from Table 2 the average for the 15 items was about the same for short-time and long-time effects, with a slight advantage (2.4 per cent) in favor of the long-time effects. However, Table 2 brings out clearly the fact that the near equality of the averages is a balance of some effects that were larger in the short-time measurement and others that were larger in the long-time measurement rather than approximate equality of individual effects at the two time intervals. This trend is perhaps somewhat exaggerated in Table 2 owing to the selection of effects that met the criterion of 10 per cent at either time interval. Thus borderline instances that just barely met the criterion at only one of the time intervals would be expected to regress somewhat in a replication of the experiment.

These findings are of considerable significance both from the standpoint of methodology of research on educational films and from the standpoint of theory as to the effects of educational programs on attitudes. Methodologically, they raise the problem as to the point in time at which effects of a film or other educational device are to be measured. From the standpoint of theory they raise the possibility of "sleeper" effects in the case of opinions and the implications of such effects for theory of attitude or opinion changes. From the standpoint either of educational film research or of the use of educational films it would be very desirable to know how generally this finding holds for documentary films of this type and also to know what factors determine whether the effects will show a loss or a gain with time. Unfortunately, studies of long-time effects were not made on any of the other orientation films, so no evidence can be given as to the generality of the results.

An analogy may be drawn between the findings reported here and the finding in studies of retention that "substance" is better retained than verbatim learning.[2] Thus the general ideas in a passage of verbal material are retained with little loss over periods in which memory for the actual wording has dropped markedly. In the present study retention for opinions—which correspond to the substance—averaged better than 100 per cent whereas memory for detailed facts dropped to only half of its initial value.

However, this analogy is somewhat superficial in view of the fact that the average for opinions was a mixture of some gains and some losses on particular items of "substance" (if opinions can be regarded as "substance"). In this connection it may be pointed out that another familiar phenomenon in learning studies—the phenomenon of "reminiscence," in which more rather than less of the original content is recalled after a lapse of time—is more frequently found in the case of substance material than in the case of detailed verbal

---

[2] Cofer, C. N. "A Comparison of Logical and Verbatim Learning of Prose Passages of Different Lengths." *Amer. J. Psychol.*, 1941, *54*, 1–20.

content.[3] Thus the present results may be regarded as a mixture of the greater retention of general ideas plus "reminiscence" for part of the material.

One hypothesis as to the source of the "sleeper" effects involving a purely methodological artifact was checked but was not supported by the data. This hypothesis was that the before-after procedure may cause a "consistency reaction" which would occur when the two questionnaires are close together in time but which would not be present for two questionnaires separated by an interval as long as eleven weeks. The possibility of a "consistency reaction" is discussed in Appendix C along with other methodological aspects of the before-after procedure. The effect of the "consistency reaction," if present, would be a tendency for the respondent, having given a particular answer to a question on one occasion, to give the same answer when questioned in a similar context a short time later. Hence the true magnitude of the change effected by the film would not be revealed at the short-time interval. Since some of the questions in the present study were asked only in the "after" questionnaire and others both before and after, it was possible to check whether after-only questions show the normal forgetting decrement with time and only the before-after questions show an increment. This finding would be expected if the "consistency reaction" were reduced where an 11-week interval is allowed between before and after tests.

However, no significant relation was found between whether the question was an after-only or a before-after question and whether it showed a decrement or an increment with time. In Table 2 the after-only questions were numbers 2, 7, 8, 11, 14, and 15. Of these six after-only items, it can be seen that two showed a decrement and four showed an increment in effects as a function of time. Of the remaining nine questions, asked both before and after, five showed a decrement and four showed an increment. Thus while the hypothetical "consistency reaction" may have functioned to some extent to reduce the size of the decrement, the data do not at all support it as the factor responsible for the delayed or augmented effects. As can be seen in Table 3 the results are in the opposite direction from the prediction of the consistency hypothesis. (The apparent difference in retention of the after-only items is not significant.)

[3] English, H. B., Wellborn, E. L., and Killian, C. D. "Studies in Substance Memorization." *J. gen. Psychol.*, 1934, *11*, 233–60. See also Buxton, C. E. " 'Reminiscence' in the Studies of Professor English and His Associates." *Psychol. Rev.*, 1942, *49*, 494–504.

TABLE 3

MEAN EFFECT (FILM % MINUS CONTROL %)

	Short-time	*Long-time*
For six after-only items	6.2%	12.5%
For nine before-after items	9.9	9.7

Relation of the Effects to Educational Level

Further information about the nature of the effects is obtained from the analysis of short-time and long-time changes among men of differing education. Analysis by education is particularly significant for the reason given in Chapter 6—namely, that opinions positively correlated with education may be considered as "informed" opinions—as "more valid" interpretations of the available facts.

Using the correlation of initial responses with education as the criterion of "validity" of opinion three sets of opinion items may be distinguished: (1) those with *positive* correlation, (2) those with *no* correlation, (3) those with *negative* correlation. A fourth kind of item may also be considered: the factual items—on which positive correlation is also generally present.

For purposes of the separate analysis of these different kinds of items the decision as to whether positive or negative correlation with education was present was based on whether the lowest and highest education groups differed significantly in a positive or negative direction. If this difference was not significant the correlation was considered "zero." In Figure 1, results are presented for the four sets of items, showing the average *initial level* of opinion in different education groups, i.e., the correlation of the opinion with education, and showing the *changes* in opinion as a function of education in both the short-time group and the long-time group. The changes due to the film are presented in terms of the "effectiveness index" to take account of differences in initial level among the different educational groups.

Two interesting relationships are revealed in Figure 1. The first is that responses initially positively correlated with education show effects of the film that are positively correlated with education, whereas responses with no significant initial correlation or with negative correlation tend to show effects that are either poorly correlated or negatively correlated with education. This is in accord

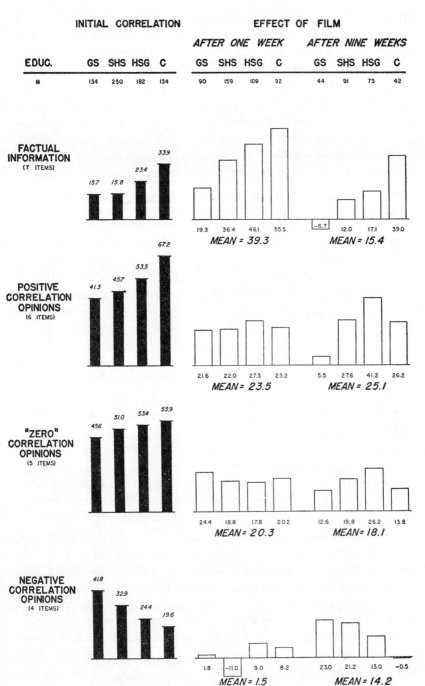

Figure 1.   Mean initial levels and effectiveness indices for four sets of items for each of four education groups.

with the findings reported in Chapter 6, and it will be noted that the relationship is present at both time intervals. The second relationship revealed by the figure is that the more negatively correlated the response with education initially the more likely it is to show a "sleeper" effect (a gain with lapse of time). This is most easily seen in the mean effects for the group as a whole, in which a marked decrement with time is obtained for fact-quiz items, while a definite gain with time is found for opinion items having a significant negative correlation initially. The increments for initially negatively correlated items are particularly notable among men with less education.

These observations suggest that perhaps the "sleeper" effects are found only for "uninformed" opinions and mainly among the less well educated. But a separate analysis of those items showing gains with time—i.e., items 8 through 15 in Table 2—reveals that some are positively and some negatively correlated with education initially and that the distribution of gains with time among the different educational groups depends on the sign of this initial correlation. This analysis is shown in Table 4 in which the eight items are subdivided into two groups of four each in which the curve of initial level with education was ascending (positively correlated) for one set of four and descending (negatively correlated) for the other set of four. These correspond to "informed" and "uninformed" opinions, respectively, in terms of the initial opinions of the different educational groups.

Here it is apparent that the "sleeper" effects were confined neither to uninformed opinions nor to the less well educated. Gains were obtained among all educational groups, but the magnitude of the gains with time was larger among the better educated for items initially positively correlated with education and larger for the less well educated for items initially negatively correlated with education. In other words, for all items on which increments were found, the "valid" interpretations or "informed" opinions showed greatest increments with time among the better educated, whereas the "invalid" interpretations or "uninformed opinions" showed greater increments with time among the less well educated.

These results suggest the hypothesis that "sleeper" effects are obtained among individuals already *predisposed* to accept an opinion but who have not yet accepted it. According to this hypothesis, a person soon "forgets" the ideas he has learned which are not consonant with his predispositions, but that he retains without loss or even with an increment those ideas consonant with his predispositions. Thus if an opinion is positively correlated with education, we can surmise that the better educated are predisposed to accept it—the factors leading to most better educated men's accepting the opinion should also be at work as predisposing factors affecting those better educated men who do not yet accept it. Conversely, an opinion that is negatively correlated with education indicates that the less well educated are predisposed to accept the opinion.

TABLE 4

SHORT-TIME AND LONG-TIME MEAN EFFECTIVENESS INDEX OF ITEMS SHOWING
GAINS WITH TIME, BY EDUCATION, FOR THE FOUR "INFORMED" AND THE
FOUR "UNINFORMED" OPINIONS

	Education	SHORT-TIME		LONG-TIME		DIFFERENCE
		Av. initial level (Percentage)	Av. effectiveness index	Av. initial level (Percentage)	Av. effectiveness index	Long-time minus short-time effectiveness index
"Informed" Opinions	GS	52.5	17.9	51.2	16.0	−1.9
	SHS	63.0	3.2	51.8	33.6	30.4
	HS	68.5	0.0	60.5	31.2	31.2
	Coll.	73.8	−5.8	64.2	38.6	44.4
"Uninformed" Opinions	GS	43.0	0.9	40.5	24.8	23.9
	SHS	34.0	−8.2	31.8	20.5	28.7
	HS	23.5	8.8	25.2	12.8	4.0
	Coll.	17.8	5.1	21.5	7.0	1.9

Of course in most cases an opinion positively correlated with education will have its counterpart that is negatively correlated. Thus, since belief that Britain was to blame for our entering the war was negatively correlated with education, belief that Britain was *not* to blame was positively correlated with education. In most cases, therefore, of a sizable correlation of opinion with education, we can say that the better educated are predisposed in one direction and the less well educated are predisposed in the other.

It is worth pointing out that education is only one of the possible indices of predisposition. Ideally one would get a multiple regression based on all the important factors associated with a particular opinion. On the basis of a *combination* of predisposing factors one could then more exactly segregate the total population into fairly homogeneous subgroups that should be predisposed to think alike because of the common influences that mold opinion. Such a segregation was not feasible in the present instance but an analysis to test the implication of the predisposition hypothesis was made using education as the basis for subdividing the sample into subsamples which were homogeneous with respect to this one variable and all of its associated predisposing factors. In view of the findings reported at the outset of Chapter 6, it seems likely that education would be the best *single* variable to use in analyzing the present data.

The logic of the analysis to test the predisposition hypothesis was as follows: the initial trend of opinion was examined for each of the four educational subgroups on each of the 15 opinion items that were significantly affected (shown in Table 2). Where an opinion is positively correlated with education we expect the opinion generally to be in the minority among the less well educated and in the majority among the well educated, and conversely for negatively correlated opinions. In line with this, the degree of predisposition of a particular educational subgroup with respect to a particular opinion was regarded as being a function of the degree to which that opinion was held by the members of that subgroup. Effects were therefore analyzed for each subgroup, on each of the 15 opinions, as a function of the initial degree of acceptance indicated by the control findings.

Specifically, the analysis consisted of breaking down the control-group results into sixty (15 × 4) subpercentages, one each for the responses of each of the four educational groups on each of the 15 items in Table 2. The effects of the film, short-time and long-time, were then analyzed as a function of the degree of initial acceptance —defined as percentage choosing the response in each of the 60 initial-acceptance levels in the total array. According to the hypothesis, an opinion which is very infrequent in a particular educational subgroup is one which that group is predisposed *against* whereas an opinion held by the great majority of the subgroup is one *toward* which they are predisposed. Accordingly, opinions should show decrements or increments corresponding to the direction of the predisposition during the lapsed time after seeing the film. The total array of 60 initial percentages, derived from the control findings of the four educational groups' responses to the 15 items, can be ranked from the highest percentages—indicating the opinions initially most strongly held by a subgroup—to the lowest percentages—indicating the opinion initially most strongly opposed by any of the subgroups. According to the hypothesis there should be, corresponding to this ranking of "predisposition," a trend in effects such that increments in effects with lapse of time are found associated with items ranking high in initial acceptance and decrements are found associated with items ranking low in initial acceptance.

The results in general confirmed the hypothesis. A trend toward being affected by the film if predisposed did not show up clearly in the short-time results, but it was quite apparent in the long-time results. However, even this latter trend was accompanied by a great deal of variability. The results are shown in Table 5 with some of the variability smoothed out to show the trend by combining the 60 separate effects to make six class intervals of differing initial acceptance. The method of combination was to arrange in rank order the 60 separate initial-acceptance levels for combined short-time and long-time control groups. The ranks therefore ranged from 1 to 60, with the rank of 1 indicating the highest initial per cent obtained for the two controls combined and 60 indicating the lowest. The data were then simply combined in successive sixths. The ten combinations in each sixth are the same for both the short-time and long-time samples although the mean acceptance-level was necessarily somewhat different in each sixth for short-time versus long-time control. The results were as follows:

TABLE 5

SHORT-TIME VERSUS LONG-TIME MEAN EFFECTIVENESS INDEX FOR
60 PREDISPOSITION CATEGORIES

	SHORT-TIME DATA		LONG-TIME DATA	
Rank order of initial acceptance	*Av. level of initial acceptance*	*Effectiveness index*	*Av. level of initial acceptance*	*Effectiveness index*
(most) 1–10	77.1%	*17.4%*	74.7%	*30.8%*
11–20	59.2	*23.5*	58.0	*28.6*
21–30	53.1	*10.0*	46.0	*25.7*
31–40	45.7	*23.8*	44.2	*19.0*
41–50	33.2	*16.6*	31.8	*14.7*
(least) 51–60	12.4	*10.0*	14.6	*9.6*

While the results show some unexplained variations, it will be observed that with a high level of initial acceptance the mean long-time effects are larger than the mean short-time effects—indicating an increment with passage of time—whereas with low initial level of acceptance the mean short-time effects are the larger—indicating decrements.[4] Also a clear trend of greater effect with greater initial acceptance is seen for the long-time results. In the short-time results no clear-cut trend is visible. It is interesting that the dividing point between the effects that increase and those that decrease after a long interval is at about the 50-50 point of initial division of opinion.

While the above results are very indirect as evidence, they support the idea that degree of retention of opinion changes and the extent to which effects increase with lapse of time is in part a function of initial predisposition to accept the opinion affected.

However, it seems likely that this "predisposition hypothesis" is not sufficient by itself to account for the "sleeper" effects observed. For one thing, while the expected trend does appear in Table 5, the closeness of the relationship is not striking. The rank order correlation of effects and initial level even for long-time is only .41 and for short-time is .09. This general lack of relationship with short-time effects—apparent in Table 5 as well as in the low rank-order correlation—is difficult to reconcile with the hypothesis. If a man is predisposed to believe an idea, he should *immediately* accept it more readily than ideas against which he is predisposed. We should therefore expect that the items that show increments over time would also show immediate effects at the short-time which might be as large or larger than the nonsleeper items. But this expectation is not confirmed in a single instance. Inspection of the data presented in Table 2 for items that showed an increment (items 8 through 15) shows that none of these "sleeper" or increment items showed a significant overall effect at the short-time interval. This failure to obtain any significant short-time effects for items where the long-time effects were greater than the short-time effects appears quite contrary to the expectations of the hypothesis. Thus while the results summarized in Table 5 are in line with the hypothesis of a predisposition factor, the operation of this factor

---

[4] In computing mean effects, the sign given to each effect is positive for the direction of change found significant in the overall results shown in Table 5, and effects have been measured in terms of the "effectiveness index" to take account of the varying initial levels.

would not by itself account for all of the findings. What is needed is some mechanism to account for *delayed* effects that do not show up at all immediately after the film. It is interesting in this connection that while a "selection ceiling," as described in Chapter 3, is suggested by the results for the short-time men, no such result is obtained among the long-time men. An elaboration of the present hypothesis might be that "sleeper" effects are likely in the "diehards" who resist the message at first but eventually change their opinion in conformity with the predisposing factors of their subgroup of the population.

Other Hypotheses

A number of other hypotheses may be advanced suggesting possible factors contributing to the increments on some of the opinion items. These hypotheses could not be checked in the present experiment but they are presented below because they may provide useful areas for future study.

1. *Forgetting of an initially discounted source.* One hypothesis that could explain the results would be that some of the themes of the presentation were initially accepted and others were initially discounted as having a biased source. According to this hypothesis, forgetting is the rule but the *source* of an item of information is more quickly forgotten than the material presented. Thus the men might have retained a feeling that the British did well in the war long after they have forgotten about seeing the film, "The Battle of Britain." The factors involved in this hypothesis would be maximized in situations where the content was very well presented but where the source was suspect, so that the main factor preventing an attitude change is nonacceptance of the trustworthiness of the source. In this case, what is remembered and what is believed may be kept separate at first, but if the content "sticks" after the source is forgotten, it may no longer be discounted. Content would of course be subject to some forgetting, so that the net result would be a decrement of effect with passage of time for those contents which are *immediately* accepted contents, but an increment of effect for those contents for which forgetting of the suspected source proceeded more rapidly than forgetting of the content.

2. *Delayed interpretation in a relevant context.* Another hypothesis is that while forgetting of content is the rule, the implications of the initially learned content may not be apparent to the audience at the outset but may become more clear later when the material

learned in the film becomes relevant to some new experience. Thus the film, "The Battle of Britain" showed the defeat of the Luftwaffe by the much smaller RAF and the frustration of the Nazi plans for the capitulation of Britain. Initial effects on fact-quiz and attitude items indicated that this content was learned. However, the film in no way presented the idea that the Nazi military machine was weak or that their strategy and tactics were inferior, and nothing in the initial effects indicated that this was a conclusion immediately drawn by the men as a result of seeing the film. However, if the men were later forced to consider the implications of these facts as to the likelihood that the Nazis could defeat the Allies, they might conclude that if the Germans could not defeat little Britain they have little chance of winning the war, as in the delayed effect on item number 14 in Table 2.

An expectation from this second hypothesis is that material directly related to the content of the film would tend to show a decrement with time in correspondence with the forgetting curve, whereas increments would occur only for indirect implications of the content that could be initiated at a later time while a fair amount of the content was still retained. However, as already noted (Chapter 6, p. 171f.), a differentiation between direct and indirect implications is one which it was not feasible to make clearly with these films.

3. *Conversion of details into attitudes.* A third hypothesis to account for the results involved a possible factor that would, if it actually functions, be of more general significance for theory concerning attitude formation. According to this hypothesis, forgetting is accompanied by loss of specificity of content—the details drop out and only the "general idea" or "substance" of the material remains. This "general idea" that is retained is in a more generalizable form, so that the individual has a greater tendency to go beyond the facts initially learned. In this sense attitudes are to a certain extent "general ideas" that lack specificity and generalize more broadly than is justified by the evidence.

An example of the interpretation from this hypothesis in the case of the film, "The Battle of Britain," would be that initially the men learned specific facts about the performance of the British, particularly the RAF, during the Battle of Britain, but as the specific facts were forgotten all that was remembered was that the British had performed well in the war. In this form the "general idea" applies to all British rather than just the RAF and to the entire war rather than just the Luftwaffe attack on England. Any opinions that dealt with specific contents would show a decrement with time, whereas those dealing with generalizations beyond the evidence would show an increment with time.

Delayed Effects on Orientation Objectives

One final question raised by the findings in this comparison of long-time and short-time effects of an orientation film is the extent to which delayed effects were found in the orientation objectives of the film. This is a question of methodological importance in the evaluation of an educational program designed to affect attitudes, because the evaluation may provide a different answer depending on the point in time at which the program is evaluated. The findings in the present study indicate a real possibility that at least in the case of the film, "The Battle of Britain," greater effects on orientation attitudes were obtained after a nine-week lapse of time than after only five days. The relevant findings are presented below.

The orientation objective most relevant to the film was that of increasing confidence in our ally, Britain. While many items about Britain were included to test the effects of the film, only six items were used for the specific purpose of determining general orientation attitudes toward Britain. The short-time and long-time effects for these items are shown in Table 6. The effects are measured as differences between before-after changes for all questions used in both questionnaires.

Results on other standard orientation items not specific to opin-

TABLE 6

EFFECTS ON THE ORIENTATION OBJECTIVE OF INCREASING MEN'S
CONFIDENCE IN THE BRITISH

| | EFFECT OF FILM | |
Content of item	Short-time effect	Long-time effect
British are doing all they can to help in the war	7%	3%
British will try to work out a just peace after the war	9	7
British are taking it easy in hope that U.S. will win the war for them (disagree)	2	9
British are doing their fair share of the fighting	2	16
British will fight on to the end (rather than seek a separate peace)	1	4
British are to blame for America's entry into war (disagree)	−2	11
Mean	3.2%	8.3%

ions of the British are shown in Table 7.   These items are of lesser relevance to the film than the above items concerning Britain as an ally.   Specific contents of individual items are not shown; only the general area of the items is given.   In the case of each area, however, the results given are the averages for all of the standard items used in that area.

TABLE 7

EFFECTS ON GENERALIZED ORIENTATION OBJECTIVES

| | AVERAGE EFFECT OF FILM | |
Content of area	*Short-time*	*Long-time*
The U.S. had to fight—war was unavoidable (3 items)	0.3%	6.0%
Resentment against the enemy (2 items)	−2.0	5.0
Confidence in home support (4 items)	−1.0	2.0
Willingness to serve (2 items)	1.5	0.5
Mean	0.5%	3.4%

In both Table 6 and Table 7 the mean effect is larger at the long-time interval.   This indicates that a greater effect of the film in achieving its orientation objectives was present after nine weeks than after one week.   However, the results are not highly consistent from item to item in Table 6 nor from area to area in Table 7.   In neither case is the result reliable at the 5 per cent level if we treat the questions used as a sample from the population of relevant items.

While inconclusive, the results have a bearing on two important problems: (1) they support the hypothesis that changes in opinions of a general rather than specific nature may show increasing effects with lapse of time, and (2) they focus attention on the methodological problem of selecting the point in time at which measurements should be made after a presentation in order to detect its full effects. At the outset of the present studies it was more or less assumed that deterioration of effects with time would be the rule; it now appears that this assumption is not warranted in the case of opinions of a general nature.

CHAPTER 8

THE EFFECTS OF PRESENTING "ONE SIDE" VERSUS "BOTH SIDES" IN CHANGING OPINIONS ON A CONTROVERSIAL SUBJECT

IN DESIGNING Army orientation programs an issue which was frequently debated was this question: When the weight of evidence supports the main thesis being presented, is it more effective to present only the materials supporting the point being made, or is it better to introduce also the arguments of those opposed to the point being made?

The procedure of presenting only the arguments supporting a thesis is often employed on the grounds that when the preponderance of the evidence supports the point being made, the presentation of opposing arguments and misconceptions merely raises doubts in the minds of the audience. On the other hand, the procedure of presenting the arguments for both sides was defended on the grounds of "fairness"—the right of members of the audience to have access to all relevant materials in making up their minds. Furthermore, there is reason to expect that those audience members who are already opposed to the point of view being presented may be distracted by "rehearsing" their own arguments while the topic is being presented and will be antagonized by the omission of the arguments on their side. Thus, presentation of the audience's arguments at the outset possibly would produce better reception of the arguments which it is desired to convey.

The present experiment was set up to provide information on the relative effectiveness of these two types of program content in changing the opinions of individuals initially opposing as compared with those favoring the position advocated in the program. Controlled variation of treatment was introduced by preparing two transcriptions with the same orientation message in alternative forms. In one form arguments were presented on only one side of the issue; in the other both sides were presented.

METHODS OF STUDY

1. THE TWO PROGRAMS USED

At the time the experiment was being planned (early 1945) the war in Europe was drawing to a close and it was reported that Army morale was being adversely affected by overoptimism about an early end to the war in the Pacific. A directive was issued by the Army to impress upon troops a conception of the magnitude of the job remaining to be done in defeating Japan. This furnished a controversial topic on which arguments were available on both sides but where the majority of experts in military affairs believed the preponderance of evidence supported one side. It was therefore chosen as a suitable subject for experimentation.

Radio transcriptions rather than films were used, primarily because of the simplicity with which they could be prepared in alternative forms. The basic outline of the programs' content was prepared by the Experimental Section. All materials used were official releases from the Office of War Information and the War Department. The final writing and production of the programs were carried out by the Armed Forces Radio Service.

The two programs compared in this chapter were in the form of a commentator's analysis of the Pacific War. The commentator's conclusion was that the job of finishing the war would be tough and that it would take at least two years after VE Day. A brief description of the two programs follows.

Program I ("one side"): The major topics included in the program which presented *only* the arguments indicating that the war would be long were: distance problems and other logistical difficulties in the Pacific; the resources and stockpiles in the Japanese Empire; the size and quality of the main bulk of the Japanese Army that we had not yet met in battle; and the determination of the Japanese people. The program ran for about fifteen minutes.

Program II ("both sides"): The other program ran for about nineteen minutes and presented all of these same difficulties in exactly the same way. The difference of four minutes between this and the "one-sided" program was the time devoted to considering arguments for the other side of the picture—U.S. advantages and Japanese weaknesses such as our naval victories and superiority, our previous progress despite a two-front war, our ability to concentrate all our forces on Japan after VE Day, Japan's shipping losses, Japan's manufacturing inferiority, and the future damage to be expected from our expanding air war. These additional points were woven into the context of the rest of the program.

Before the preparation of these programs, pretests had been conducted in which men were individually interviewed on questions relating to the length of the war with Japan. The purpose of this was to discover what arguments were actually used by the soldiers who took the position that the war would soon be over. At the same time, the phrasing of questions for the final questionnaire to be used in the study was worked out. This qualitative pretest was followed by a quantitative pretest on 200 men to discover the approximate distribution of men's estimates of probable length of the war and the approximate frequency of the various arguments for and against a short or long war. The information thus gained was then used as a basis for preparing an outline of the factual material to be used in the program, greatest weight being given to the material relevant to countering the arguments most frequently offered by the men as a basis for expecting an early end to the war in the Pacific after VE Day.

In preparing the programs, the sequence and manner of presenting the various arguments was guided, in so far as possible, by principles thought to be those which would most effectively utilize the arguments on both sides so as to convince the men initially opposed to the orientation message. The major hypothesis governing the preparation of the presentation giving "both sides" was that those who were opposed would be stimulated by a one-sided argument to rehearse their own position and seek new ways of supporting it. A further aspect of this hypothesis was that those opposed to the position taken would discount a one-sided presentation as coming from a biased source that had failed to consider the arguments on the other side. The introduction of the arguments "on the other side" was designed to minimize such tendencies among those opposed. In line with these considerations, the following provisional rules or principles of presentation were formulated.

(1) *All of the main arguments on the other side should be mentioned at the very outset.* This was designed to have the effect of indicating to the opposed members of the audience from the very beginning that their point of view and supporting arguments would not be

neglected. As a consequence it was expected that they would be less likely to start rehearsing their own arguments to themselves, more likely to credit the presentation as having the authenticity that usually goes with unbiased interpretations, and less likely to have their own emotional motivations aroused against accepting the conclusion of the communication.

(2) *Any appeals to the motives of the opposed audience members should be presented early.* On the assumption that appeals to motives are the most important determiners of opinion change, it seems likely that with opposed audience members the rational arguments would be more influential if the emotional appeal had already been made as far as possible. This timing would be less important with individuals already emotionally predisposed to accept the conclusion —the latter group would be highly receptive to the rational arguments that backed up their position.

(3) *Opposed arguments that cannot be refuted should be presented relatively early.* Such arguments actually tend to weaken the conclusion, but they serve to satisfy the opposition and thus reduce antagonism. By high-lighting them fairly early in the communication, the maximal advantage in reducing aggressive tendencies is obtained, but they should also be expected to be remembered less at the conclusion of the communication.

(4) *An attempt to refute arguments on the other side should be made only when an obviously compelling and strictly factual refutation is available.* Here the expectation is that any attempted refutation will have a tendency to antagonize the opposed members of the audience, and may motivate them to seek new arguments to support their position. Therefore, direct refutation should be considered only when it is based on factual evidence so strong that it will be accepted even by those who are opposed.

(5) *An unrefuted opposed argument should be followed by an uncontroversial positive argument.* The inference here is that a negative argument can be offset by an equally strong or even stronger positive argument. It may even be true that the effect will often be greater if a refutable negative argument is left unrefuted in order not to arouse any antagonistic motivation—in order to avoid getting the opposed listener's "ego" involved—and is instead offset by a positive argument that is accepted as valid by the opposition. The order of negative, then positive, should serve to indicate that the negative point is being considered, but that despite this important point on the negative side, the positive point swings the balance in

the direction of the conclusion endorsed. This sequence should take advantage of the appearance of impartiality and satisfy the opposition as to the correctness and relevance of their own considerations, but still leave the weight of evidence against their position.

(6) *The timing in presenting counter arguments of the opposition should be: positive argument leading, objection raised by an opposed counter argument, and then positive argument offsetting the objection.* One purpose of this sequence is to state the negative argument exactly at the time that it is most likely to be aroused implicitly in the opposition group. They therefore should not be so likely to rehearse the argument in an antagonistic frame of mind, but instead be gratified to hear their own position voiced. At the same time their argument is presented in a context of doubt, and the argument that is favored by both primacy and recency is the positive argument that is used to refute or offset the negative counter argument.

(7) *Any refutations, and those positive arguments which are potentially most antagonizing, should come late in the presentation.* This follows from the expectation that a potentially antagonizing refutation will elicit less antagonism if the opposition has already been changed in a positive direction by the preceding portions of the communications. If they have already been partly "won over" to the position of the communication, they may not be at all antagonized by an idea that would have aroused aggression at the outset.

(8) *Members of the opposition should not be given a choice to identify themselves as such.* This principle is perhaps more difficult to utilize than the others. The basis for the principle is that a person is easier to change if he does not have his "ego" involved in supporting a particular point of view. If he feels that he belongs to a group that is being attacked by the communication, he is more likely to respond with aggressive resistance. Anything that can be done to present the communication as if it represented the views of each member of the audience, or to prevent the listeners from taking sides on the issue, should make those initially opposed more susceptible to change.

Not all of these "rules" could be adhered to strictly in the preparation of the actual scripts. However, an outline of the factual material to be presented was organized in such a way as to follow rather closely the implications of the first five rules, and in general to introduce the negative arguments at those points where, as determined by pretests, they seemed most likely to occur spontaneously to the opposed members of the audience. In these pretests, interviewers had actually presented the case for a long war in a face-to-face situation and had attempted to elicit counter arguments from interviewees who felt that the war would be short. In the final scripts used, refutations of the opposed arguments were in general avoided. Counter arguments rarely took the form of trying to *disprove* or *deny* the truth of an important argument; rather, the truth of the argument was admitted but its force was weakened by immediately bringing in additional relevant facts.

The outline of factual material thus organized was used by the script writers as the basis for preparing the program that used arguments on "both sides" of the question. The script for the "one-side" version was identical with that for "both sides" except for the omission of all facts or arguments supporting a short war, plus a very few wording changes necessary for transitional purposes.

At the time of preparing the scripts, the writer knew the purpose of the experiment and the actual wording of the main question to be used in measuring the effects of the transcriptions.

It should be pointed out that while Program II gave facts on *both sides* of the question, it did not give equal space to both sides, nor did it attempt to compare the case for thinking it would be a long war with the *strongest possible case* for believing it would be an easy victory and a short war. It took exactly the same stand as that taken by Program I—namely, that the war would be difficult and would require at least two years. The difference was that Program II mentioned the opposite arguments (e.g., U.S. advantages). In effect it argued that the job would be difficult, even when our advantages and the Japanese weaknesses were taken into account.

2. CONDUCT OF THE EXPERIMENT

The general plan of the experiment has been discussed in another connection in Chapter 5. The procedure was to give a preliminary "opinion survey" to determine the men's initial opinions about the Pacific War and then to remeasure their opinions at a later time, after the transcriptions had been played to them in the course of their orientation meetings. In this way the *changes* in their opinions from "before" to "after" could be determined. A control group, which heard *no* transcription, was also surveyed as a means of determining any changes in response that might occur during the time interval due to causes other than the transcriptions—such as the impact of war news from the Pacific.

Since the purpose of the study was to analyze differential effects of two kinds of content on individuals with differing initial opinions, it was desirable to obtain for analysis the maximum overall effects possible. For this reason the effects were measured immediately after the presentation of the programs. It is, of course, conceivable that the effects might have been even greater after a longer time interval, and further that with the longer time interval the pattern of effects might have been different from the immediate effects observed.

The preliminary survey was administered during the first week of April 1945 to eight Quartermaster training companies. One week later eight platoons, one chosen at random from each of the eight companies, heard Program I (which presented only one side) during their individual orientation meetings. Another group of eight platoons, similarly chosen, heard Program II (which presented both arguments). Immediately after the program the men filled out the second questionnaire, ostensibly for the purpose of letting the people who made the program know what the men thought of it. Included in this second questionnaire, with appropriate transitional questions, were some of the same questions that had been included in the earlier survey, asking the men how they personally sized up the Pacific War. A third group of eight platoons served as the control with no program. They filled out a similar questionnaire, during their orientation meeting, which, in addition to asking the same questions on the Pacific War, asked preliminary questions about what they thought of their orientation meetings and what they would like in future orientation meetings. For the control group, the latter questions—in lieu of the questions about the transcriptions—were represented to the men as the main purpose of the questionnaire.

While 24 platoons were used for this experiment, the units were at only about 70 per cent of full strength at the preliminary survey and at the orientation meetings. The "shrinkage" was therefore quite large as to number of men present *both* times, and the sample available for "before-after" analysis was consequently small (a total of 625 men, with 214 in each experimental group and the remaining 197 men in the control group). In view of the rapidly changing picture in the Pacific, however, it was considered inadvisable to repeat the experiment at another camp.

3. ADMINISTRATION

For proper administration of the experiment there were three major requirements: presentation of the transcriptions under realistic conditions, preventing the men in the sample from realizing that the experiment was in progress, and getting honest answers in the questionnaires. For realism in presentation, the transcriptions for the experimental groups were incorporated into the training program and scheduled as part of the weekly orientation hour. This not only insured realistic presentation but also helped to avoid indicating that effects of the transcriptions were being tested.

The preliminary "survey." The preliminary "survey" had been presented as being part of a War Department survey "to find out how a cross section of soldiers felt about various subjects connected with the war," with examples being given of previous Research Branch surveys and how the findings had been used. Questionnaires were administered to all the men in a company at once, the men being assembled in mess halls for the purpose. The questionnaires were administered by "class leaders" selected and trained for the job from among the enlisted personnel working at the camp. In an introductory explanation of the survey the class leader stressed the importance of the survey and the anonymity of the answers. No camp officers were present at these meetings and the men were assured that the surveys went directly to Washington and that no one at the camp would get a chance to see what they had written. The questionnaire used in this preliminary "survey" consisted mainly of check-list questions plus a few questions in which the men were asked to write their own answers. The content of most of the questions was the point system for demobilization and the Army's plans for redeployment. This was a convenient context for the questions that formed the measuring instrument per se which dealt with the difficulty of defeating Japan. The questions about the point system and redeployment were not necessary for the actual experimental measurements but were used to give scope to the "survey" and to prevent a concentration of items dealing with material to be covered by the transcription. This was done partly to help make the survey seem realistic to the men but mainly to avoid "sensitizing" them to questions about the topic of the subsequently presented orientation material through placing too much emphasis on it in the survey.

The second questionnaire. To prevent the men from suspecting that an "experiment" was in progress because of the administration of two questionnaires within a short space of time, the second questionnaire differed from the first one both in its form and its announced purpose.   Thus the first questionnaire was given as a general War Department "survey" while the second one was given during the orientation meetings to "find out what men thought of the transcriptions" (or, in the control group, "what they thought of their orientation meetings").

An additional difference in the administration of the two questionnaires, which was also designed to reduce the appearance of similarity, was that while the first had been given by company in mess halls the second was administered by platoon in the men's barracks where the orientation meetings were held.

While the ostensible purpose in giving the men the second questionnaire was to get their opinion of the program, appropriate "tie-in" questions, such as whether or not they thought the commentator too optimistic or too pessimistic, were used to lead to the questions as to how long they thought the war would last and on the other topics concerning the difficulty of the job.

As in studies of opinion changes described in earlier chapters, it was considered necessary in the case of the present study to obtain opinions anonymously, and also to measure the effects of the program without awareness on the part of the men that an experiment was in progress.   These precautions were dictated by the type of effect being studied—it was felt that if the men either thought their questionnaires were identified by name or if they knew they were being "tested," some men might give "proper" or otherwise distorted answers rather than answers expressing their true opinions in the matter.

ANALYSIS OF RESULTS

The results to be presented are based on an analysis of the responses of men whose preliminary survey could be matched with the "after" questionnaire given in the orientation meetings.   Although all of the questionnaires were anonymous, the "before" and "after" questionnaires of the same individual could be matched on the basis of answers to such personal-history questions as years of schooling, date of birth, etc., with handwriting serving as an additional factor among men whose personal history was similar.

1. *Overall Effects of the Two Programs on the Marginal Distribution of Estimates of the Length of the War*

As previously stated, the main question used to evaluate the effectiveness of the two programs was a question asking men for their estimates of the probable length of the war with Japan after VE Day.   The wording of this question was the same in both the "before" and the "after" questionnaire and was as follows:

> What is your guess as to how long it will probably take us to beat Japan after Germany's defeat?   (Write your best guess below.)
>
> About _____ from the day of Germany's defeat.

The men's answers to this question tended to be in half-year intervals and were accordingly coded by steps of one-half year each.

A marked overall shift in an upward direction in the distribution of estimates was obtained.   The results are shown below with the answers dichotomized into those estimating one-and-one-half years or less versus those estimating more than one-and-one-half years.

TABLE 1

OVERALL EFFECTS OF THE TWO PROGRAMS ON DISTRIBUTION
OF ESTIMATED LENGTH OF WAR

| | PERCENTAGE ESTIMATING A WAR OF MORE THAN ONE-AND-ONE-HALF YEARS | | |
| | *Experimental groups* | | |
	Program I "One side"	Program II "Both sides"	*Control group*
Before	37%	38%	36%
After	59	59	34
Difference	22%	21%	−2%
Probability	<.01	<.01	

The effectiveness of both programs is revealed by the marked change shown for both experimental groups (with practically no change for the control group).   However, no advantage for one program over the other for the audience as a whole is revealed.

While changes in overall frequencies of response, such as those shown above, are often useful in evaluating the effectiveness of a program at achieving its educational objective, they are not usually the most sensitive measure of effects. In the present case if the orientation objectives were specifically to prepare the men to expect a war of at least one-and-one-half years after VE Day, the above analysis does reveal the increase in the number of men holding this desired point of view. However, an analysis of this form often conceals other effects important for a more complete description of the changes that occur. Thus shifts occurring within the region below the point of dichotomy (e.g., from an estimate of six months to an estimate of one year) or within the region above this point (e.g., from two-and-one-half years to three years) are not revealed. A more sensitive analysis of the overall effects is described in the next section.

2. *Analysis in Terms of Net Proportion Who Change*

Since measurements on the same men were made both before and after the programs it was possible to get each man's individual change in estimating the length of the war. As already stated, the answers tended to be in terms of half-year units, so the minimum change occurring with a sizable frequency was a change of one-half year. Accordingly, the results were analyzed in terms of whether a man increased or decreased his estimate—from "before" to "after" —by one-half year or more. This analysis gets at individual shifts all along the time continuum, irrespective of whether they cross a particular cutting point along the marginal distribution.

Using this analysis procedure it was found that in all groups some men increased their estimates and others decreased their estimates. This is to be expected merely from the knowledge that most opinion questions are not perfectly reliable. In addition, a certain amount of "turnover" of opinion is expected because of various individual experiences during the interval between the two measurements.

The results showed, however, that in the control group the positive shifts (increased estimates) were about equal in number to the negative shifts, but that in both experimental groups the positive shifts greatly exceeded the negative shifts. These results are shown in Table 2.

Here the programs are seen to have resulted in a net proportion of *two-fifths* of the men increasing their estimates. On the basis of the analysis procedure used in Table 1 we could only have been sure that a net of around *one-fifth* was affected.

TABLE 2

EFFECTS OF THE PROGRAMS IN TERMS OF NET PROPORTION
CHANGING THEIR ESTIMATES

| Kind of change | PERCENTAGE WHO CHANGED THEIR ESTIMATE BY ONE-HALF YEAR OR MORE | | |
| | Experimental groups | | |
	Program I "One side"	Program II "Both sides"	Control group
No change	46%	45%	63%
Increased estimate	47	47	18
Decreased estimate	7	8	19
Net change (increase minus decrease)	40	39	−1
Net effect (experimental change minus control change)	41	40	
*Probability**	<.01	<.01	

* The method for determining the significance level of the "net effect" utilizes the fact that the net *change* for each group is the difference between two mutually exclusive proportions in the same sample—namely, the proportion P_1 who gave an increased estimate and the proportion P_2 who gave a decreased estimate. The net *effect*, is the difference between two such differences—i.e., the difference between the net change for an experimental group and that for the control group. Its standard error is given by the formula:

$$\text{Est. } \sigma_{\text{diff} - \text{diff}} = \sqrt{[P_1 + P_2 - (P_1 - P_2)^2]\left[\frac{1}{N_E} + \frac{1}{N_C}\right]}$$

where P_1 and P_2 are the above stated proportions computed for the experimental and control groups *combined*, and N_E and N_C are the N's for the experimental and control groups. (See Appendix, B, pp. 303-304.)

3. *Effects of the Programs on Men Initially Opposing and Initially Favoring the Commentator's Conclusion*

The results already reported indicate no greater effectiveness of either program on the audience *as a whole*. However, as mentioned earlier, a critical feature in the theory underlying the experiment was the expectation of adverse effects of the "one-sided" program on men initially opposing the commentator's view that the war would take at least two years after VE Day. In line with the theory, therefore, the results were analyzed separately for men who initially opposed and those who initially favored the stand taken by the programs. The basis for distinguishing these two groups was whether their initial estimate of the length of the war in the "before" questionnaire was, respectively, less than two years, or was two years or more. The measure used in the analysis was the "net effect" described in the previous section for changes of one-half year or more.

The net effects of the two ways of presenting the orientation material are shown below for these two subgroups of men; those initially estimating a war of less than two years (the "opposed" group) and those initially estimating a war of two or more years (the "favorable" group). Control results are omitted for simplicity since the present concern is with comparing the two programs, both of which had the same control.

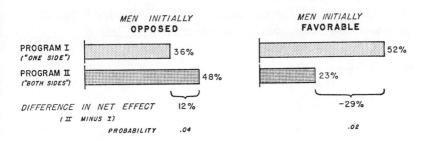

Figure 1. Differential effects of the two programs on men initially opposing and men initially favoring the commentator's position.
See supplementary Table A, p. 226, for subgroup *N*'s and control results.

The above chart shows that the *net effects* were different for the two ways of presenting the orientation material, depending on the initial stand of the listener. The program giving some of the U.S. advantages in addition to the difficulties was more effective for men initially opposed, that is, for men who, contrary to the programs, expected a war of less than two years. On the other hand, the program giving the one-sided picture was more effective for men initially favoring the stand taken, that is, for the men who agreed with the point of view of the programs that the war would take at least two years. The initial division of opinion was roughly three men opposing to every man favoring the stand taken, but since the differential effect was greater in the latter group the overall net effects on the men as a whole were almost equal for the two programs.[1]

4. *Effects on Men with Different Amounts of Education*

In line with theoretical considerations and data presented in Chapters 4 and 6, it would be expected that the better educated men would be less affected by a conspicuously one-sided presentation and would conversely be more likely to accept the arguments of a pres-

---

[1] The statistical test used to assess the reliability of the differential effects is exactly analogous to that used in the previous section. In the above case, however, the control is not involved since the experimental subgroups can be directly compared.

entation that appears to take all factors into account in arriving at a conclusion.   On the other hand, the consideration of both sides of an issue could weaken the immediate force of the argument for the less well educated insofar as they are less critical and more likely to be impressed by the strength of the one-sided argument without thinking of objections.

When the results were broken down according to educational level, it was found that the program which presented both sides was more effective with better educated men and that the program which presented one side was more effective with less educated men. Figure 2 shows results comparing the effects on men who did not graduate from high school with the effects on high school graduates. This breakdown by education divides the sample into approximately equal halves.

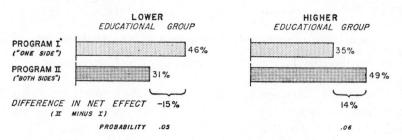

Figure 2. Differential effects of the two programs on men of different educational backgrounds.
See supplementary Table B, p. 226, for detailed computations.

The above results show that the program giving both sides had *less* effect on the nongraduates but *more* effect on the high school graduates.

5. *Effects When Both Education and Initial Estimates Are Considered*

The interesting question arises as to how initial position on the issue presented by the transcription is related to effects among men in each educational group.   Definitive results on this point could not be obtained because of the small number of cases involved when the sample is broken into the eight subgroups required for this analysis.   The data available are presented, however, to indicate the trends and to suggest a hypothesis deserving further study: that the argument giving both sides is more effective among the better educated regardless of initial position whereas the one-sided presentation is primarily effective with those who are already convinced among the less well educated group (Figure 3).

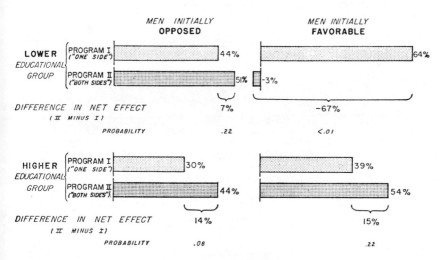

Figure 3.   Differential effects of the two programs on men initially opposing and men initially favoring the commentator's position, shown separately for men with different education.

See supplementary Table C, p. 227, for detailed computations.

The conclusions suggested by the pattern of results presented thus far may be summarized as follows: Giving the strong points for the "other side" can make a presentation more effective at getting across its message, at least for the better educated men and for those who are already opposed to the stand taken.   This difference in effectiveness, however, may be reversed for the less educated men and, in the extreme case, the material giving both sides may have a negative effect on poorly educated men already convinced of the major position taken by a program.   From these results it would be expected that the total effect of either kind of program on the group as a whole would depend on the group's educational composition and on the initial division of opinion in the group.   Thus, ascertaining this information about the composition of an audience might be of considerable value in choosing the most effective type of presentation.

6. *Men's Evaluation of the Factual Coverage*

One factor that should tend to make a presentation taking into account both sides of an issue more effective than a presentation covering only one side is that the men might believe the former treatment to be more impartial and authoritative.

In the present study, however, the group as a whole did not consider the factual coverage more complete in the program giving U.S. advantages in addition to the difficulties faced. This is illustrated below.[2]

Per cent of men saying that the program did a good job of giving the facts on the Pacific War

Program I
("one side")   61%
Program II
("both sides")   54

Per cent of men saying that the program took all of the important facts into account

Program I
("one side")   48%
Program II
("both sides")   42

It can be seen above that the factual coverage was not considered better in the program giving U.S. advantages as well as the difficulties. The difference obtained was in the opposite direction, although not reliably so. Essentially the same results were obtained for each of the two educational subgroups analyzed.

The explanation of this unexpected result apparently lies in the fact that both programs omitted any mention of Russia as a factor in the Pacific War, and *this omission seemed more glaring in the presentation that committed itself to covering both sides of the question.* This somewhat paradoxical conclusion is well supported by results to be shown shortly and while it was not anticipated it is quite understandable in retrospect.

At the time that the Pacific War was chosen as the orientation subject for the experiment it was recognized that a weakness of this topic was that under existing informational policy no stand could be taken on the help to be expected from Russia. Thus maximum content difference between the two presentations could not be achieved because they *both* had to omit mention of an important argument on the "other side," namely, that Russia might enter the war against the Japanese. It was not anticipated, however, that

[2] The N's on which these percentages are based are 214 for Program I and 214 for Program II.

this omission would be more noticeable in the program that otherwise covered both sides. That this actually happened was indicated by the men's answers to the "write-in" question: "What facts or topics that you think are important in the war with Japan are not mentioned in the program?" The percentages writing in that aid or possible aid from Russia was not mentioned are shown below.

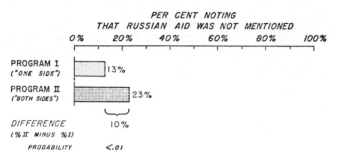

Figure 4. Frequency with which the omission of the topic of Russian aid was noted by the men.

As shown above, almost twice as many men mentioned the omission of Russia in the program covering "both sides." The difference was even more pronounced among *groups that would be expected to be especially sensitive to this omission*, such as men who were initially optimistic about the length of the war, men with more education, and men who had indicated in the "before" questionnaire that they expected a great deal of help from Russia in the job against Japan.

7. Relative Effectiveness of the Two Programs on Men Most Likely to Note the Omission of the Topic of Russian Aid

In the preceding section it was shown that the program giving "both sides" was *not* considered more adequate than the one-sided program in its factual coverage and that it caused more men to note that Russia was not mentioned. The question now to be considered is whether this actually detracted from the effectiveness of this program that otherwise took all factors into consideration. A direct answer to this question cannot be given, but indirect evidence indicates that the omission did detract from this program's effectiveness.

The indirect evidence comes from a separate analysis of the results among men who initially opposed the point of view of the commentator. These were the men for whom the program giving both sides was more effective, even with the omission of the topic of Russian aid. The question is, would it have been still more effective if this topic could have been included? To get evidence on this question this subgroup of opposed men was further subdivided according to whether or not they were predisposed to note the omission of Russia. The logic of the analysis was that men especially sensitive to the omission (because they were opposed and thought Russia might help) would not accept the commentator's argument, whereas those men who were opposed to his position but did *not* have Russian aid as one of their own important arguments for a short war would show less detrimental effect of the omission. The following question in the "before" questionnaire was used to subdivide the initially opposed men into those anticipating and those not anticipating substantial aid from Russia.

"How much help do you think America will get from other countries when it comes to the job of defeating the Japs?" (Check one)

_____ very little
_____ some, but not a great deal
_____ a great deal (Which countries? _____)

The breakdown on this question among "opposed" men put about two-fifths of the men in the "sensitive" subgroup, that is, about two-fifths of the "opposed" men said they expected a great deal of help and *wrote in Russia* as one of the countries from which they expected a great deal of help.

When these subgroups of the "opposed" men were compared it was found that the men who counted on a great deal of help from Russia gave a relatively poorer evaluation of the factual coverage in the program giving "both sides" and were relatively less influenced in the direction of increasing their estimates of the probable length of the war.

The results for the men's evaluation of the factual coverage, based on two items, are shown in Figure 5.

The implication of the results in Figure 5 is that the authenticity of the program which presented both sides suffered from the omission of the subject of Russia. Men who counted on Russian aid had a lower evaluation of the factual coverage of this program than of the one-sided program.

The presumption from this indirect evidence is that if the program covering both sides had dealt with the subject of Russia, it might have been considered more complete in its factual coverage, particularly among men who expected Russian aid. This inference receives corroboration from the fact that in a fairly large-scale pretest of the two programs, conducted at a time when possible aid from Russia was a less important news topic, the program covering "both sides" had been found to be *reliably more accepted* in its factual cov-

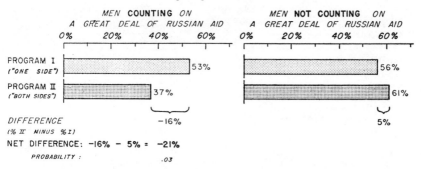

A. Per cent saying program did "a very good job" of giving the facts.

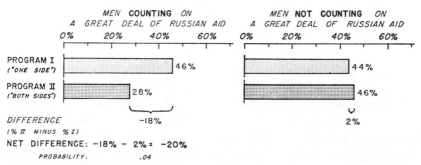

B. Per cent saying program "took all of the important facts into account."

Figure 5. Differences in evaluation of factual coverage in the two programs, *among men opposed to the commentator's position*, comparing those who did and those who did not count on Russian aid.

For subgroup *N*'s, see supplementary Table D, p. 227.

erage, just the reverse of the results shown on page 216. This pretest was conducted with a sample of 347 Infantry reinforcements in March 1945 and practically no difference was obtained between the two programs in the percentages of men noting the omission of Russian aid. In the present study, however, the programs were played during the second week of April, about a week after the Russians announced that they would not renew their nonaggression pact with Japan.

Not only did the omission of the topic of Russia affect men's evaluation of the factual coverage in Program II in the subgroups above, but it may have reduced the effect of the program on the men's estimates of the length of the war.   This is suggested by an analysis of the net effects of the programs on opinions of the men in the same subgroups as those used in Figure 5.   The results of this analysis are shown in Figure 6.

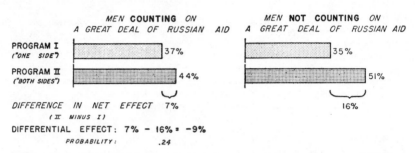

Figure 6.   Differential relative effect of the two programs among men initially opposed but differing as to whether they had counted on a great deal of help from Russia. See supplementary Table D, p. 227, for N's and control group results.

These results are in line with the expectation that among the men for whom the presentation with both sides is most effective (i.e., the men initially opposing the idea of a two-year war) the advantage of the "both-sides" presentation was less among those counting on a great deal of help from Russia than among those not expecting much help.   The differential effect is too small to be reliable with the small number of cases involved in the above subgroups, but they are consonant with the interpretation that the effects of the program giving some of the "other side" would have been even greater on those opposed to the stand taken if *all* of the other side could have been covered.

All of the results dealing with the omission of the topic of Russian aid seem to support one important conclusion, namely, that if a presentation supporting a particular conclusion attempts to take both sides of the issue into account, it must include *all* of the important negative arguments; otherwise the presentation may "boomerang" by failing to live up to the expectation of impartiality and completeness.

Apparently the fact that the commentator in giving "both sides" indicated that he was trying to take *all* factors into consideration in drawing his conclusion prepared the men to expect the inclusion of possible Russian aid as one of the factors to be considered.   Thus the omission in the context of considering all factors stood out more than in the context of the one-sided program where only the difficulties were being considered.   The general conclusion seems to be that a one-sided presentation in which the conclusion is stated in advance and the reasons for this conclusion are then given will be accepted as the argument for a given point of view without much loss of authenticity resulting from failure to cover the other side.   However, if a presentation commits itself to taking everything into account, either by announcing this in advance or by actually covering parts of each side of the issue, it will seem less authentic than a single-sided presentation if any important facts known to the audience are not included in the discussion, and its effectiveness at changing opinions will be reduced among those who are most aware of the point omitted.

8. *Relation of the Results to the Contention That the Initially Opposed Will Be Negatively Affected*

The results of this experiment have an obvious bearing on the frequently made assertion that "propaganda" merely reinforces the opinions already held, i.e., that those initially favoring a point of view tend to be made more favorable, whereas those initially opposed may tend to become even more opposed than at the outset.[3] This would be predicted on the grounds that a person is receptive to arguments having the conclusion he himself has already reached, but that arguments counter to a strongly held opinion serve as the occasion for an individual to rehearse the arguments favoring his side, to think up new arguments to combat the ones presented, to "get his ego involved" in his position, and so forth.

In all of the results shown comparing the net effects of the programs on men "initially opposing" the point of view presented by the commentator, it will be observed that "opposed" men were influenced in the direction of the "message" presented rather than against it.   Thus regardless of educational level or expectation of aid from Russia the "opposed" men were influenced to accept the point of view of the commentator with either program.   This is definitely contrary to the contention that "propaganda" merely reinforces existing beliefs.[4]

[3] Cf. e.g., Murphy, G., L. B. Murphy and T. M. Newcomb, *Experimental Social Psychology* (rev. ed.) New York: Harper, 1937., p. 874f. and 963f.

[4] A word should also be said concerning the interpretations here placed on such expressions as "more opposed."   The frequently stressed distinction between "intensity" of opinion and "content" or "direction" of opinion is relevant to this interpretation. Thus, changes in the direction of "more favorable" or "more opposed" might refer either to changes in the direction of a more extreme position on a content continuum, or to greater intensity of feeling on a given position, or both.   However, the present discussion is limited to the former kind of change because of the absence of adequate measures of intensity.

It might be contended that in the results shown so far the men in the "opposed" group were not sufficiently opposed for the alleged phenomenon to be revealed. Thus the opposed group contained a sizable proportion who were close to the borderline of two years in their estimate of the length of the war and these could not be said to be very strongly opposed. But a finer breakdown of initial estimate reveals the same general result. This is shown below in Table 3 which shows net effects as a function of initial position for less broad categories than those used so far. The most opposed group possible with the coding used—that is, the group estimating a war of less than six months—is not shown because the number of cases was so small; only about one man in twenty fell in this category. However, even in this tiny group the results come out in the same direction. The results presented are for both programs combined.

TABLE 3

THE EFFECTS OF RADIO TRANSCRIPTIONS ON OPINIONS ABOUT DURATION OF WAR, FOR THOSE WITH VARIOUS INITIAL OPINIONS

	NET PERCENTAGE CHANGING ESTIMATE BY ONE-HALF YEAR OR MORE AMONG MEN WHOSE INITIAL ESTIMATE WAS:			
	Less than 1 year	*1 year up to 1½ years*	*1½ years up to 2 years*	*2 years or more*
Net change in experimental groups	58%	53%	26%	2%
Net change in the control group	20	6	−12	−34
Net effects	38	47	38	36

It will be seen that the familiar "regression" phenomenon occurs in the control group, that is, because of the imperfect reliability of the question on length of the war the men who initially made long estimates tend to make shorter ones and the men who initially made short estimates tend to make longer ones.[5] The changes due to regression as indicated by the changes in the control group must be subtracted from the changes in the experimental group to obtain the net effect of the program, shown in the third line of figures in Table 3.

It can be seen from the net effects shown in Table 3 that even with the finer breakdown of initial estimate, all of the subgroups

---

[5] This regression phenomenon, which may be unfamiliar to some readers, is discussed in Appendix D, p. 329ff.

were influenced in the direction of revising their estimates upward. This was true even of the men with the most extreme opposition— that is, men whose initial estimate was only one year or less.

These results are consistent with the results of analyses of data obtained in other studies reported in this volume. Several analyses were made in connection with the orientation film studies to see how opinion change was related to initial opinion. In all cases it was found that men initially opposed to a particular opinion were nevertheless influenced in the same direction as the men as a whole rather than being driven further in the direction of their original position. An example of such an analysis is adduced here to illustrate the general conclusion.

A scale of five opinion items was used to measure confidence in the "British War Effort" in the before-after study of "The Battle of Britain." This gave six categories of initial response according to whether the individual accepted none of the opinions expressed, one of them, and so on up to accepting *all five*. For the analysis, all men in the film group were sorted into these six categories as determined from their responses on the questionnaire administered *before* the film. The mean scale value for the "after" responses of each of these six subgroups was then determined, and these values compared with similar values for the control group. The mean changes for film and control groups are shown in the tabulation below.

Again we see the phenomenon of regression toward the mean in the control group. Thus men whose initial scale position was 0 re-

TABLE 4

MEAN CHANGE IN SCALE VALUES FOR FILM AND CONTROL SUBGROUPS
GETTING EACH SCALE SCORE BEFORE THE FILM
(SCALE OF 5 OPINION-ITEMS CONCERNING "BRITISH WAR EFFORT")

	0 (opposing)	1	2	3	4	5 (favoring)
Mean after-minus-before differences for those with each initial position:						
Film group	1.14	0.93	0.35	0.17	−0.10	−0.44
Control group	0.70	0.34	0.15	−0.45	−0.84	−0.91
Film-control difference	.44	.59	.20	.62	.74	.45

gressed *up* to an average of .70 and men whose initial scale position was 5 regressed *down* to an average value of 4.09. But just as in the study of the radio programs *all* groups were affected in the direction of accepting the "message" of the communication, even the most extreme subgroup that had initially been so anti-British that they did not check a single response favorable to the British in the five items making up the British war effort scale.

It may be further argued that the contention that opposed men would be made more opposed applies not to the extremeness of their content position but rather to the intensity with which they hold their opinion or the extent of emotional involvement in supporting their point of view. No answer is available from the present studies on this interpretation of degree of opposition because measurements of intensity of feeling independent of content were not feasible. To the extent, however, that intensity and content are correlated, the present study and all other analyses that were made show negative results regardless of how "opposition" is defined for the type of communication investigated.

This qualification concerning the type of communications investigated is made because it seems theoretically possible that opposition would be fostered with some kinds of "propaganda." This seems especially likely for face-to-face situations in which the communicator and the communicatee become involved in a give-and-take argument. In such a case the individual who constitutes the "audience" himself takes a stand and is likely to have more "ego involvement," actively to seek new arguments in support of his position, and so forth. A similar situation would be the debate form of communication in which there is a protagonist for each side of the issue. If the audience is initially divided in opinion on the issue individual audience members would be expected to identify with the protagonist representing their own initial stand, and a situation similar to the face-to-face argument is created.[6]

9. *Summary of Results*

(1) Presenting the arguments on both sides of an issue was found to be more effective than giving only the arguments supporting the

---

[6] Exposure to debates has been shown to strengthen the initial opinions of those audience members initially expressing an opinion and to reduce the neutral, no-opinion category by shifting some people in one direction and others in the opposite direction. (Cf. Millson, W. A. D., "Problems in Measuring Audience Reaction," *Quart. J. Speech*, 1932, *18*, 621–37.)

point being made, in the case of individuals who were *initially opposed* to the point of view being presented.

(2) For men who were *already convinced* of the point of view being presented, however, the inclusion of arguments on both sides was less effective, for the group as a whole, than presenting only the arguments favoring the general position being advocated.

(3) Better educated men were more favorably affected by presentation of both sides; less well educated men were more affected by the communication which used only supporting arguments.

(4) The group for which the presentation giving both sides was least effective was the group of poorly educated men who were already convinced of the point of view being advocated.

(5) An important incidental finding was that the absence of one relevant argument against the stand taken by the programs was more noticeable in the presentation using arguments on both sides than in the presentation in which only one side was discussed. Furthermore, advantage of the program giving both sides among men initially opposed was less for those who regarded the omitted argument as an important one.

(6) Men who were initially very opposed to the point of view being presented—as measured by their deviation in *content* from the position taken by the communication—were nevertheless influenced to alter their opinion in the direction of the "message" rather than being shifted further in the direction of their initial opinion.

SUPPLEMENTARY TABLE A

BREAKDOWN OF CHANGES IN ESTIMATES AMONG MEN INITIALLY FAVORING
AND MEN INITIALLY OPPOSING THE STAND TAKEN

	PER CENT OF MEN					
	PROGRAM I "one side"		*PROGRAM II* "both sides"		*CONTROL* no program	
	initial estimate		*initial estimate*		*initial estimate*	
	Less than 2	2 or more	Less than 2	2 or more	Less than 2	2 or more
No change	45	46	41	56	65	56
Revised estimate upward	50	36	58	16	22	5
Revised estimate downward	5	18	1	27	13	39
Net change (% up minus % down)	45	18	57	−11	9*	−34*
Control net change*	9	−34	9	−34		
Net effect (program net minus control)	36	52	48	23		
Number of cases in each subgroup**	152	45	150	55	140	41

* The net changes in the two subgroups of the *control* represent the familiar "regression" phenomenon due to unreliable test answers. (See p. 329ff., Appendix D.) The greater degree of regression in the subgroups estimating a war of 2 or more years is accounted for by the extent of their deviation from the average estimate of less than 1½ years.

** The numbers of cases given here add to 583 instead of the total of 625 men studied because the analysis could not include the 42 individuals who failed to write legible estimates of the length of the war in either the "before" or the "after" survey. The omission of such individuals applies also to the three following tables.

SUPPLEMENTARY TABLE B

BREAKDOWN OF CHANGES IN ESTIMATES AMONG MEN
WITH DIFFERING EDUCATION

| | PER CENT OF MEN | | | | | |
| EDUCATION: | *Non-graduates* | | | *High school graduates* | | |
PROGRAM:	I ("One side")	II ("Both sides")	Control	I ("One side")	II ("Both sides")	Control
No change	40	45	64	51	45	62
Revised estimate upward	54	44	19	40	50	17
Revised estimate downward	6	11	17	9	5	21
Net change	48	33	2	31	45	−4
Control net change	2	2		−4	−4	
Net effect (program net minus control)	46	31		35	49	
Number of cases in each subgroup*	93	105	104	104	100	77

* See second footnote to Table A.

SUPPLEMENTARY TABLE C

BREAKDOWN OF CHANGES IN ESTIMATES IN THE SUBGROUPS SEPARATED BOTH
ACCORDING TO INITIAL ESTIMATE AND ACCORDING TO EDUCATION

	PER CENT OF MEN							
EDUCATION:	Non-graduates				High school graduates			
INITIAL ESTIMATE:	Less than 2 years		2 or more years		Less than 2 years		2 or more years	
PROGRAM:	I	II	I	II	I	II	I	II
	"One side"	"Both sides"	"One side"	"Both sides"	"One side"	"Both sides"	"One side"	"Both sides"
No change	35	40	52	57	53	41	41	56
Revised estimate upward	59	60	39	3	43	56	32	32
Revised estimate downward	6	—	9	40	4	3	27	12
Net change	53	−60	30	−37	39	53	5	20
Control net change*	−9	9	−34	−34	9	9	−34	−34
Net effect	44	51	64	−3	30	44	39	54
Number of cases in each subgroup**	70	75	23	30	82	75	22	25

* The control net change used above to eliminate the effects of regression is the same as that used in Table A. This procedure assumes that regression was the same at the two educational levels, but it was considered a better estimate than could be obtained from the small separate subgroups of the control. In any case, chief interest is attached to the *differences* between the effects of the two programs; these differences are independent of the estimate of regression used.
** See second footnote to Table A.

SUPPLEMENTARY TABLE D

BREAKDOWN OF CHANGES IN ESTIMATES, AMONG MEN INITIALLY OPPOSED TO
THE STAND TAKEN, FOR THOSE WHO HAD AND THOSE WHO HAD NOT
COUNTED ON A GREAT DEAL OF HELP FROM RUSSIA

	PER CENT OF MEN					
	Men who had counted on a great deal of help from Russia			Men who had not counted on a great deal of help from Russia		
	Program I	Program II		Program I	Program II	
	"One side"	"Both sides"	Control	"One side"	"Both sides"	Control
No change	46	48	66	45	34	64
Revised estimate upward	50	52	21	50	63	23
Revised estimate downward	5	0	13	5	2	13
Net change	45	52	8	45	61	10
Control net change	8	8		10	10	
Net effect (program net minus control)	37	44		35	51	
Number of cases in each subgroup	66	71	62	86	79	78

CHAPTER 9

THE EFFECT OF AN AUDIENCE-PARTICIPATION TECHNIQUE IN FILM-STRIP PRESENTATION

IN THE usual method of presenting motion pictures or film strips, participation by the audience is limited to implicit, symbolic responses. In the experiment here reported, a technique for obtaining greater participation was introduced by requiring the audience to recite aloud during parts of a film strip, thus achieving more active rehearsal of the material by each learner.

Increased participation would be expected to result in greater learning because it guarantees overt practice of the actual responses to be learned rather than merely relying on implicit practice of symbolic responses. Participation also is likely to function as an incentive to learn, since the learner soon finds out that if he has to perform the response himself at the appropriate intervals he must try harder to learn the material as it is being presented. Since it is likely that the effects of procedures for increasing participation are achieved in part through motivational factors, the effectiveness of the participation would be expected to depend on the learner's initial motivation. For this reason in the present study the additional variable of motivation, induced by announcing an exam, was introduced in order to determine its interaction with the effects of audience participation.

PROCEDURE

1. THE FILM STRIPS USED

Two film strips with sound accompaniment were used in the study. The educational objective of the film strips was to teach Signal Corps men the phonetic alphabet and pronunciation of numerals. The film strip presented to the *experimental* group used the aforementioned technique for increasing audience participation; the film strip presented to the *standard* group was exactly like the experimental strip in every respect except that it did not use the recitation procedure for increasing audience participation.

In both film strips, after a few preliminary frames to show the nature and importance of the phonetic alphabet, the phonetic names ("Able" for "A," "Baker" for "B," etc.) corresponding to each letter were shown in a printed list and pronounced by the narrator. Then, successively, each letter and phonetic name was presented in an individual frame showing a picture to illustrate the phonetic name, with accompanying sound effects and narration designed to facilitate the formation of an association between the letter and the name. Two illustrative frames are shown below in Figure 1.

Sound effect: German band playing "O where, O where, has my little dog gone," with dogs barking.
Narrator: "Dog."

Sound effect: Oboe music.
Narrator: "Oboe—An oboe, it's clearly understood, is an ill wind no one blows good."

Figure 1. Frames excerpted from film strips to illustrate type of presentation used.

Interspersed after about every six individual frames was a frame showing a review list of the preceding group of phonetic names. When all 26 of the individual frames and the four review lists had been shown, a complete review list of all 26 letters and phonetic names in alphabetical order was shown. After a digression on the pronunciation of numerals, another complete review list, this time in scrambled order, was shown.

In all aspects described thus far the two film strips were identical in both the sound track and the frames shown. The only difference between the two was that in the "standard" film strip all *review* lists presented each phonetic name with its corresponding letter and these were pronounced by the narrator, whereas in the experimental strip the letters in the review lists were followed by question marks and the names were to be recalled and pronounced by the audience. A correlated difference was the additional statement in the introductory narration that from time to time the audience would be asked to recite the names aloud; also, each time a review list was shown, the frame title and the narrator instructed the audience to recite the names aloud. Examples of the standard and experimental review-list frames are shown below.

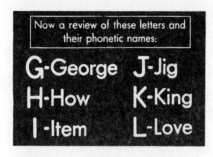

Review-list frame from *standard* film strip.   Review-list frame from *experimental* film strip.

Figure 2.   Examples of the review-list frames.

In the instructions to both the experimental and the standard groups prior to the film, a very brief statement was made describing the content of the film strip they were to see and its importance as a part of a soldier's training. This approximated what would normally be said by the training officer or noncom in charge of presenting a sound film strip. The experimental subjects were given the additional instruction that from time to time they would be required to recite the phonetic names out loud, at which times they were not merely to mumble to themselves but should "sing out" so they could be heard.

2. DESIGN OF THE EXPERIMENT

The general plan of the study was to show the film strips to a number of platoon-size audiences of enlisted men, and to administer tests to the men immediately afterward, to find out how well they had learned the phonetic alphabet. By comparing the test performance of men who had seen the experimental film strip with the performance of men who had seen the standard film strip, the effects of the procedure for increasing audience participation could be evaluated.

Because motivation was expected to be a variable that would modify the effects of the participation procedure, the men were told in half of the showings that they would be tested after the film strip; the other half were told only that they were going to see a film strip that was part of their training. The purpose of this difference in treatment was to make possible an analysis of the relative value of the increased audience participation under conditions of greater and lesser motivation. Thus in this study two experimentally controlled variables were studied in combination.

For convenience, the individuals who knew in advance that they were going to be tested will be referred to as the "motivated" group, and the individuals who were not informed in advance of the test will be referred to as the "nonmotivated" group. This terminology is intended to imply nothing more than a difference in the *relative* amount of motivation expected for the two groups; there would clearly be considerable motivation operative in the "nonmotivated" group, even though they were on the average less well motivated than the other group.

The men used in the study were new recruits at a Reception Center. An important purpose in using a Reception Center was that the men had no previous military experience, "company organization" was purely temporary, and the recruits were moved through the center so fast that their entire stay at the camp was only a few days. These properties of a Reception Center were all considered important to the experiment because they insured: (1) little previous experience with the phonetic alphabet; (2) few communication lines along which knowledge of the experiment could spread among the men not yet used—particularly the knowledge that a test was given at the end of the film, which would have eliminated the motivational differences; and (3) little realization that some aspects of the experiment were not typical of the Army.

The aspect of the experiment that was particularly not typical of the Army was the method used for determining whether a man would serve in the experimental or in the standard group. A "company" roster was divided into two halves—about 100 men each—on the basis of alphabetical order, and men in the first half were ordered to assemble at one hour and the remainder to assemble at the next following hour. When each of these halves had assembled, they were lined up in a formation in which they chose their own positions. They were then counted and the half of the group on the left (about 50 men) was sent to one theater and the half on the right was sent to the other. Since the two theaters followed a balanced pattern of alternate presentation of experimental and standard film strips, the resulting choice of experimental-group and standard-group men was a random selection of individuals rather than the usual company-unit selection used in the other film studies. To reduce any possible concern of the men about the arbitrary division as to who went to what theater, they were told that they would see a training film, but that the theaters would accommodate only 50 men. Since there was no platoon organization, the method used seemed as reasonable as any. By scheduling the two halves of a "company" for successive hours, the communication problem was further controlled. One half was marching to the theaters while the other was marching back to the company area by a different route.

Sixteen audiences of approximately 50 men each were used, the number of men totaling 742. Name and serial number were recorded on each man's test blank so that the number of years of schooling and the AGCT score of each man in the sample could be subsequently obtained from the classification office. This latter information provided a basis for equating the learning ability of the groups used for the final analysis of results and a means of analyzing the relative value of the increased audience participation of men for differing learning ability as indicated by AGCT and education.

3. THE TESTING PROCEDURE

Immediate rather than deferred testing was employed, partly in order to maximize sensitivity of the experiment to effects of the participation procedure. Introduction of a delay period between training and testing would presumably have yielded results in the same direction as those obtained with immediate testing, but with differences attenuated through intervening forgetting and possible voluntary rehearsal by individuals in both the experimental and standard groups. This would operate to reduce the effects obtained from the overt rehearsal given the former group during the training session. The rehearsal problem was particularly crucial in view of the communication problem already mentioned, especially since half of the men (the "motivated" group) were told a test would follow. If time were allowed between film and test, these men might have communicated their knowledge about the coming test to "nonmotivated" men.

Another advantage of immediate testing was related to the stated purpose of the film. According to the film-makers the function of the film strip was to give preliminary familiarization with the phonetic alphabet and an opportunity to learn it well enough to be able to carry out further rehearsal. Extensive further drill would of course be required to attain high proficiency in the use of the alphabet in later field situations, but presumably Signal Corps men would have strong motivation to rehearse the material afterward. The purpose of the film was to provide sufficient learning to permit further effective practice.

Five men from each of the sixteen audience groups were given *individual oral tests* of their ability to recall the phonetic names. In these tests each letter was presented singly as a visual stimulus stamped in large type on a card, and the men were required to respond orally with the phonetic name. The correctness of each response was recorded and the time required for a man to give his response was timed by stop watch, with a limit of 15 seconds for each letter.

Space and personnel limitations forced the number of the individual tests to be smaller than might have been desirable. Ten individual testers, made available by the camp's classification office, were used for each hour of the experiment. The number of individuals tested was therefore limited to 5 men from each audience, or a total of 80 from the 16 audiences involved. The men to be tested individually were selected in such a manner as to give roughly equivalent distributions of education in the four experimental conditions. The rest of the men in each audience group were given a *written test*. In these tests the men received a sheet with a mimeographed list of the letters, with blanks beside each letter for writing in the phonetic names.

Both types of tests presented the twenty-six letters of the alphabet in a random sequence. Varied orders of presentation were used in a balanced fashion in testing different subjects, there being five different test orders in all, used with equal frequency.

RESULTS

The results obtained with the individual oral tests will be presented first, followed by presentation of relevant portions of the data from the written tests. Conclusions from the two sets of data were in all cases in agreement as to direction, but differences were smaller in the case of the written tests. Use of the oral-test data was considered preferable because of the superior sensitivity and realism of this measure.

The individual tests were more *sensitive* both because the measurement of the exact time taken by each individual to recall each letter is a precise measure of learning and because the individual administration provides better control of the conditions of testing. The individual tests were more *realistic* in that they more closely approximated the conditions under which the phonetic alphabet would actually be used, that is, with men making an oral response to each individual letter. However, since only 20 men were given oral tests for each of the four conditions of the experiment, presentation of the written-test results has been included when recourse to these data was necessary to afford a sufficient number of cases in some of the subgroups used for analysis.

An important difficulty of the written test was the opportunity given the men to divide up the time allowed in such a way that an individual could concentrate much more time on the phonetic names he had difficulty in remembering. Another factor was the possibility that additional cues were provided by being able to see all the letters at once and to see all the names that had been remembered and written in. This supposition is supported by the finding that the smaller differences among the experimental groups taking the written tests were accompanied by a considerably higher average performance on the tests.

Results for Individual Tests

1. OVERALL EFFECT OF PARTICIPATION

Figure 3 gives a comparison of the individual-test results for men who saw the experimental film strip and for men who saw the standard film strip. The difference in performance represents the effects of the increased audience participation provided by the active nature of the reviews in the experimental strip. The curves in the chart show the average number of phonetic names remembered correctly with various limits on the time interval allowed to remember each phonetic name. These results are for men who did not know in advance that they would be tested after the film strip (the "non-motivated" group). This was the group which was shown the film strip under conditions typical of use in the Army—that is, with no test announced. Comparison with the motivated group will be made later.

The figure shows that there was a marked superiority in the test performance of men who had seen the film strip with the active participation technique. This superiority shows up at each of the various time intervals that could be used as the limit allowed for thinking of the phonetic name after being shown each letter.

From the standpoint of actual use of the phonetic alphabet, proficiency should probably be such that every name can be recalled almost immediately when the letter is shown. To approximate these conditions, a two-second time interval was used as one criterion of effectiveness. Within this time limit it is seen from Figure 3 that

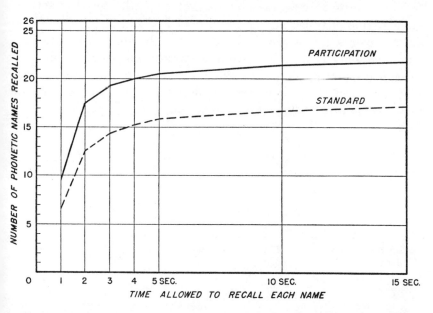

Figure 3. Average number of phonetic names correctly recalled within designated periods of time per name.

the men who had active participation recalled an average of 17.6 phonetic names or about 68 per cent of the 26 names, whereas the men who had the standard form of the film strip recalled an average of 12.6 names or only about 48 per cent. Thus the technique for increasing audience participation increased the number of words learned *proficiently* from a level of 48 per cent to a level of 68 per cent.

From another standpoint, the training objective of the film strip was to provide sufficient memory of the correct phonetic names to permit their being recalled and practiced later. A single showing of a 25-minute sound film strip would not be expected to teach the phonetic alphabet to the level of complete proficiency.   From this standpoint a longer time limit for remembering each phonetic name would be desirable in evaluating the training value of the increased audience participation.   Preliminary oral tests indicated that very few names required more than 15 seconds to be recalled if they could be recalled at all.   Therefore in the conduct of the individual tests in the main experiment the men were given a maximum of 15 seconds in which to try to recall the phonetic name after each letter was presented.   It can be seen in Figure 3 that there was very little gain during the last 5 seconds of this interval.   With the 15-second time limit as a criterion, the data show that men who saw the active-participation strip learned an average of 21.9 out of the 26 names, whereas men who saw the standard form of the film strip learned an average of only 17.2 names.   In other words, when a 15-second criterion is used for recall of each name, the active participation procedure increased the amount of learning exhibited from a level of about 66 per cent of the names to a level of about 84 per cent.

TABLE 1

EFFECT OF PARTICIPATION ON NUMBER OF PHONETIC NAMES RECALLED

	WITHIN 2 SECONDS AFTER SEEING LETTER		WITHIN 15 SECONDS AFTER SEEING LETTER	
	Mean number recalled	*Percentage recalled*	*Mean number recalled*	*Percentage recalled*
Participation	17.6	68%	21.9	84%
Standard	12.6	48	17.2	66
Difference	5.0	20%	4.7	18%
	$t = 3.5, df = 38$		$t = 3.0, df = 38$	
	$p < .01$		$p < .01$	

The results showing the effectiveness of the participation procedure from the two points of view are summarized in Table 1.   A test for the significance of the effect of audience participation is also shown in Table 1.   It can be seen that the mean differences in number of phonetic names given correctly by standard and participation groups are highly reliable at both the 2-second and the 15-second criteria.

2. VALUE OF ACTIVE PARTICIPATION WITH MATERIAL OF VARYING DIFFICULTY

Some of the phonetic names were more easily learned than others. For example, "X-ray" for "X" was remembered by a higher pro-

portion of the men than "Tare" for "T." By dividing the 26 phonetic names into an easier half and a more difficult half on the basis
of combined test performance with both film strips, a comparison
could be made of the relative gain from increased audience participation with the easier names as compared with the more difficult
names. Figure 4 shows the results of this comparison for the individual tests, using the 15-second time limit:

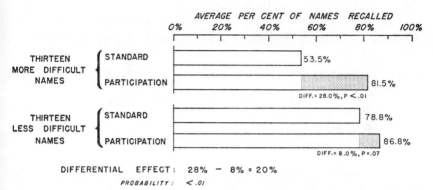

Figure 4. Average per cent of easy and difficult words learned.

In the analysis of the results as a function of ease or difficulty of
the material, the problem of equivalence of units arose—is an increment of one phonetic name as a result of audience participation the
same for easy as for difficult items? Without participation, the
average was about 14 names for difficult items and about 20 names
for easy items. Since the initial level is different, some ratio (e.g.,
per cent improvement, per cent reduction of wrong answers, etc.)
might be appropriate. While such proportional measures might be
meaningful, the measure used for analysis in the present study was
the actual number of words answered correctly.

The above comparison shows that the gain from the increased
audience participation procedure was much greater with the more
difficult half of the phonetic alphabet. The effect attributable to
participation was small and not very reliable for the easy material,
but it was large and highly reliable for the difficult material. The
difference between the effects (differential effect = 20%) was also
highly reliable.[1] The results indicate that *active participation is
most important when the material to be learned is most difficult.*

---

[1] The reliability of the mean differential effect was tested from the distributions of
differences between each man's score on the 13 "easy" items and his score on the 13
"difficult" items. The mean difference was 3.3 words for the standard group and 0.7
words for the participation group. The difference between these would have arisen by
chance less than one time in a thousand.

3. EFFECT OF INCENTIVE ALONE ON AMOUNT LEARNED

As mentioned earlier, the men in half of the audience groups were told in advance that they would be tested subsequently on the material, while half of the audiences were not told. The effect of the added motivation to learn provided by the announcement of the quiz can thus be analyzed without regard to its interaction with the participation procedure. The relevant group for this analysis is the standard group which did not actively participate since the active participation technique was not typical of the Army training films and film strips.

In the instructions the men were told: "During this hour we're going to show you training slides on the phonetic alphabet. The slides will be projected on this screen. There is a recording that plays along with the slides and explains each one. The phonetic alphabet is an important part of military training, so pay close attention."

In half of the audience groups (the "motivated" groups) the following additional announcement was made: "After the training slides have been shown, we will pass out a test paper to each of you. We are going to give each of you a test to see how much you have learned. It's to your own advantage to do as well as possible, so be sure that you pay close attention to the training slides and learn as much of the phonetic alphabet as you can."

The chart below, using the 15-second criterion and the standard group, shows the average amounts learned by the men who were told in advance that they would be tested, compared with the amounts learned by those who were not told in advance about the test.

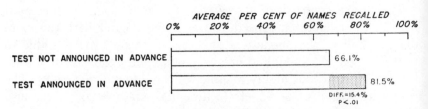

Figure 5. Effect of added motivation on amount learned.

It can be seen in the chart that the announcement of a test significantly increased the amount of material learned under standard conditions.

4. VALUE OF ACTIVE PARTICIPATION WITH AND WITHOUT INCENTIVE

Active audience participation is one way of insuring that the task to be learned is actually rehearsed by the audience members. However, under conditions of high motivation the audience members may rehearse the material to themselves as it is presented even though overt rehearsal is not formally required. Thus, if there is a high level of motivation to learn, relatively little additional benefit from audience participation may be obtained. Under these conditions the amount of additional benefit of active participation would depend mainly on the relative advantage of overt practice as contrasted with only implicit or symbolic rehearsal.

Figure 6 compares the percentage of words learned with and without active participation for men who did and who did not have advance announcement of the test. As before, these results are based on the 15-second criterion.

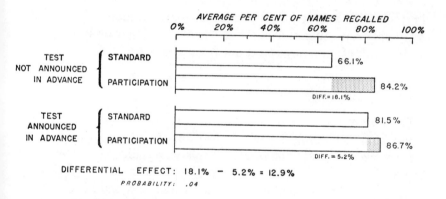

Figure 6. Amount learned by active-participation and control groups, under two conditions of motivation.

As anticipated, the difference between the active-participation and standard procedures was less when the men were motivated by knowledge that they would be tested. The difference of 18.1 per cent for the nonmotivated group is considerably larger than the corresponding difference of 5.2 per cent for the motivated group. Second-order differences as large as this in the expected direction would occur only about four times in a hundred. These results indicate that *active participation is most important when individuals are least motivated to learn.*

RESULTS OF WRITTEN TESTS

From the 662 men who answered the written tests, four groups—one for each of the four experimental conditions—were selected so as to be exactly matched by education and AGCT category. This stratification resulted in a reduction of the total group from 662 to 504, or 126 men in each of the four groups.

As stated earlier, the results of the written tests conformed in every respect to the findings of the individual tests except that in the written tests the average number of phonetic names answered correctly was higher under all conditions and the differences between active participation and standard forms of the film strip were smaller. Since only two minutes or less are required to write in all of the phonetic names, if they are well learned, the ten minutes allowed for the written test permitted the men to go back and fill in names not initially remembered but recalled at a later point in the series. However, the ten-minute time interval rather than a shorter period was required to minimize any tendency for the men to try only a portion of the letters because of lingering too long trying to think of one they could not remember easily.

1. VALUE OF ACTIVE PARTICIPATION AT DIFFERENT
   LEVELS OF ABILITY

The number of men tested individually was too small to permit subdivision according to initial learning ability. However, this analysis was made for the larger sample who took the written tests. As noted earlier, each man wrote on the test sheet the number of years of schooling he had completed. He also signed his name and serial number, so his AGCT score could later be obtained from the personnel records. AGCT scores were used as the best available measures of the men's learning ability.

When test performance was analyzed according to AGCT scores it was found that *the less intelligent groups profited most from the increased audience participation.* It was found that AGCT groups I, II, and III all gave fairly similar results, but the results for groups IV and V differed markedly from those for the upper three groups.[2] The results for this breakdown into "more intelligent" (classes I, II, and III) and "less intelligent" (classes IV and V) are shown in Figure 7. The results are for the standard conditions in which the

---

[2] There were very few cases in groups I and V, so the analysis was essentially of groups II, III, and IV.

men were not motivated by the knowledge that they would be subsequently tested.   The AGCT breakdown subdivides the 126 men in the active-participation group and the 126 men in the standard group into 101 "more intelligent" men and 25 "less intelligent" men per group.

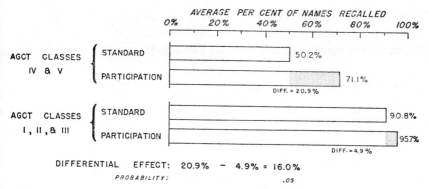

Figure 7.   Comparative contributions of active-participation procedure for those of different intelligence levels.

It is seen in Figure 7 that the differential effect on the two intelligence groups is 16 per cent.   The critical ratio of this second-order difference was 2.0, indicating a difference that would occur in either direction by chance about five times in 100.

2. EFFECTS WITH DIFFICULTY, MOTIVATION, AND ABILITY OPERATING IN COMBINATION

The preceding results have shown separately the value of the increased audience participation procedure under varying conditions of difficulty of material, motivation to learn, and learning ability. By dividing the results into the appropriate subcategories of all three of these variables, their effects when operating in combination can be seen.   Figure 8 shows these effects of participation—that is, the *differences* between amount learned under active participation and under standard conditions—for all the different subcategories.

It can be seen from Figure 8 that the importance of audience participation increased cumulatively as a function of each of the factors analyzed.   Active participation was most effective when intelligence and motivation were lower and difficulty was greater. At the one extreme, the more intelligent men (regardless of motivation) benefited only 3 per cent from participation on the easy words; at the other extreme, the less intelligent, nonmotivated men showed an increase due to participation of 23 per cent in the case of the difficult material. Thus the participation procedure tended to bring the amount learned under all conditions up toward the level ordinarily achieved only under the most favorable circumstances. Another way of describing the results is that the participation procedure helps most where it is most needed, that is, where individuals with little ability or motivation are learning difficult material.

It will be noticed that the results presented in Figure 8 are in terms of the gains attributable to participation, and do not show

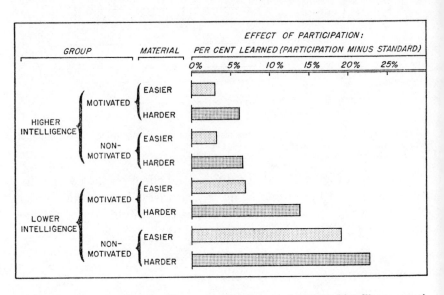

Figure 8.   Contribution of audience participation as a function of intelligence, motivation, and difficulty of material.

total amounts learned.   The total amount learned was, of course, greatest for the intelligent, motivated men in learning easy material, and least for the unmotivated, unintelligent men in learning difficult material.   Thus the results, as presented, do not take into account a "ceiling effect" due to the fact that the maximum amount of gain possible from participation varied from condition to condition.   The reason for presenting the results in this form—without taking the ceiling factor into account—is because the picture as shown seems more meaningful in terms of educational objectives. A gain from 95 per cent without participation to 98 per cent with participation, which was obtained for motivated intelligent men in learning easy material, is a gain of 60 per cent when one divides the

3 per cent increase by the 5 per cent maximum possible gain. But while such a large relative improvement may be of theoretical significance, it would probably be of much less interest to an educator than the increase from 44 per cent without participation to 66 per cent with participation which was obtained for unintelligent, unmotivated men with difficult material.

The question arises as to what extent the findings reported in this chapter are of general applicability. It seems a fair assumption that the device of reciting aloud can probably be used with about equal effectiveness for other films of the same general character as the one studied—i.e., films in which the learning materials are simple paired associates, such as might be used in teaching the vocabulary of a foreign language, a new nomenclature, recognition of aircraft types, and the like. But the recitation procedure as here used would seem less readily applicable to films having other kinds of learning objectives—for example, those involving motor learning or substance learning rather than rote memorization. An important problem is therefore to determine what alternative procedures might be used in such instances to utilize the same basic factors that are responsible for the demonstrated effectiveness of participation. Here the crucial question is: What are the "basic factors" that account for the results obtained with the present procedure of reciting aloud? The answer to this question determines what alternatives to reciting aloud would be suggested where group recitation is not appropriate.

In terms of learning theory, several factors can be mentioned as possible contributors to the advantages of active participation. These are discussed in the following paragraphs.

Direct rehearsal. The worst aspect of passive "learning" is that the learner may not actually be practicing any relevant responses. He may be daydreaming or he may be making some irrelevant observations concerning the material presented. Active participation is one way of insuring that the learner actually practices relevant responses that will be needed in later performance.

In the present experiment the response practiced during participation was identical with the response to be learned—that is, saying the correct phonetic name—so that the concept of "direct rehearsal" is entirely appropriate. However, it is apparent that in many cases little could be done to get *direct* rehearsal during actual film instruction where the responses to be learned were nonverbal ones. Occasionally such direct participation might be feasible—for example, in a film about the use of the slide rule the audience members might be given slide rules to manipulate as per instructions during the film showing. But probably in the majority of film subjects the responses to be learned could not be directly rehearsed during the film. Instead, symbolic responses must be learned during the film showing and later translated into the response to be performed. In such cases the problem is inevitably one of "transfer of training"—the symbolic responses learned during passive instruction must subsequently "transfer" to the actual responses which are the object of instruction. In such a case, the "active participation" procedures available are those which insure that relevant symbolic responses are practiced during the film showing. Thus even though active practice of the overt act is not possible, participation procedures that insure rehearsal of appropriate symbolic responses could still be employed.

A relevant consideration in the problem of transfer from symbolic response to overt responses is the ease with which the symbolic responses learned can be translated into the desired performance. Even with active participation in the learning of the symbolic responses, little transfer to actual performance would be expected unless the symbols are readily translated into the desired overt action.

In the study reported in the present chapter these problems of translating symbolic responses into action did not arise. The overt response was in this case itself a symbolic response—a word—and there is little reason to believe that the implicit vocalization of a word differs much in form of response from its overt vocalization. Thus in the present case we probably have an example of nearly perfect transfer of the symbolic response into overt action. This feature of the present subject, however, makes it unrepresentative of many instructional films.

A related aspect of the problem of transfer of training is the advantage of having present during training a stimulus situation closely approximating that in which the response is subsequently to be performed. This is an important advantage in the typical "learning by doing" situation, but it offers real difficulties in the case of film instruction where, aside from what is seen on the screen and heard on the sound track, the stimulus situation is one involving passively sitting still in a darkened room. However, the important factor of connecting the correct response to cues that are later to elicit it might often be taken into account in a movie by use of scenes that duplicate as many elements as possible of the stimulus situation in which it is desired that the response be elicited later. In the present experiment this was done by using review frames in the film strip which showed the letters of the alphabet without accompanying them by the correct word. Thus, unlike the passive control group, the active learners saw only the stimulus letter and had practice reciting the phonetic name while seeing the letter presented alone—a situation which tends to duplicate the conditions under which performance was to be required later.

Motivation. A perhaps less obvious basis for advantage in the active participation procedure is a motivational factor that appears to be involved. What is the effect on the learner of being required to reproduce the material to be learned? If he has a desire to avoid seeming stupid, the effects of active recitation or active participation should be to make him apply himself more diligently during the passive parts of the presentation. In other words, a likely effect of the participation procedure is to provide a series of "examinations" in which the learner is immediately required to show what he has learned. If his "ego" is involved in his ability to learn —that is, if he is shamed by poor performance—these "examinations" should produce an additional motivation to learn. This may be particularly true in the case of the procedure used in the present study, in which audience members recited aloud: each subject would be aware that his immediate neighbor could tell whether or not he had remembered the correct phonetic name. The present findings fit in well with the expectations from the postulated operation of a motivational factor in that when an independent source of motivation was applied the participation procedure had relatively less effect.

Although the factors of direct rehearsal and motivation have been discussed separately, it may be that they actually achieve their effects through the same mechanism. In each case the critical factor could be the rehearsal of the response to be learned. In typical human learning situations it seems very likely that the effectiveness of "motivational" procedures is in part brought about by the fact that they provide incentive for practice. Nothing is learned without some practice, and the individual who has no incentive to practice will therefore not be expected to learn. The procedure of participation and the procedure of announcing a test may simply be alternative ways of getting the subjects to practice the correct symbolic responses during the film showing. Furthermore, the efficacy of the participation procedure may lie in part in the motivating effects of these recitations on the learner's subsequent implicit practice as the material is presented in later portions of the film, rather than being entirely due to the practice occasioned during those portions of the film in which the subject is required to recite aloud.

The results obtained in the present study and the foregoing theoretical considerations have a number of implications for those engaged in the preparation and use of instructional films. The most obvious implication is that, to the extent possible, the actual response to be learned should be actively practiced during the film showing. If the actual response to be learned cannot feasibly be practiced during the film showing, appropriate symbolic responses should be actively practiced, the most appropriate symbolic responses being those most readily translated into the overt responses the film is attempting to teach. Further, the film should as nearly as possible duplicate, in its visual and auditory presentation, the stimulus situation in which the audience members later will be expected to perform the responses to be learned. Finally, since it is theoretically possible that motivational devices achieve all of their effects through providing an incentive to practice, attention should be given to insuring that whatever incentives are provided actually lead to the practice of appropriate responses. The motivation should not just provide a "motive to learn"; rather, it should provide an incentive to perform (as voluntary "active practice" during the film showing) implicit or overt responses that will transfer readily to the performance situation that defines the objectives of the film.

At the present stage of knowledge, these implications serve mainly as guiding principles rather than as "rules of thumb" that can readily be applied in the preparation and utilization of instructional films. They leave a considerable need for ingenuity and good intuition in successfully applying them to a particular case. It is expected, however, that as research findings accumulate as to what particular devices are successful in achieving the desired effects, these general principles will break down into subprinciples that can be more directly applied to a particular film.

CHAPTER 10

SUMMARY AND EVALUATION

O NE of the primary tasks of the Experimental Section of the Research Branch was to provide evaluations of the motion pictures prepared by the Information and Education Division of the Army. These films included the "Why We Fight" series, designed for indoctrination of members of the Armed Forces concerning the events leading up to American participation in the war. In addition, a number of experiments were carried out in cooperation with other divisions of the War Department to study training films.

The experimental studies of the "Why We Fight" films constituted a large-scale attempt to utilize modern socio-psychological research techniques in the evaluation of educational and "indoctrination" films. The methods used in these studies and the results obtained are described in the present volume in the belief that there will be increasing use of such procedures both for determining whether motion pictures and similar media really do succeed in attaining their objectives and for modifying the products in accordance with the results obtained by research.

RESEARCH DESIGN

The principal criteria of "effectiveness" used in evaluating these films were whether they succeeded in imparting information, in changing opinions in the direction of the interpretations presented, and in increasing men's motivation to serve. It would have been of considerable interest to use changes in overt behavior as an additional criterion of effectiveness. It would have been interesting, for example, to find out whether troops who had seen the "Why We Fight" series would have been more highly motivated in combat than those who had not. But it was not found possible to set up such long-range experiments as would be involved in answering such a question. At the same time, no acceptable behavioral index of "morale" or motivation to serve was developed that could be used in determining the relatively immediate effects of films. In only

247

one study was an overt behavioral criterion possible—in a study where the purpose of the film was to teach a verbal response and it was not difficult to use overt verbal responses as the criterion. This was the study reported in Chapter 9 concerning the effects of "audience participation," in which actual performance in using correctly the letter-name associates in the phonetic alphabet was used as the criterion of effectiveness.

While it was not possible to use overt *behavioral* changes as criteria in testing most of the films, the criteria used were nevertheless such as to reveal actual *changes* produced in the audience by the films. For example, the "Why We Fight" films were evaluated in terms of the extent to which factual knowledge and opinions concerning the war were altered by seeing the film. This criterion contrasts with others commonly used in programs of public information and education. Most frequently no check is available save the fact that a certain quantity of material was prepared and released. In the case of newspaper and radio media, such data are commonly supplemented by market surveys to determine readership or listening indices, since it is realized that unless the material is seen or heard it cannot become effective.

In commercial motion-picture research the most important criterion is usually the "box office," commonly predicted from "previews" in which audience approval is the crucial criterion. This criterion is obviously much less relevant in the case of educational and informational films of the type studied here. However, on the grounds that unless interest is aroused close attention is not apt to be achieved in educational films, most studies did obtain information about soldier evaluation of the films both through questionnaires and through interviews. Here the purpose was to supplement the findings on the film effects—that is, actual changes produced—with evidence concerning things liked and disliked about the film. In the informal interviews conducted for this purpose an attempt was made to get ideas for product improvement. This turned out to be quite unproductive of suggestions. The men readily enough expressed liking or disliking for the films but were quite inarticulate as to their reasons and had few suggestions of ways in which the films could be improved.

In other studies, interest was the only response considered relevant; these studies were concerned with films whose objective was described as that of satisfying the interests of the soldiers. For these studies, more elaborate methods of recording interests were used, including use of the "program analyzer"—a polygraph record of "likes" and "dislikes" registered during the presentation of the film—which is familiar as a technique for recording audience evaluation of radio programs.

It is clear that the amount of interest or extent of approval provides only supplementary information about a film with an educational purpose and does not constitute a measure of its effectiveness at achieving its educational objective. Even intensive interviewing of sample audiences "to get their reaction" to detailed aspects of the material presented was found to be misleading as an indication of what effects were produced. What appeared to be an "effect" of the film often turned out, when the results of the controlled experiments became available, to be a reaction as prevalent among men in general as among those who had seen the film.

It was necessary to develop new techniques for the purpose at hand. Earlier studies had either restricted their measurement to information tests or had used only a few attitude scales to determine overall effects. For the present purposes, information tests were necessary but a much more comprehensive analysis of opinion change was fundamental. The objectives of the orientation program encompassed a large number of areas of belief, and considerable effort was devoted to developing measuring instruments and studying the interrelation between the various opinion scales used. In some studies as many as a dozen scales of opinion were necessary in addition to miscellaneous single opinion items and a battery of information test items. It was also desirable to investigate the interrelation of opinion changes produced by the films. A number of methodological problems were encountered in these attempts to analyze opinion changes as a function of other opinions and other changes.

The general procedures used in the investigations are described in Chapter 2. The starting point was a content analysis of the film to be studied, together with intensive discussion with the individuals preparing the script as to their objectives in producing the film. The success of measurement was felt to be directly related to the precision with which the intended objectives were formulated. Unfortunately, in the case of the orientation films precision was sometimes lacking in the definition by the producers of what their films were intended to accomplish. As a result the criteria used in evaluating these films were the overall objectives of the orientation program, combined with inferred objectives based on the content analysis of the films as an index of what the producers were trying to accomplish.

On the basis of the above information, tentative fact-quiz and opinion items were developed. These were then pretested for interpretation and intelligibility by including them in intensive interviews with typical soldiers. The importance of this step in the process can hardly be overestimated. After any revision necessitated by this procedure, a "dress rehearsal" was employed in which questionnaires containing the revised items were administered as an "opinion survey" to soldier groups. The results from this step, the "quantitative pretest," enable advance analysis of the interrelation of opinions and the discarding of items which would be insensitive to change because either a very large or very small proportion selects the key response.

After revision in the light of the qualitative and quantitative pretests, the questionnaires were employed in the actual film evaluations. The typical procedure involved administration of questionnaires to two comparable groups before and after the presentation of the film to one of the two groups. The group shown the film constituted the "experimental" group whose responses reflected the effects of the film. The other constituted the "control" for any changes in knowledge or opinion that might have been occasioned by events external to the film presentation. An alternative procedure used in some studies has been termed the "after-only" procedure. In this procedure the administration of the questionnaire before the film showing is omitted. Here the control group reveals the knowledge and opinion of a group which has not yet seen the film and the experimental group reveals the knowledge and opinion of a comparable group after exposure to the film.

Each of these two alternative procedures was found to have its advantages and disadvantages. The "before-after" procedure—with administration of the questionnaire both before and after the film showing—requires special precautions to prevent the first questionnaire from revealing the purpose of the study and from biasing the answers obtained in the second. But it has definite advantages in permitting more detailed analysis of effects and compensation for inequalities between the groups arising from lack of random sampling in selecting control and experimental groups. In the present studies, completely random sampling was not possible—instead, to get naturalistic conditions of film showing, it was necessary to sample by company units rather than to use random selections of individuals. In the early studies it was not known to what extent this would lead to lack of comparability between control and experimental groups. As it turned out, the methods used by the Army in assigning men to companies were in most cases essentially random, that is, company units were found to differ in most cases no more than would be expected in random samples of about 200 men (the typical size of a company). In the earlier studies, both the "before-after" procedure and the "after-only" procedure were used in testing the same films. Because of the apparent comparability of the results obtained with the two procedures and because of the general lack of wide variation from company to company, the "after-only" procedure was considered sufficient in some of the later studies. It is to be remembered, however, that the "after-only" procedure always sacrifices completeness in the description of changes produced because it cannot isolate individual changes in opinion. The relative advantages and disadvantages of the two procedures are discussed in Appendix C.

In testing the orientation films, an interval of about one week was allowed before administration of the "after" questionnaire. At the outset of the orientation film studies the experimenters more or less implicitly assumed that effects would be maximal immediately after the film showing and that opinion changes as well as learning of factual knowledge would show a forgetting curve as time passed after the film showing. The standard time interval of about one week after the film showing as the interval before testing for effects was adopted simply on the grounds that it was judged a sufficiently long lapse of time to be on the more flat portion of the forgetting curve. It seemed that waiting a week would avoid including any transient immediate effects in the evaluation of the extent to which the film achieved its purpose. Eventually a systematic study was set up to test the assumptions involved in the use of the one-week interval. The results, which are described in detail in Chapter 7, indicated that while the expectation of gradual decrement with time appeared justified in the case of factual information, there was a tendency for many opinion items to show increments rather than decrements with the lapse of time. This finding is of considerable theoretical and methodological interest and will be discussed later in the present chapter.

One of the principal methodological problems revolved around the necessity of making measurements of the individual's opinions in such a way that they would be represented without bias and obtained without the individual's knowing that the measurements were connected with the showing of the film or part of an experiment. As discussed more fully in Chapter 2, many precautions were required to insure that this bias was avoided. A procedure that let the men know the effects of the film were being studied might have led to "Army-approved" answers rather than honest answers to opinion questions. Therefore, complete anonymity was maintained and the questionnaires were presented as having a purpose very different from the actual one of testing the film. In using the "before-after" procedure, it was particularly important to prevent the first questionnaire from being recalled when the film was subsequently shown and to prevent the repetition of the questionnaire after the film from suggesting to the men that a test of the intervening film was in progress. To prevent this, the second questionnaire was "revised" as much as possible and it was necessary to provide a carefully worked out rationale for the administration of a second questionnaire similar to the earlier one.

Another methodological problem that must be solved for an evaluation experiment to be maximally useful is insuring that the conditions of the experiment closely approximate those under which the product is later to be used. This was rather easily achieved in the Army situation. Attendance at training films and orientation films was compulsory in the Army, so attendance at the films tested was as close to 100 per cent as possible, exceptions being those on sick call, those on leave, and those on various special duties such as KP. The important point here is that self-selection was kept at a minimum without introducing any procedure that seemed out of place. The groups used attended the films as part of their regular training, and while attendance was compulsory it was in this respect no different from any other aspect of Army life. This handled neatly one of the bugaboos of civilian media research in which either those who attend a film showing are self-selected for initial interest in such a way as to make results obtained for them very atypical of the entire population, or in which a certain degree of unusualness is introduced by forcing individuals to attend.

Several problems of method also arose in connection with expressing the amount of change in information or opinion produced by the films. The procedure used in the studies expressed effects in terms of the percentage of individuals affected on each questionnaire item. Measurements were not made in terms of changes in the degree of conviction with which an individual held the particular opinion. A particular statement of opinion was agreed upon for each opinion question as the opinion consonant with the objectives of the orientation program, just as a particular answer was designated as the correct answer to fact-quiz items. Effects were then measured in terms of the difference in the percentage of individuals endorsing this statement before and after the film.

In expressing the amount of change produced by a film, a straight percentage difference between film and control groups was found to have certain limitations. While the percentage difference in the number knowing a particular fact or endorsing a particular opinion may provide an adequate description of a single effect, it leads to difficulties when different effects are compared. The difficulty arises because of a ceiling that is placed on the size of an effect by the initial percentage picking the key response. Thus if 90 per cent initially chose the key response, only a 10 per cent change is possible, whereas if 10 per cent initially chose the key response, the maximum possible effect is a 90 per cent change. This is particularly important in comparing different groups with differing initial levels or in comparing different effects where the questions used for different effects start at different initial levels. Thus the problem arises when one attempts to compare a change from 50 per cent to 60 per cent in those knowing the correct answer on a fact item among the less well educated with a change from 80 per cent to 90 per cent on the same question among the well educated. In each case, the change is 10 per cent of the total group, but the less well educated increased only 20 per cent of the total possible change whereas the better educated increased 50 per cent of their total possible change. In other words, 50 out of 100 poorly educated men did not know the correct answer, and of this 50, 20 per cent learned the correct answer from the film. On the other hand, only 20 out of 100 well-educated men did not know the correct answer, and of these 20, 50 per cent learned the answer from the film. To permit comparisons of change with differing initial percentages, an index—labeled the "Effectiveness Index"—was developed. This index measures the percentage change occurring as a function of the total possible change. In essence, this index is defined by the following formula:

$$\text{Effectiveness index} = 100 \times \frac{\text{Change obtained}}{\text{Maximum change possible}}$$

More specifically, when the "after-only" procedure is used and the effect to be expressed is an increase in the percentage giving a particular response, the effectiveness index is:

$$\text{E. I.} = 100 \times \frac{\text{Film } \% \text{ minus Control } \%}{100 \% \text{ minus Control } \%}$$

It can be seen that this index permits comparison of effectiveness for opinions that differ in initial acceptance level, for subgroups that differ in initial acceptance level, and so forth, and the size of the effects calculated is not restricted by the original percentage subscribing to the particular opinions. The chief disadvantage is that so far its sampling distribution has not been satisfactorily worked out. A check on statistical significance of an effect can of course be obtained from the straight percentage difference test for the group as a whole, but this does not permit determining whether two effectiveness indices differ significantly.

It should be noted that the "effectiveness index" takes into account only the statistical ceiling introduced by the approach of the initial level to 100 per cent. Other ceiling effects, which the effectiveness index is not designed to take into account, are produced by psychological factors discussed in Chapter 3, such as the likelihood that when the initial acceptance of an opinion is high (e.g., 90 per cent accept the opinion and only 10 per cent hold a different opinion), the few individuals who differ in their opinion are "die-hards" who would be especially resistant to change. A further psychological factor that is not taken into account by the effectiveness index is the likelihood that an extremely unpopular opinion also reflects special resistance to change. Thus an opinion held by only 10 per cent of the general population will very often be one that the population is predisposed *against* believing, and, therefore, especially resistant to change by a film.

RESULTS OF EVALUATIVE RESEARCH

Results of the research on one of the orientation films, "The Battle of Britain," are described in considerable detail in Chapter 2, and general conclusions derived from the series as a whole are discussed in Chapter 3. The results may be briefly summarized as follows:

The films had marked effects on the men's knowledge of factual material concerning the events leading up to the war. The fact that the upper limit of effects was so large —as for example in the cases where the correct answer was learned and remembered a week later by the majority of the men—indicates that highly effective presentation methods are possible with this type of film.

The films also had some marked effects on opinions where they specifically covered the factors involved in a particular interpretation, that is, where the opinion test item was prepared on the basis of film-content analysis and anticipated opinion change from such analysis. Such opinion changes were, however, less frequent and, in general, less marked than changes in factual knowledge.

The films had only a very few effects on opinion items of a more general nature that had been prepared independently of film content, but which were considered the criteria for determining the effectiveness of the films in achieving their orientation objectives.

The films had no effects on items prepared for the purpose of measuring effects on the men's motivation to serve as soldiers, which was considered the ultimate objective of the orientation program.

A number of hypotheses are discussed in Chapter 3 to account for the lack of effects of the films upon general opinions and upon motivation. It may be, for example, simply that a single 50-minute presentation is too small an influence to produce noticeable changes in deep-seated convictions—although this was certainly not out of line with expectations of the film producers. No studies were done in which the entire series of orientation films were studied in combination to check the possibility of sizable cumulative effects. A study in which the cumulative effects of two films were studied did not, however, show sizable effects on general opinions or motivation. Certainly it was to be expected that the amount of men's motivation which could be influenced by a film was very small in relation to the other motivational factors present in their immediate and total life situation. It may be that the amount of change which could be influenced by indoctrination had already been achieved through civilian sources even before the men entered the Army. In some cases the lack of effects may have been due to the diffusion of coverage rather than the concentration upon a few well-chosen targets. Finally, it is possible that the lack of effects may be due simply to the fact that the attitudes and motivations investigated in these studies cannot be appreciably affected by an information program which relies primarily upon "letting the facts speak for themselves." It may be that such a program will prove effective with only a small segment of the population whose attitudes are primarily determined by rational considerations. For most other individuals, motivations and attitudes may generally be acquired through nonrational channels and may be highly resistant to rational considerations.

This last hypothesis calls into question the basic assumptions of the Army orientation program. The rationale of the orientation program—of which the orientation films were a part—rested primarily upon two basic assumptions concerning mechanisms for affecting motivation by means of "orientation." The first assumption was that giving men more information about the war and its background would produce more favorable opinions and attitudes. The second related assumption was that improvement of opinions, attitudes, or interpretations about the war would lead in some measure to higher motivation or greater willingness to accept the transformation from civilian to Army life and to serve in the role of soldier.

The results just summarized cast considerable doubt on the first of these assumptions. The films produced sizable increments in information but effected almost no significant changes on the more general opinion items designed to measure changes in the orientation program's objectives. This negative conclusion was also supported by data from other studies which indicated only a slight correlation between scores on information tests and orientation opinions. In addition, increases in information were only slightly correlated with changes in the opinions designated as subobjectives of the orientation program.

No evidence was provided by the experimental studies of films bearing on the second assumption, concerning the relationship between changes in opinions and in motivation, since the films produced almost no increments in the opinions considered significant. Even if there had been changes in opinion and motivation, it would be difficult to know whether to attribute the change in motivation to the change in opinion. Indeed, it is difficult to see how the relevant experiments can be performed. The chief difficulty is the attempt to vary independently the causal variables in the hypothetical relations, since here the "independent" variables are themselves *reactions of the individual* and as such require a stimulus.

Hence it is difficult or impossible to know whether the dependent variable was affected by this reaction or whether it was directly affected by the stimuli used to bring about the reaction.

Results were also obtained concerning the relation between the audience's evaluation of a film and its effects on their knowledge and beliefs. It was found that men who most liked a film tended to be most affected by it, but it is difficult to rule out the possibility that those who liked the films were different initially in other respects from those who did not like them. The problem raised is one of which is cause and which effect. Did those who were influenced by the film like it, or were those who liked the film more influenced by it? To demonstrate a correlation between liking and amount of effect does not answer the question either way since, as just noted, audience responses or evaluations cannot be treated as independent variables. They are responses that can be related to other responses or to changes in response, but there remains the possibility that both responses of the audience are direct effects of the film rather than that one response has a causal effect on the other. Similarly, it was found that men who regarded the film as propagandistic were somewhat less affected, but again the nature of causal relationship is difficult to establish from these results, since the groups compared may have been initially different in resistance to change.

EVALUATIVE RESEARCH VS. CONTROLLED VARIATION

As a by-product of the testing of a number of films, it was hoped that it would be possible to reach a number of generalizations about the factors governing the effectiveness of films. Particularly it was hoped to obtain generalizations that would specify what kinds of presentation devices would be most effective for various kinds of material. As it turned out, the drawing of such generalizations from the data obtained was possible only to a limited extent. There were two reasons for this relative paucity of generalizable conclusions from the studies.

The first reason lay in the nature of the Research Branch's mission and purpose, which was defined as a program of "applied" research intended to find answers to immediate "practical" questions rather than to attack long-range scientific problems. This meant that priorities as to what kind of film studies would be undertaken were usually decided in favor of testing completed products or making experimental comparisons between existing alternative products. The former kind of experimental evaluation of a film's effect, well illustrated by the studies of orientation films in the "Why We Fight" series, is obviously tied to the specific content of the film studied as far as experimentally demonstrated findings are concerned. But it is conceivable that, over a series of studies covering a number of films in which a variety of presentation techniques were repeatedly used, it might be possible to educe generalizations by relating the size of gains produced on specific points to the techniques used to present each point. The number of films experimentally evaluated was actually not large enough to give this possibility a fair test, but as time went on the experimenters became increasingly convinced of the relative inefficiency of such an inductive approach as compared with what might be learned through experimental comparisons specifically set up to test hypotheses about the effectiveness of various presentation methods.

Another reason for the paucity of generalizations obtained from the studies has already been in part implied by the foregoing, and is related also to the applied purpose of most of the studies. This is the inherent limitation, as a source of generalizations, that would appear to be characteristic of evaluative studies. The limitation, which is evident in the case of studies seeking to evaluate single films, applies also to those which compare alternative products, examples of which are described in Chapter 5. In each case these studies gave a fairly clear-cut answer as to the superiority of the specific products compared, but in no case did they provide any very widely generalizable conclusions. For example, the study on the relative effectiveness of a motion picture on map reading and an alternative series of still slides ("film strip") presenting information on the same subject shows clearly that the particular film strip studied was just as effective as the particular movie used in presenting the material. But this finding does not help much in generalizing about the relative effectiveness of the two media represented by the presentations compared, because these presentations differed in content and manner of presenting the material as well as in the fact that one employed moving pictures and the other employed still pictures.

By contrast, the study of the relative effectiveness of presenting "one side" versus "both sides" of an issue, reported in Chapter 8, and the study of the advantage of audience participation, reported in Chapter 9, are of considerable general significance. The advantage of the latter studies is that instead of comparing alternative existing products they compare presentations specifically designed to exemplify alternative *procedures*. In doing this, an attempt is made to control all factors except the ones under investigation. Consequently, any differences or lack of difference in effectiveness may be clearly interpreted as evidence of the importance of the factor that differentiates the two procedures. With this method of study, particularly if the experimental variable is related to theory, there is afforded a more secure basis for generalizing to other products using the same procedures than can be gained from comparison between available existing alternatives that differ with respect to a number of factors in addition to the one presumably differentiating them.

However, purely evaluative research—despite the above-indicated limitations on generality—does appear to have some merit both in relation to immediate problems of an educational film producer and in terms of its potential contribution to theory. Its potential theoretical contribution is primarily as a fruitful source of hypotheses concerning factors affecting film effectiveness. Theoretical expansion cannot proceed in a vacuum, and an abundant body of specific results on a number of films may provide the necessary catalyst to development of theory. Thus the obtaining of an unusually large effect or the absence of effects which were expected in an evaluative study requires explanation and provides a suitable occasion to examine possible hypotheses These, in turn, will—since they are merely hypotheses rather than established conclusions—usually require specially designed experimental study for validation.

The contribution of evaluative studies to the immediate practical problems of the film producer appears to lie primarily in their use for improving or checking on the effectiveness of the particular film studied. In the rapid tempo of the war situation, where a completed film could only be changed or withdrawn if it was seriously unsatisfactory, the utilization of evaluative studies was not particularly efficient. Generally the research findings could only indicate the successes and failures of a film without its being possible to remedy any defects as far as the film itself was concerned. The stage at which evaluative research would appear to have its greatest potentiality for product improvement is well prior to the completion of a film, when suggestions derived from the research can readily be incorporated into the final film production.

One kind of research analysis having general application which can be done as a by-product with the data obtained in an evaluative study is that in which the primary interest is in individual differences. That is, as part of the analysis of evaluative experiments, one can provide information as to the differential effect of a presentation upon different segments of the audience, expressing the differences in terms of "population variables" (see Chapter 1). Generalizations concerning the influence of population variables may be possible even from the data obtained from the evaluative studies of a single film. This is partly because the presentation is constant for all population groups and partly because a single film may have a number of specific effects each of which can be related to a particular population variable, so that considerable replication of effect as a function of population variables is possible even within the confines of one film.

From such analysis have come a number of interesting results concerning the relationship between intellectual ability and effects of films on knowledge and opinion. These are summarized in the two remaining sections of the present chapter, together with other more general findings obtained in the few studies where it was possible to employ controlled experimental manipulation of presentation methods. In these latter studies, the factors manipulated experimentally were either "content variables" (characteristics of the content or manner of presentation within a film) or "external variables" (e.g., conditions of utilization). The effects of these two kinds of variables, which are more fully characterized in Chapter 1, are generally considered also in relation to the population variable of intellectual ability in the findings discussed in the remainder of the present chapter.

COMMUNICATION OF FACTUAL INFORMATION

Results bearing on factors affecting the communication of factual material were derived from two types of investigation: studies of the learning of factual material presented in the orientation films, and studies of the learning of material presented in training films. These will be discussed under three headings: (1) relation of learning to intellectual ability, (2) relation of learning to motivation, and (3) relation of learning to participation by the learner.

1. RELATION TO INTELLECTUAL ABILITY

In the learning of factual material it was uniformly found that those with greater intellectual ability learned more, on the average, from a given exposure than those with less ability. This was true whether the index of intellectual ability was educational level attained or performance on the Army General Classification Test (AGCT).

In investigating this problem, an analysis was made of the relationship between intellectual ability and the amount of learning for varying degrees of difficulty of material as indicated by the amount learned by the group as a whole. Variations in difficulty tended simply to raise or lower the per cent learning a particular fact, without greatly altering the slope of the relation between intellectual ability and amount learned. It was anticipated on theoretical grounds that the relationship for easy material would show a negatively accelerated function and that for difficult material positive acceleration (see Chapter 6, p. 154). This expectation was borne out only to a slight degree. The curves are more impressive for their approximate linearity at all levels than for the slight differential curvilinearity of the curves of easy and difficult material. The differences in curvilinearity might have been greater if a wider range of intellectual ability had been available, but it is difficult to see how this could have been of general significance in view of the very wide range of ability actually represented in the Army population studied.

2. RELATION TO MOTIVATION OF THE AUDIENCE MEMBERS

It is well known that the amount that an individual learns from a given exposure is a function of the degree of motivation present. It is even possible that part of the relationship just described between intellectual ability and degree of learning is attributable to differences between the more able and less able individuals in their motivation to learn, produced by differential reward during schooling in learning new material. Thus motivation often tends to be a matter of individual difference based on lengthy past experience and not an easily manipulated variable in a teaching situation. All educators know that motivation is important; the difficult problem is to do something about it.

An opportunity to study the role of motivation was available in connection with a study of an audience-participation procedure (Chapter 9). It was found that by simply announcing in advance that a test of amount learned was to be given immediately after the showing of the film strip, the amount learned increased under standard conditions (no audience participation) from 66 per cent to 81 per cent. This seems a very large increase for such a simple device —in some schools it would correspond to a change from a D grade to a B grade. The results furnish a demonstration of the importance of motivation, as well as showing the possibility of actually manipulating motivation in an instructional situation. However, the specific effects just described may well exaggerate the amount of improvement likely to be obtained in the usual school situation by merely announcing a quiz. Quizzes following a film were not a routine aspect of Army instruction, and special importance may have been attached by some of the men to the film because of the quiz announcement in this case. In a school situation where pupils generally assume that some form of examination will be given on all instruction, considerable habitual motivation to learn is likely to be present even without a specific announcement of a test preceding the instructional film. In this case less effect would be expected from the pre-film announcement of the quiz.

The device of announcing a quiz is, of course, well known to educators. One of its limitations is the additional time that must be devoted to testing and to the grading of the quizzes in order to maintain their motivational value. However, as a motivational device to be used in conjunction with instructional films, the announcement of a quiz seems to offer some promise at the present time, particularly when the burden of testing can be lessened by use of easily scored objective tests supplied as a standard accompaniment to film distribution.

Some incidental results in connection with a study of training films are also relevant to the discussion of motivation. In this study, reported in Chapter 5, an introductory discussion of what the film was about, what to look for, and so forth, was presented just prior to showing the film. The result that emerged in the analysis of the data was that the introduction improved learning of items of information in the film that were *not* covered in these introductory comments as well as items specifically mentioned as things to look for. The implication seemed to be that an important effect of the introduction was to give *significance* to the film—heightening the motivation of the audience members to feel that it was worth paying attention to and to try to learn the contents. These incidental results make it appear desirable to study this aspect in greater detail by controlled experimentation.

3. RELATION TO PARTICIPATION BY THE AUDIENCE MEMBERS

Almost as well known in educational circles as the importance of motivation to learning is the importance of participation by the learners. "Learning by doing" has been a widely recognized educational principle ever since E. L. Thorndike found that little was learned from imitation or passive exposure. The role of participation has also been emphasized by numerous studies which have found that recall of verbal material is greatly facilitated by dividing the time spent in studying between reading the material and attempting to recall it. The active participation principle is intuitively utilized by most individuals engaged in practical training problems and has been a standard precept in Army training doctrine for many years. A problem is posed, however, in applying this principle to film instruction, which is characteristically carried on by presenting material to members of an audience who sit back and receive the instruction passively.

The device that was tested in the experiment reported in Chapter 9 was a simple one to utilize for the kind of material being taught by the film strip. The topic of instruction was the phonetic alphabet ("Able for A," "Baker for B," etc.), making the learning task comparable to the simple paired-associates learning problem that has been widely used in psychological experimentation. To such a task an active recitation method was readily applied. At the end of every half dozen letters, the film strip presented a review list of the letters without the names, and the audience members practiced aloud the correct names. As was seen in Chapter 9, this participation procedure increased markedly the amount learned as compared with a standard presentation that was identical except for the instructions to recite aloud.

The effect of participation was found to be greater for the more difficult phonetic names than for the easier names. The results also showed that the individuals with lower mental test scores profited more from the audience participation procedure than those at the higher levels of mental ability. Finally, more improvement in learning was attributable to the participation when men were not given special motivation to learn, and less when motivation was increased by announcing that they would be tested on the material covered. These various factors appeared to operate cumulatively in modifying the contribution brought about by the active participation procedure: at the one extreme, the participation procedure added little in the case of the bright, motivated men learning easy words, and at the other extreme considerable benefit from active participation was obtained among the less intelligent, nonmotivated men learning difficult words. Since high intelligence, strong motivation, and easy material are all factors favoring rapid learning, these results suggest the generalization that active participation will contribute relatively more as other conditions of learning become progressively less favorable.

The specific device of reciting aloud as a means of providing participation cannot, of course, be used in connection with all types of material. It seems a fair assumption that the device of reciting aloud can probably be used with about equal effectiveness for other films of the same general character as the one studied—i.e., films in which the learning materials are simple paired associates, such as might be used in teaching a foreign language vocabulary, nomenclature, recognition of aircraft types, and the like. But the recitation procedure as here used would seem less readily applicable to films having other kinds of learning objectives—for example, those involving motor learning or substance learning rather than rote memorization. An important problem is, therefore, to determine what alternative procedures might be used in such instances in order to utilize the same basic factors responsible for the demonstrated effectiveness of active recitation in rote verbal learning.

The factors responsible for the improvement produced by participation are discussed in Chapter 9. The most obvious advantage of active participation is that it insures rehearsal of responses which are to be learned. The present experiment involved learning by doing directly the very thing that was to be learned. With other subject matters (for example, teaching an athletic skill) such direct practice during the presentation of a film is generally not feasible, so that during a film the learner can at best be practicing verbal or other symbolic responses which can later be translated into the kind of action to be learned. Even in these cases, however, a participation procedure requiring *overt* performance of such mediating symbolic responses has the advantage of insuring that some relevant response is being practiced—and insuring at least that the audience is not merely day-dreaming.

A second factor of potential advantage introduced by the participation procedure is that it may motivate the learner to try to do well by providing, in effect, periodic examination on each segment of the material that has just been presented. With the procedure used in the study described in Chapter 9 this motivational factor may be particularly effective, since with oral recitation each member of the audience would realize that his immediate neighbors are aware of how well he is performing.

A third factor of probable importance in contributing to the superior effectiveness of the participation procedure is that practice is required under stimulus conditions very similar to those obtaining at the time when the response is subsequently to be performed. Thus, the learners' practicing of the proper phonetic word was done during the presentation with much the same visual stimulus as was later presented to test their knowledge of the material—i.e., the letters were presented without being accompanied by the visual presentation of the word which was present in the control strip.

FACTORS AFFECTING OPINION CHANGE

The reader will probably have noted in the previous chapters that responses to questions which do not deal with factual subject matter were generally referred to as "opinions" and that the term "attitude" was usually avoided. This usage reflects in part the fact that no satisfactory way was found of distinguishing between attitude questions and questions of opinion. As treated in Chapter 6, the outstanding feature of an "opinion" as distinguished from a statement of fact is that opinions are *interpretations* of available facts, which interpretations are difficult to verify or disprove directly. From this point of view it is obvious that whether or not a statement is regarded as a fact or as an opinion is a matter of degree dependent on how convincing is the proof or disproof of the statement. It is also clear that what is an opinion for one individual may be a fact for another, depending on the amount of information available to each individual. In the present studies the experimenters usually judged whether a particular item would be regarded by most of the men as a factual question or as a question of opinion, and then reinforced the classification decided upon by separating the two kinds of items in the questionnaire, one group of items being labeled as "factual" and the other group being labeled as "matters of opinion" on which disagreement was to be expected from person to person.

Several generalizations concerning the effects of mass-communication devices on opinions are indicated by the findings reported in the preceding chapters. These fall primarily under three major headings: the relation of changes to intellectual ability, the relation of changes to initial opinion, and the relation of changes to the amount of time elapsing after exposure to the communication. A further section discusses the nature of "propaganda."

1. RELATION TO INTELLECTUAL ABILITY

A very consistent finding in the present studies was that both the initial opinion held and the changes in opinion obtained were generally related to the men's educational level. Other population variables or demographic characteristics were also investigated, but they were much less often related to the initial opinion held than was educational level and they were almost universally unrelated to the size of opinion changes resulting from exposure to a film or other communication. Educational level on the other hand turned out to be so commonly related to initial opinion and to opinion change that eventually the exceptional instances in which no relation was obtained came to be regarded as meriting special investigation.

As indicated in Chapter 6, the educational level attained by the men was found to be a useful index of general intellectual ability. The availability of this index made it possible to investigate a variety of theoretical relationships between intellectual ability and the effects of communications upon opinions.

The key concepts found useful in a theoretical framework relating intellectual ability to opinion changes may be called learning ability, critical ability, and ability to draw inferences. Learning ability enters in that the more intelligent learn more from a given exposure. Thus if everything else were constant, greater changes in opinion would be expected in the case of the brighter men simply because they learn and remember more of the things presented in the communication. However, because of greater critical ability they are less likely to *accept* an interpretation which is unsound, given the facts at hand. That is, they are better able to judge whether the interpretation goes too far beyond the evidence, whether the conclusions follow logically from the assumptions made, and so forth, so that they may refuse to accept an unsound interpretation no matter how well they have learned the interpretation given. Moreover, their critical ability, by enabling them to recognize prejudice in their own thinking, makes them less likely to resist accepting a sound interpretation.

The third factor postulated—ability to draw inferences—would be expected to affect opinion change by enabling the individual to arrive at an interpretation as a result of a communication despite the fact that the interpretation was not part of the direct content of the communication. That is, this ability would facilitate an individual's being influenced by the unstated implications of a communication as well as by the statements explicitly made in it. This ability is probably also related to the aforementioned critical ability since if an individual were able to draw his own correct inferences from the factual material presented he would notice any invalid interpretations presented in the communication.

All of the foregoing factors would be expected to affect the relation between intellectual ability and the size of opinion change achieved by a particular communication. The form of relation obtained would be determined by which factor or factors was most relevant in a particular case. For example, an ascending curve similar to the curve for learning of factual information would be expected in relating opinion change to intellectual ability if the interpretation was directly made in the communication, and if in addition it was the most reasonable interpretation of the facts presented. If the interpretation was the most reasonable one but was not directly stated in the presentation, an ascending curve would also be expected but perhaps one which was positively accelerated, showing effects only among the most intelligent. If, on the other hand, the interpretation was not reasonable but was clearly presented, a descending curve would be expected—the interpretation would be easy for even the less intelligent to learn but it would not be accepted by the more intelligent. With a large range of intelligence, curves which first rise and then fall would be expected if there were an "inference" of only moderate difficulty to be drawn from the communication but one that was not acceptable on logical grounds. In such a case the least intelligent would not get the inference at all, the most intelligent would get the inference but not accept it, and only those in between would have enough ability in drawing inferences, and little enough critical ability, to accept the interpretation.

All of these different kinds of relationships were obtained in the present studies in comparing opinion changes at different intellectual levels. Because of the heterogeneity of the relationships obtained with different items, an overall "average" relationship between intellectual ability and opinion changes is relatively meaningless since it obscures the separate relations—some positive, some negative, etc.—obtained for separate items.

Most of the results obtained for individual items could be interpreted "after-the-fact" in terms of the theoretical framework described above. Unfortunately, it was not possible to do much experimentation to test "before-the-fact" the utility of this conceptual scheme. One experiment, that comparing a one-sided argument with one that took both sides of the question into account provides an example. The prediction from the factor of "critical ability" was that the more intelligent would be more influenced by the presentation taking both sides into account. This prediction was borne out, as was seen in Chapter 8.

Testing of hypotheses that could be derived from such a theoretical framework relating intellectual ability to effects of a communication in changing opinion seems like a promising field for future research. Unlike the relation of intellectual ability to learning of factual information, the relation to opinion change appears to be quite complex. Understanding the relation is important because of the likelihood that very different kinds of communications would be most effective depending on whether the audience members were of high, low, or of mixed intellectual ability.

2. RELATION TO INITIAL POSITION HELD

It seems highly probable that the effectiveness of a particular communication at changing opinions will depend in part on the initial opinions of the members of the audience. This consideration suggests two valuable ways of using research in developing effective communication methods. One is the continuing use of research in establishing general principles concerning how initial opinion affects the reaction to communications; the other is the use of opinion research prior to the preparation of a particular communication, as a means of providing information concerning the initial opinions of the intended audience so that the applications of principles to the design of a communication can be made in terms of the opinions actually held.

One of the opportunities to check on general principles about the relation of opinion change to initial opinion was in connection with the assertion sometimes made that the effect of "propaganda" or any attempt to persuade a person to change his beliefs serves primarily to reinforce his initial position—to make him all the more convinced of his belief. Another way in which this point of view is expressed is that "propaganda" has its intended effect only on those individuals whose initial position was already the same as that of the communication—i.e., it has positive effects only on those already positive.

In the present studies intensity of conviction was not measured, so it was not possible to determine whether some individuals were made more firmly convinced of their initial position by a communication designed to change their position. But in terms of whether a communication has positive effects only on those already positive, the present studies failed to confirm the expectation. Instead it was found—wherever an appropriate analysis could be made—that the communication had its intended effects over the entire range of initial position. That is, whether a man was initially for or against the stand taken in the communication, his opinion tended to be influenced in the direction of *more acceptance* of the point of view argued for in the communication. In no case was there found a significant change opposite to the intended effect of the communication among those initially opposed, and in all cases where the audience as a whole showed a positive change, the change was positive among those initially opposed.

However, initial position of the audience members was found to be an important determiner of what kind of communication was most effective in changing opinions. In Chapter 8, it is shown that while the members of the audience who were opposed to the communication's point of view showed significant positive changes both for the one-sided communication and the communication giving "both sides," they were more likely to change their opinion if the arguments supporting their own initial stand were included (i.e., with the program giving "both sides") than if only the arguments against their position were included. In other words, it was found that a man was more likely to accept a new point of view, opposed to his initial point of view, if the case is made for his previous opinion as well as the case for his adopting the new opinion. At the same time it was found that making the case for "both sides" of the issue was less likely to produce a change than a "one-sided" argument among those who initially had the same point of view as that endorsed by the communication. Here again both forms of presentation produced positive effects, but the effect was less if arguments for the other side were mentioned.

This experiment was designed to study a common contention that a communication should never mention the other side of the argument. The purpose of the experiment was to test the alternative hypothesis that among those initially opposed to the point of view fostered by the communication, and particularly those familiar with important opposing arguments, it would be more effective at least to mention the arguments on the other side. This hypothesis is somewhat related to the above-noted assertion that propaganda may have negative effects on those initially opposed. If there is any situation in which those initially opposed would be made all the more opposed by a communication, it would probably be one in which a one-sided presentation—which left out all of their own important points—antagonized them and served only to give them further rehearsal of their own position. As it turned out, however, even the one-sided presentation produced positive effects all the way along the scale of preference for, or opposition to, the point of view of the communications used.

The most significant finding, noted earlier, that did emerge from the study was that the presentation giving both sides was—as expected—more effective among those initially opposed. It should be realized that the method of utilizing the arguments on both sides of a question is probably very important in determining the relative effects of the communication on either those initially opposed or those initially favoring a particular point of view. In the experiment reported in Chapter 8, the utilization of arguments on "both sides" was with the specific purpose of producing the maximal positive effect among those initially opposed. The experiment was initiated in the expectation that a one-sided argument would be less effective with this subgroup than would a presentation that used judicious inclusion of the arguments on their side—and a one-sided argument might even have negative effects. On the assumption that not all ways of presenting the arguments for both sides would have the same effect, it is desirable to consider the theoretical basis for the initial expectation, and how the theoretical factors were incorporated in the communications used.

The main theoretical consideration was that those opposed would already be familiar with the chief arguments on their side, so no harm could be done by mentioning these arguments; on the contrary, a favorable effect of such mention seemed likely by preventing the opposed individuals from practicing, in an antagonistic mood, their own arguments as refutations of the validity of the arguments presented in the communication. Thus a communication that omitted their arguments at points where they were relevant would thereby seem unfair, and the audience members would be implicitly rehearsing their own arguments instead of attending to the communication. This would be expected to have the effect of making them (1) feel the presentation was invalid because biased; (2) motivated to reject rather than to accept the conclusion endorsed; (3) practice implicitly their own opposed arguments and conclusions; (4) learn less of the content of the communication because of the distracting effects of their preoccupation with implicit incompatible responses. All of these factors, if present, would interfere with the effectiveness of a one-sided communication. The utilization of arguments on the "other side" was aimed at minimizing their negative effects.

The chief implication from these theoretical considerations is that the arguments on the "other side" ought to be explicitly mentioned. Various subsidiary inferences may be drawn with respect to the timing and manner of presenting these arguments on the other side. Such inferences led to a series of "rules" of presentation which appeared likely to maximize the effectiveness of a presentation that commits itself to giving "both sides" of an issue, for the purpose of converting as many as possible of those initially holding the point of view opposing the one advocated. Some of these rules were followed in preparing the transcription covering "both sides," as described in Chapter 8, p. 203f. Two examples of rules followed are: (1) that all of the arguments for "the other side" should be mentioned at the very outset (in order to let the opposed members of the audience know at once that their arguments would not be ignored), and (2) that attempts to refute opposing arguments should be made only when an obviously compelling and purely factual refutation is available (on the grounds that strong positive arguments are likely to be convincing whereas an attack on opposing arguments which have previously been accepted will tend to have mainly the effect of antagonizing those who hold them).

The experiment reported in Chapter 8 also has relevance to the second aspect of research on the role of initial opinion mentioned earlier—that is, the experiment has a bearing on the use of research in determining the nature of the opinions of the intended audience, prior to the preparation of the communication. For example, in preparing the presentations used in the experiment reported in Chapter 8, an advance survey was made to find out which arguments against the conclusion were most common, and a special pretest was made in an attempt to discover the conditions under which these arguments were elicited. In this special pretest, the experimenters sought to engage representative subjects in a controversy —using the main positive arguments as stimuli—in order to determine which positive arguments elicited which negative arguments.

As a result of this pretest, there was an empirical basis for knowing when, in the course of the presentation, the various arguments of the opposition were likely to be elicited. A subsequent quantitative survey provided information as to which of these arguments of the opposition were common enough to be worth taking into account in the communication used. Such a sequence of pretests would appear to be a necessary preliminary to the most effective use of the principles utilized in the present study, or of similar principles which depend on taking into account the arguments, prejudices, and motives of persons opposed to the stand being advocated.

It will have been noted that the preceding discussion deals only with a mass-communication situation. It is assumed that the audience members are not themselves allowed to participate, that they are merely passive receivers of whatever is presented. A different set of principles might apply in a different situation, although it seems likely that most of the same principles would hold and the difference would be chiefly one of emphasis. For example, in a face-to-face situation it would probably be of paramount importance to apply the last principle discussed on page 205 of Chapter 8 —that is, the avoidance of opportunity for the opposed individual to identify himself as a member of the opposition. In a face-to-face situation we would expect "ego involvement" to become a greater factor and would therefore expect considerable importance to attach to preventing the listener from taking a stand at the outset—otherwise the effect of the communication might only be to strengthen his motivation to accept his initial belief and to find new arguments to rationalize his position. Also, it is not surprising that a common result of the debate form of communication is to make each individual more convinced in adhering to his initial position, especially when the audience members are required to express their initial position.

Obviously, the results obtained cannot be regarded as verification of any particular one of the theoretical principles used in preparing the arguments presented, since all of the principles that could be incorporated were used simultaneously in an attempt to maximize the effectiveness of the program giving both sides among the initially opposed view. An important area for future investigation is the experimental determination of the comparative efficacy of presentations which utilize the various specific "rules" derived from the theory here employed. It is in line with the point of view expressed in Chapter 1 of this volume to expect that progress in the development of a real science of communication will, in fact, stem primarily from experimental study of this kind and from revisions in theoretical formulation such as the accumulation of experimental results is likely to dictate.

3. TEMPORAL COURSE OF EFFECTS FOLLOWING A COMMUNICATION

It has been previously noted that there was, at the outset of the orientation film studies, a more or less implicit assumption on the part of the experimenters that effects of a film would be maximal immediately after the film showing. A related assumption was that opinion changes as well as factual knowledge learned would show a forgetting curve as time passed after the film showing. As mentioned earlier, a standard time interval of about one week after the film showing was adopted as the interval before testing for effects simply on the ground that this was judged a sufficiently long lapse of time to be on a relatively flat portion of the assumed forgetting curve.

The only data obtained to investigate the validity of these assumptions came from a special study of the fourth orientation film, "The Battle of Britain," reported in Chapter 7. In this study two points on the presumed "forgetting" curve were investigated, by measuring the film's effects nine weeks after the showing as well as at the standard interval of about one week. At the outset, the phrasing of this investigation's purpose was in these terms: How much of the one-week effects will still be *retained* nine weeks after the showing?

However, as was seen in Chapter 7, while the word "retention" applied well in the case of factual knowledge, it did not turn out to apply to the results for most opinion changes because, on the average, these were somewhat *larger* after nine weeks than after one week, and in some cases they were very much larger. This result was clearly contrary to the initial expectation, even though it had been anticipated that opinion changes would be somewhat better retained than changes in factual knowledge. This expectation was based on the grounds that opinion changes should correspond to "substance" learning, which is usually well retained, whereas changes in factual knowledge would correspond more nearly to rote learning of details, which ordinarily shows a relatively rapid rate of forgetting. But it was not expected that the opinion changes would tend to show an actual increase with passage of time.

Unfortunately, this finding was discovered too late in the series of orientation film studies to make it possible to check the results in other films. It is unknown, therefore, whether the same general finding would have been obtained with the other films in the series. Consequently, the results for Film 4 and for the film series as a whole have been presented in Chapters 2 and 3 only in terms of the findings at the end of about one week after the film showing, as if these were *the* effects of the films. It should be kept in mind, however, that further long-time studies might have revealed a tendency for some of the opinion changes produced by each film to be greater after a lapse of several weeks following the film showing. A further possibility suggested by the data for Film 4 is that some opinion changes might not show up at all until several weeks after the film showing.

As was noted in Chapter 7, the slight average increase in the opinion changes during the nine-week interval did not reflect a general trend for *all* opinion changes to increase with passage of time. Rather, the average trend resulted from a composite of some significant increases and some significant losses, which in the present case resulted in a slight average increase overall. Analysis indicated that the increases in opinion changes with passage of time were more likely to occur in the case of "uninformed" opinions— i.e., opinions more prevalent among the less well educated—and that the changes occurred more frequently among the less well educated and among individuals who seemed predisposed to accept a particular opinion prior to the film showing. In the actual analysis, these factors are inextricably interrelated and could not be disentangled as entirely separate variables; however, the overall impression is definitely suggested that some "projective" factor is at work—that over a period of time the individual utilizes the material shown to modify his opinion in a direction toward which he is already predisposed.

The results bear out the expectation that forgetting occurs for factual material, but suggest that little forgetting occurs for "reasonable" opinions (interpretations of facts positively correlated with education) and that, in the case of highly "questionable" interpretations, an actual increase with time is found instead of a loss. Since the specific-versus-general continuum is one of the dimensions along which facts are differentiated from opinions or attitudes, it would be interesting to know whether the increases were primarily obtained in the case of the less specific items. An attempt to rate the items with respect to their specificity was made, and significantly greater increments of effect with passage of time were found in the case of items rated less specific. However, these subjective ratings were not considered sufficiently reliable for the results of the analysis to deserve presentation. But the hypothesis is suggested that increments in opinion change with lapse of time are in part a function of predisposition for belief in a certain direction, and that this projective factor is more likely to show up in the case of general statements than in the case of highly specific statements. This may be related to the usual finding that immediate projective factors have greater influence when the stimulus is more vague and undefined.

In addition, it may be that the increments with time reflect a change in memory content. To the extent that specific material tends to become more general with lapse of time, the acceptance—after nine weeks—of opinion statements that were not accepted immediately may indicate that the content of what is retained has shifted from specific to general. The operation of a projective factor and a shift from specific to general would work in combination to produce increments on the "more attitudinal" items, and in the direction toward which the individual was already predisposed. These highly speculative suggestions indicate some very interesting areas for future research. As speculations they would appear to fit in well with the findings of Bartlett, as reported in his well-known book, *Remembering*, that after original learning, that which is recalled tends to be progressively modified with lapse of time, the modifications being predominantly in the direction of omission of all but general content and the introduction ("impartation") of new material that is in line with the individual's initial attitudes toward the content.

The Determination of What Constitutes "Propaganda"

In the foregoing discussion and throughout the preceding chapters the notion of "informed" and "uninformed" opinions has been used, and in Chapter 6 this notion is tied in with a proposed method of defining "propaganda" operationally on the basis of its content. Working from the definition of opinion as "interpretation of available facts," it was proposed that the valid interpretations are those which can be shown to be positively correlated with an index of ability to make valid interpretations, and that attempts to foster "invalid" interpretations (i.e., those negatively correlated with this ability) might be classed as "propaganda."

In assessing an individual's "degree of ability to make valid interpretations," it is suggested that account be taken of the following factors: (a) intellectual ability, (b) knowledge of the relevant facts, (c) freedom from emotional bias.

The assumption here is that in order to make valid interpretations an individual would not only need to have the capacity for generalizing from facts and knowledge of all of the relevant facts that were available, but that also the interpretation should as nearly as possible be uninfluenced by nonrational considerations. If people were scaled along these three dimensions, with the scale values weighted appropriately to yield a single index of interpretive ability, plotting the index thus obtained against the frequency with which a given opinion is held would afford a valuable and definitive empirical basis for distinguishing informed interpretations from invalid interpretations ("propaganda").

It is believed that this procedure can generally, however, give a definitive answer concerning an item of opinion if either a positive or negative correlation is obtained between the index and the extent to which the opinion is accepted. It might be argued that an interpretation held by a great majority of the best informed and most capable intellectually would be a valid interpretation, regardless of the opinion held by the less informed and capable. However, unless it is shown that greater knowledge and intelligence makes the opinion *more likely* to be held than in cases of less information and ability, there is no very secure evidence that the interpretation is any more valid than any other. This is because the acceptance of the interpretation may in all groups be based on an irrational bias. But if a positive correlation is shown it would appear to be extremely likely that the interpretation can be supported by an intelligent assessment on the basis of relevant facts.

It is evident that a number of assumptions are implicit in the foregoing proposal for an objective procedure to assess the validity or propaganda character of interpretations classified as opinions. For example, it is assumed that satisfactory agreement can generally be obtained as to what facts are the ones "relevant" to the ability to make a sound interpretation in each instance. In the absence of available data to test such assumptions and their implications, the procedure proposed still appears to have at least the merit of objectivity and reasonableness; it would seem, at any rate, to offer a criterion superior to the haphazard and unsystematic judgments that are usually the basis for deciding whether statements of opinion are considered as being sound or are labeled as "propaganda." A limitation of the procedure which deserves mention is the possibility that a particular conclusion could be validly drawn only by having available certain facts known by only a very few individuals. In this case the overall correlation between opinion and an index of general intellectual ability might be irrelevant.

An important practical limitation lies in the difficulty of obtaining a satisfactory scaling of the three criteria proposed. The most difficult of the criteria to scale would almost certainly be that of freedom from emotional bias. Presumably, nonrational bases for making interpretations would be less frequent or influential among those better qualified intellectually, but on some questions an emotional bias might be more prevalent among the more intelligent. In lieu of a scale of degree of prejudice on a particular interpretation, it might in some instances be possible to circumvent this difficulty by getting sufficient representation from all subgroups of the population that nonrational considerations would in effect largely be "balanced out."

The procedure proposed here for identifying propaganda is directed at the content of the interpretations fostered by a communication rather than at the methods of persuasion used. The proposal does, however, have implications concerning the aspect of propaganda stressed when attention is being called to the use of unscrupulous and nonrational methods as characteristic of propaganda. Thus, if invalid interpretations are those which do not follow from the relevant facts, attempts to foster such interpretations must almost inevitably resort to nonrational methods such as emotional appeals, concealment of facts, etc. The proposed procedure does not, however, have relevance for the ethical problem involved in the converse, i.e., using nonrational methods to convince others of a valid interpretation.

In the absence of measures of all three factors suggested as criteria of the ability to make valid interpretations, it was found useful to employ educational level attained as a crude index of "ability to make valid interpretations." This use was justified on the grounds that educational level is a rough overall index of general intellectual ability, access to general factual knowledge of all kinds and, to a lesser extent, freedom from irrational bias. It was found that some items were highly positively correlated with this index. For example, the opinion (in 1942) that the German ground forces ranked at the top in strength among the major nations was accepted by only 29 per cent of the grade school men but by 70 per cent of the college men, indicating that the opinion was a "valid interpretation" of available facts. On the other hand, some opinions were negatively correlated. For example, belief that in Germany babies are taken away from parents and raised by the state was found in 63 per cent of grade school men but only in 33 per cent of college men, indicating an "invalid interpretation" which would constitute "propaganda" if fostered by a communication. It was also found that these two kinds of opinions—the positively correlated and the negatively correlated—were differentiated with respect to the effectiveness with which they were communicated among men of different ability. "Valid interpretations" tended to be acquired as a result of seeing a film to a greater extent by those with higher intellectual ability; "invalid interpretations" tended to be more readily acquired by those of lower than by those of higher intellectual ability. A further finding was that the two kinds of opinions behaved differently with passage of time after exposure to the communication: positively correlated items tended to show decrements in time while negatively correlated items, indicative of invalid interpretations, were more likely to show increments with passage of time, the increments in such cases occurring mainly among the men of lower intellectual ability.

Although the use of educational level as a rough index of ability to make valid interpretations appeared justified for the subject matter covered in the present studies, it is recognized that this single index may have more serious limitations with other topics, particularly those dealing with economic issues. Here the positive correlation between educational level and socio-economic status may introduce considerable bias even among the better educated group.

An important area for future research lies in exploring further the relations between the effects of communications and the operationally defined "validity" of the interpretations made. Especially to be desired would be replication in a new context of the study in which effects were analyzed as a function of passage of time with use of a more complete index of ability to make valid interpretations.

PRACTICAL VALUE OF SYSTEMATIC STUDIES

As a final evaluative comment, a word should be said concerning the relative contribution to the solution of practical problems made by the types of research described in the present volume. The studies reported in Chapters 8 and 9 were designed primarily to extend our scientific knowledge rather than to provide immediately practical information. But the results were of considerable use in providing practical suggestions concerning effective methods of preparing mass communications. Equally useful suggestions were rare in the studies presented earlier, which aimed at "practical" evaluation of specific film products or comparison of existing products. There thus arises the interesting paradox that the most useful practical conclusions obtained arose from the few studies designed and executed to answer more general scientific and "long-range" questions rather than from studies that were fostered for the purpose of giving answers to "immediate, practical problems."

This apparently greater immediate practical value of the more "scientific" or "long-range studies" is here interpreted as indicating that, at the present stage of research on factors determining the effectiveness of mass communications, studies predicated on theoretical considerations involving the possibility of considerable generality are very likely to have more immediate practical value, as well as greater long-run scientific importance, than are studies aimed solely at solving immediate practical problems. In terms of the considerations discussed in Chapter 1, this superiority of studies closely related to theory seems likely to be particularly great where such studies are set up so as to involve not only the controlled manipulation of any single variable but simultaneously its interaction with other relevant factors which are experimentally varied in combination. It is believed that research of this kind, closely related to theory, will have greater practical value until a point is reached at which general principles have been established in the field and there remains only the working out of details of how most effectively to apply these principles to specific content.

APPENDICES

APPENDICES: MEASUREMENT PROBLEMS ENCOUNTERED

SOME of the measurement problems that were encountered in the film studies were of minor importance or specific to a particular study. Most of these have been presented in connection with specific studies to which they were relevant. Several recurrent problems of a more general nature were also encountered. Some of these are discussed in the appendices that follow. These measurement problems are not specific to film research but would be encountered in practically any experiment that attempts to quantify qualitative data.

THE BASELINE FOR MEASUREMENT
OF PERCENTAGE CHANGE

A COMMONLY used method of measuring effects of an experimental variable on qualitative responses is to show the percentage making the key response in the control group, the percentage making this response in the experimental group, and the difference between these two percentages. The "effect" is therefore indicated by the difference between the percentages.

However, this measure of effect is a function of the existing level of frequency of the key response prior to the experiment. If nearly all members of the population are unfamiliar with a particular fact prior to a film showing, a very effective film can yield a numerically large change when effects are expressed in this way. But if nearly everyone is already familiar with the fact, the effect is limited in size because only a small proportion did not know the fact initially and therefore only a small "effect" of the film can be obtained.

Thus the measure has serious disadvantages for determining the relative effectiveness of a film in teaching two different facts that are not equally well known initially. A different ceiling is imposed on the magnitude of effect for each different initial level, and the comparison is biased against items that are well known initially. Similarly, the measure introduces a bias if used for comparing the effects of a film on two or more groups that differ in initial level prior to the film. For example, if nearly all of the better educated know a particular fact, they can show little learning if effects are measured as the difference between control and film percentages, whereas the poorly educated, who are in general poorer learners, can show a large effect because they knew so little to begin with that there was considerable room for improvement.

This "ceiling" artifact is even further exaggerated if effects are measured as "percentage improvement," in which the baseline is the initial level and effect is expressed as the proportion of increase in this initial level. Thus a change from an initial level of 10 per cent to a final level of 20 per cent exhibits 100 per cent improvement, whereas a change from 80 per cent to 90 per cent—with the same 10 per cent difference in percentages— is only a 12 per cent improvement. Since the baseline and the ceiling are inversely correlated, the ceiling effect is exaggerated by the use of per cent improvement.

The "Effectiveness Index"

Both of these measures of effects—the difference in percentage and the proportionate increase in the initial level—are inadequate in comparisons in which the baseline varies for the two things being compared. In many cases a more appropriate measure is the increase in number checking the correct response divided by the *maximum increase possible* as a baseline. Thus if the initial level is 10 per cent correct answers and the film increases the number to 20 per cent, the difference between the percentages is 10 per cent. But since the initial level was 10 per cent, the maximum change possible is 90 per cent. Therefore the increase, divided by the maximum increase possible is 10 per cent divided by 90 per cent, or 11 per cent. Similarly, if the initial level is 80 per cent and the film increases the level to 90 per cent, the increase is again 10 per cent; but 10 per cent out of a maximum possible increase of 20 per cent (i.e., 100 per cent minus 80 per cent), gives a film effect of 50 per cent of the total possible increase.

This measure of effect is termed the "effectiveness index" in the present volume. It is so named because it is a measure which indicates the extent to which the film achieves maximum effectiveness in the particular area involved and with the particular measuring instrument used. If P_1 is used to indicate the initial per cent and P_2 the final per cent, the effectiveness-index is expressed by the following formula:[1]

$$\text{Eff. index} = \frac{P_2 - P_1}{100 - P_1}$$

This measure of effect may be interpreted as the effect of the film in increasing the frequency of correct responses among those initially having the wrong response. The major argument in favor of the effectiveness index is that the relative value of a particular instructional technique is thus ascertained on the basis of those individuals who do not already know the content of the instruction; therefore, any comparisons that are made to determine relative effectiveness should be free of distortion due to lack of effects among those who already know the material.

The per cent who check wrong answers initially is of course not actually the per cent who did not *know* the right answer initially. An indeterminant number of individuals will check the correct answer initially because they merely guessed, and happened to guess correctly. However, the increase

---

[1] The above formula applies for responses that are increased by the film. If the film decreases a particular response and it is desired to express this negative effect, the analogous formula is $\frac{P_2 - P_1}{P_1}$. This will give an effect with a negative sign and which measures the decrease as the proportion of maximum decrease possible.

in per cent is also not the actual number who changed as a result of seeing the film, because the increase would be generally accompanied by a reduction in the number who get the answer right by guessing. Thus the number who actually learned the material is really greater than the increase in correct responses, depending on the initial amount of guessing. Provided the film does not change the proportion who guess correctly among those who do not know the correct answer, the two factors above exactly balance each other so that the increase in frequency of correct responses divided by the initial frequency of errors gives the proportion who were changed of those who initially did not know the correct answer. This may be shown as follows:

Let k_1 and k_2 represent the percentages of the sample that actually *know* the correct answer before and after the film respectively. Then $100 - k_1$ is the percentage who did not know initially and $100 - k_2$ is the percentage who still do not know after the film. Now if X is the proportion of those who do not know who will guess correctly, then the obtained percentages of correct responses before and after the film, P_1 and P_2, respectively, will be as follows:

$$P_1 = k_1 + X(100 - k_1)$$

$$P_2 = k_2 + X(100 - k_2)$$

The effect, as computed from the increase in correct responses divided by the initial number of wrong responses, is equal to $\dfrac{P_2 - P_1}{100 - P_1}$. Substituting from above,

$$\frac{P_2 - P_1}{100 - P_1} = \frac{[k_2 + X(100 - k_2)] - [k_1 + X(100 - k_1)]}{100 - [k_1 + X(100 - k_1)]}$$

$$= \frac{k_2 (1 - X) - k_1 (1 - X)}{100(1 - X) - k_1 (1 - X)}$$

$$= \frac{k_2 - k_1}{100 - k_1}$$

It can be seen that this final expression is exactly the expression desired, namely, the increase in number *knowing* the correct response divided by the total who did not know it originally. In other words, it is the percentage who learned the answer among those who previously had not known it.

It will be noted that no assumption was made about the value for X, the proportion of correct guesses among those not knowing the correct answer. It was assumed, however, that X stays the same after the film, that is, that the correct choice is still just as attractive a guess among those who did not learn the correct answer.

In any case, the measure of effect obtained is unbiased by statistical ceiling effects. It always measures the increase as the proportion of the total increase possible.

Two illustrations from a study of "The Battle of Britain" are shown below, comparing "effects" as measured in the three different ways discussed above. The comparisons are made for the type of situation in which change as a function of maximum change possible appears to be the most appropriate measure. The examples illustrate how the conclusion is altered by using less appropriate measures that are biased by ceiling effects. In the first example the "effects" are compared for two different fact-quiz items with different initial levels; the second example compares "effects" at four different educational levels.

First Example

		PER CENT ANSWERING CORRECTLY	
		Reason British Navy could not be used	British military equipment after fall of France
	Control	36%	5%
	Film	55	18
Effect measured as difference between per cents		19	13
Effect measured as per cent improvement		53	260
Effect measured from base of maximum increase possible (effectiveness index)		30	14

In this example the effects are roughly the same for the second item as for the first if only the differences between per cents are considered, and the effect on the second item is about five times as great if "per cent improvement" is used, whereas the effect on the second item is about half as great as for the first item if the ceiling is equalized for the two groups by using the effectiveness index.

Second Example

		PER CENT ANSWERING CORRECTLY THE ITEM ABOUT THE BRITISH NAVY			
		Grade school men	Men with some high school	High school grads.	College men
	Control	31%	29%	38%	55%
	Film	32	57	60	78
Effect measured as difference between per cents		1	28	22	23
Effect measured as per cent improvement		3	97	58	42
Effect measured from base of maximum increase possible (effectiveness index)		1	39	35	51

In the above example the effect of the ceiling is to produce marked curvilinearity in the curve of effects expressed as differences, which is greatly exaggerated by the use of "per cent improvement," whereas the expected positive correlation between magnitude of effects and learning ability is found if the ceiling effect is equalized.

These examples were chosen to illustrate situations in which the appropriate base line is the maximum effect possible. In other types of situations the other base lines might be adequate. For example, in a comparison of two alternative presentation methods in teaching the same material, the same questions would be asked of samples from the same population, and the conclusion about relative effects from the comparison of the two presentations would be the same whichever of the three base lines is used. However, a distorted picture of the absolute magnitude of the effects might result from improper interpretation of the measure used. This is particularly true of the per cent improvement measure in which huge "improvements" may reflect only a small educational accomplishment merely because the starting level was very low.

The preceding considerations of base lines for measuring effects have been discussed from the standpoint of measuring instructional effects of a film on factual information. The same considerations apply, however, in the measurement of changes on opinion items. In this case the concept of "guessing" is not as appropriate as the more general concept of "unreliability," and the concept of "believe" is more appropriate than the concept of "know." Otherwise, the argument in the case of fact-quiz items may be directly transferred to the case of opinion items.

An important limitation to the utility of the effectiveness index as a measure for comparing changes lies in the fact that its sampling distribution has not been satisfactorily worked out, so that at present there is no adequate method available for determining whether two effectiveness indices *differ* reliably. Therefore, to the extent that the use of the index is desirable for this comparison of changes starting from different initial levels, the development of the sampling distribution of the measure becomes a problem for future statistical research.

Special complications arise if it is desired to extend the concept underlying the effectiveness index beyond the case of single qualitative measures such as percentages so as to cover *averages* of several responses. If one wishes to use the effectiveness index in representing a film's effect on the average number of correct or desired responses to a small (or at least finite) number of items, there are two alternative procedures possible. Either one may compute an effectiveness index separately for each item and average the obtained separate effectiveness indices, or an "effectiveness index" may be computed in terms of average change divided by "average change possible." The two procedures will in general lead to somewhat different numerical results unless the size of the effectiveness indices for individual items is uncorrelated with initial level of response over the range of items involved.

With the first procedure, experience indicated that obtained distributions permitted comparisons of means by the t-test, treating each effectiveness index as a raw "score." The main difficulty encountered with this procedure was that, with small samples, the value of a mean effectiveness index can be grossly influenced by a single deviant E.I. value such as is likely to occur with an initial level that leaves very little room for change and consequently gives a very unstable denominator in the E.I. formula.

Possible gross distortion of the average value by an aberrant and unstable component item is much less likely with the second procedure suggested above—i.e., computing a single effectiveness index based on the average obtained and "average change possible" for a set of several items. But this alternative introduces special difficulties of its own. In the first place, use of single effectiveness indices instead of averages over several observations leaves one without a measure of variability from item to item. Second, such an application of the logic of the effectiveness index necessitates defining E.I. in quite general terms as "obtained change divided by maximum change possible" rather than more specifically as "obtained number of individuals changing divided by maximum number who could change." This makes the unit of measurement a response rather than an individual, and consequently fails to differentiate changes in one or two items for a large number of persons from changes on more items by a small number of persons.

Attempts to Correct for Guessing

The foregoing discussion of the use of the "effectiveness index" deals with the problem of measuring changes that can be interpreted as the *per-cent-who-change* out of the group that could change. A more difficult problem is posed if it is desired to determine the *per-cent-who-know* the correct response before or after the film. It will be remembered that on page 286 an unspecified proportion, X, was used to represent the proportion of correct guesses among those not knowing the correct answer. This proportion does not need to be determined to calculate the per-cent-who-change among those not knowing initially, but it must be determined in order to calculate the per-cent-who-know the correct answer either before or after the film.

Assumptions can be made about the distribution of guesses in an attempt to express the effect of the film more accurately in terms of the per-cent-who-know out of the total sample, as a result of seeing the film. Thus in a four-choice item about which some individuals know nothing at all and only guess, it might be assumed that each choice is equally likely to be guessed, so that the distribution of guesses would be 25 per cent on the correct choice and on all others. If k is used to designate the percentage who know the correct answer, then $100 - k$ is the per cent who guess and

$1/4$ $(100 - k)$ is the per cent who guess correctly. If p is used to designate the total per cent who choose the correct response, then $p = k + 1/4$ $(100 - k)$, and k may be solved for, giving $k = 4/3$ $(p - 25)$. Thus if 50 per cent check the correct answer on such an item, 33 per cent know the correct answer; or if 80 per cent check the correct answer 73 per cent know the correct answer. With a three-choice item k would be equal to $3/2$ $(p - 33)$; with a five-choice item k would be equal to $5/4$ $(p - 20)$; and so forth.

The difficulty with this attempt to correct for guessing is that there is usually little confidence in the assumption that guesses are distributed equally over the different choices. Various factors cause the men who really do not know the correct answer to favor particular choices. This sometimes follows from the purpose of the instruction, which may be to correct a popular misconception. In this case, a wrong alternative that is highly favored is likely to be included in the choices written for the question. In such a case there may be little actual guessing although none of the group knows the correct answer. Also, the correction leads to a special difficulty when the correct choice initially receives fewer than the "chance" expectancy for guessing—as when only 10 per cent check the correct answer to a four-choice item. In this case a negative per cent is obtained for those knowing the correct answer.

In general the necessary assumptions are so infrequently justified that "corrected" results are about as likely to be less representative as they are to be more representative of the actual number who know the correct answer as a result of the film.

It should be pointed out again that this same difficulty is not present when it is only desired to express the per cent who change out of the group who could change initially, as shown earlier. The attempt to correct for guessing makes assumptions as to the *amount* of guessing of the correct answer, together with the assumption that this amount is a fixed proportion of those who do not know before and after the film. The interpretation of change divided by the maximal change possible as being the per cent who learn among those who do not know initially, on the other hand, makes only the latter assumption, namely that the same proportion of those who do not know will pick the correct response before and after the film.

Selection Effects

The "ceiling effects" discussed so far are purely statistical effects that influence the obtained measure of the effectiveness of the experimental variable. However, an additional type of ceiling may also be encountered, as the result of the selection of individuals, that may be a function of the initial level. If no one in the sample knows the correct response to a fact question at the outset, there is no selection involved in the group that can learn from the film. But if part of the group already knows the correct answer, there is the likelihood that this portion who already know the correct answer is not a random subsample of the group but rather is a select group in terms of important variables. Conversely, therefore, the remainder who can learn the correct answer because they do not already know it will also be a select group.

For example, if half of the population knows a particular fact, it is likely that as many as three fourths of the better learners in the population know the fact whereas as few as only one fourth of the poorer learners may know the fact. Positive correlation of knowledge of well-publicized information with learning proficiency is the rule and was typically found in the fact-quiz items used in the orientation studies. But the implication of such positive correlation is that those who do *not* know a well-publicized fact are a select group, likely to be biased in the direction of poorer learning proficiency. In the above hypothetical case it would include 75 per cent of the poorer learners and only 25 per cent of the better learners. For relatively little-known material the selection effect would not be great, but for very generally well-known material a *selection ceiling* is imposed in that the small proportion who do not initially know the material—and therefore could learn it from the film—are a selection of the very poorest learners in the population. In an extreme case in which, say, 90 per cent of the population already knows the fact, the remaining 10 per cent who can learn it from the film is likely to be a very backward group.

When the content of a film or other educational device is purely factual and only effects on factual knowledge are measured, the most important selection variable probably is learning proficiency. But in the case of a film designed to affect emotionally toned opinions, well-established opinions, and so forth, other selection factors may loom as of greater importance than learning proficiency. Prejudice and emotional involvement, for example, might be important selection variables.

In the studies of the orientation films, many of the orientation objectives were points of view held by the great majority of the men. Thus it was found that over 80 per cent of the men believed, at the time they came into the Army, that it was desirable to send American troops overseas to fight rather than merely waiting to defend America's shores in case of an enemy attack on the home soil. It seems likely that the remaining 20 per cent who could still be changed to this point of view by the orientation films were a very select, recalcitrant group, who would be very hard to "sell" on this point of view. Correlations with other variables and responses indicated that this was the case, such men tending to have been isolationists before Pearl Harbor, to have foreign-born parents originating in Axis countries, and so forth.

While no definite facts can be mustered in support of the contention, it seems likely that any opinion held by the great majority of the population represents a point of view that has been well publicized in the population.

Many of the cultural forces are at work to mold opinion in this particular way, and the majority of the group conforms. In such a case the small remainder that do not conform to the group opinion are likely to be "die hards" who have been exposed to all the usual forces and still will not change their opinion. If true, a selection ceiling would be present in the group who could be affected by an educational program designed further to affect opinions already held by the great majority of the population. Such a selection ceiling, if present, would mean that for a film to increase a response from 85 per cent to 95 per cent would, other things being equal, be a more difficult achievement than effecting an increase from an initial level of 55 per cent to a final level of 65 per cent. Under these circumstances there would tend to be a negative correlation between the prevalence with which an opinion is initially held and the ease with which a communication can effect an increase in the number holding the opinion.

On the other hand, an opinion or belief initially held by only a small minority may frequently be an "unpopular" opinion against the wider acceptance of which there are strong predisposing factors operative. In this case the effect of the psychological factors involved would tend to produce a *positive* rather than a negative correlation between initial prevalence of the opinion and its susceptibility to change in the direction of wider acceptance. An analysis of opinion changes as a function of initial acceptance level in population subgroups, reported in Chapter 7, shows results which can be interpreted as supporting this supposition.

As noted earlier, the use of the effectiveness index is not designed to correct for selection effects of the kind just discussed. Such selection effects involve differential susceptibility to change from a psychological standpoint, whereas the purpose of the effectiveness index is restricted to providing a statistical correction for differential possibility of change, or room for improvement.

"MARGINAL" VERSUS "INTERNAL" EFFECTS

THE effects discussed so far have all been in terms of a net shift in the proportion answering with a particular response, i.e., the "key" response. This was the most commonly used way of expressing effects in the evaluative studies carried out by the Experimental Section. The measure was usually appropriate because for any item the response desired by the makers of a training film could be specified in advance, and the evaluation of the film in a particular content area was in terms of the extent to which it increased the frequency of this response.

However, this way of describing the effects of the film may often be very incomplete in terms of all the changes produced by the film in the particular area. In studies with scientific aims it is more likely that the experimenter will seek more complete description of the effects than is provided by the marginal increase for a particular response category.

An additional degree of completeness of description of effects is provided by analysis of the marginal *distribution* of all of the response categories used in the particular content area. For example, in a multiple-choice item with several response categories, the complete distribution of responses provides additional information. Thus the complete marginal distribution indicates what responses showed a net increase and from what response categories the increase was derived, i.e., what responses showed a net decrease in frequency as a result of the film.

"Internal" Changes

The above-mentioned "more complete" degree of description is still limited to a *marginal* distribution—it shows the end product or net effects of a variety of possible shifts in response that could have brought about the end product. For some purposes this would be sufficient, but for a detailed analysis of the factors determining the effects of a film it would generally not be. A more complete analysis requires a description of the "internal" changes that brought about the net shifts in the marginal distribution. This can be done only by determining the response before and the response after the film presentation for each individual in the sample and comparing the distribution of *changes* of response with that of a control group that

APPENDICES

was subjected to the same determination of responses "before" and "after" but was not exposed to the experimental variable.

In this case the effects may be analyzed in terms of the differences between the cross-tabulation of responses before and after in the experimental group as contrasted with the same cross-tabulation in the control group. The distribution of changes of response in the control indicates changes occurring because of unreliability of response and other causes external to the film, and the difference between this distribution and the distribution of changes occurring in the film group indicates changes produced by the film. This procedure for determining effects shows the changes in the marginal distributions, which are the algebraic sums of the appropriate individual changes, but it also shows all of the individual changes that contribute to the end result of net changes on the marginals.

An illustration of this method of measuring effects is shown below from a study of the effectiveness of different kinds of radio programs in achieving orientation objectives. The purpose of the programs was to counteract overoptimism about the ease of defeating Japan, and the item used in the illustration below measured the effect of one kind of transcription at reducing overoptimism concerning the damage done by U.S. air raids. The study is described in more detail in Chapters 5 and 8; the programs used for the illustration below are the dramatic programs, which had the greatest effect on the question used in the illustration. The responses to the three answer categories given a week prior to the use of the programs are shown cross-tabulated against the responses to the same question after the program, for both experimental and control groups.

The wording of the question was:

> What is your idea of how much damage our air raids in Japan are doing to the Jap war effort? (Check one)
>
> —— *Already* have done a great deal of damage
> —— Not doing much damage so far but will do a great deal *soon*
> —— Not doing much damage so far and *will not* do a great deal *for quite a while* yet.

The breakdown of before and after responses is shown below with these responses paraphrased as "already," "soon," and "will not," respectively.

The cells comprising the descending diagonal in the cross-tabulation of the control group give the proportions who did not change their responses; they reflect the stability of responses during the time interval between before and after measurements. The sum of the three cells in this diagonal is the total percentage who did not change, and the remaining six cells give the "turnover" that reflects the instability of the responses to the question. The differences between control and experimental cells, shown in the last three-by-three table, show the effects of the transcription, that is, the changes of response in the experimental group with the values to be expected from chance and other causes subtracted out. From this table the net effects of the transcription on any particular response category can be determined from the appropriate marginal total, as well as the net effects on the marginal distribution of the three responses. At the same time, however, the net changes can be broken down into the various individual effects whose algebraic sum determines the net marginal change.

PER CENT CHECKING EACH RESPONSE COMBINATION
BEFORE AND AFTER PROGRAM

ANSWERS BEFORE

ANSWERS AFTER	Control—did not hear program				Experimental— heard program				Effects— exp. minus cont.			
	Already	Soon	Will not		Already	Soon	Will not		Already	Soon	Will not	
ALREADY	40	9	–	49	19	1	–	20	−21	−8	–	−29
SOON	4	38	5	47	28	35	1	64	+24	−3	−4	+17
WILL NOT	1	1	2	4	2	10	4	16	+ 1	+9	+2	+12
	45	48	7	100%	49	46	5	100%	+ 4	−2	−2	0%

The findings in the above example show, first of all, an increase in the total proportion changing their response as a result of the radio programs. This is seen by summing the descending diagonal in the "effects" table. Thus 22 per cent fewer in the experimental sample gave the same response before and after. If individual cell changes of 5 per cent or more are assumed to be statistically significant, four significant specific effects can be stated:

1. A decrease of 21 per cent in the number adhering to the most optimistic opinion of "already have done a great deal of damage."

2. An increase of 24 per cent in the number shifting from the most optimistic to the more moderate "soon" response.

3. A decrease of 8 per cent in the number going from the "soon" interpretation to the most optimistic "already" response.

4. An increase of 9 per cent in the number changing from the "soon" response to the most pessimistic idea that damage could not be expected for quite a while.

Finally, by summing the horizontal rows in the "effects" table we see that there was an overall decrease of 29 per cent in the most optimistic response and increases of 17 per cent and 12 per cent in the moderate and pessimistic responses, respectively.

Significance Test for Distribution of "Internal" Changes

The question may be raised as to the method of calculating the statistical significance of an "effect" of the film as determined in this manner. The meaning of an "effect" in this case is a *difference between the distributions* of before-after changes in the experimental group as contrasted with the control group. If the two cross-tabulations (experimental cross-tabulation versus control cross-tabulation) differ as a whole, an "effect" is demonstrated. An appropriate test is a Chi-square test of the significance of the differences between the two distributions, taken as a whole. If a significant difference is found for the distribution as a whole, the appropriate Chi-square or percentage tests of significance may be applied to the differences obtained in the sub-portions of the distribution, which differences serve to describe the nature of the "effect" obtained.

With this Chi-square test any differences at all between the two distributions contribute to the value for the total χ^2, even including such effects as an increase in the number *keeping the same opinion* as they had before. A short-cut procedure that is sometimes useful for locating items significantly affected by the film is simply to sum the changes of response and compare the per cent who change their response in the experimental group with that in the control group. Thus in the preceding example it can be seen that 42 per cent of the experimental group and only 20 per cent of the control group changed their responses. Thus the cross-tabulation can be used to dichotomize the samples into "changed" and "did not change," and the significance of a difference between the experimental and control percentages changing is a simple test of whether the experimental variable caused significant amounts of opinion change. This test may prove particularly useful if a question has a large number of categories so that many of the cells have expected frequencies too small properly to use χ^2 (e.g., expected values less than 5) with the size of samples used. Also with a large number of categories the amount of computation in using χ^2 is much greater, so the simpler test of percentage who change is a useful short-cut if it detects the effect.

In general, however, the Chi-square test is more sensitive in determining an effect than is the per-cent-who-change test described above. This is mainly because one possible type of effect is to *prevent changes* of response, which effects add to χ^2 but subtract from the per cent who change. When samples are small but the number of response categories is large, it is usually possible to make combinations of answer categories that are meaningful and at the same time sufficiently increase the expected frequencies that the χ^2 test may be used.

In applying the Chi-square test, the simpler procedure is to combine the frequencies in the experimental and control cells and use the combined distribution as the basis for obtaining the predicted frequencies, the predicted value being obtained by multiplying the experimental or control N by the ratio of the combined cell-frequency to the combined N. In this case the number of degrees of freedom of Chi-square is one less than the number of cells in the cross-tabulation.

However, this procedure is strictly applicable only with random sampling of subjects. If there are significant differences in the marginal proportions of the cross-tabulation because the experimental and control groups are not a random selection of individuals, a significant Chi-square may be obtained simply because the marginals differ significantly before the application of the experimental variable. In such a case the expected values should be computed from the ratio of combined cell frequencies to combined *marginal N*'s in the "before" data rather than the ratio to total N. The ratios should correspondingly be applied to the separate "before" marginal N's, and the number of degrees of freedom is reduced accordingly to $r(r - 1)$ where r is the number of "before" marginal totals (i.e., the number of response categories).

As stated earlier, if the Chi-square test reveals a significant overall deviation in the control and experimental distributions, the distributions may then be examined for the nature of these effects. In general in this type of analysis it would be required that a reliable effect be obtained for the total Chi-square before it would be permissible to examine the reliability of separate subgroups of response combinations before and after. This would be particularly important where the response categories are numerous. For example, if a question has four response categories, the total number of cells in the before-after cross-tabulation would be 16. This multiplies considerably the number of comparisons that would meet the significance test even though chance were the only factor operating, and therefore it increases the probability of finding a false "effect" of the experimental variable on the question. The probability of "detecting" a false "effect" is greatly reduced if it is first shown that a significant difference exists in the total array of comparisons.

"Internal" Effects That Cancel in the Marginal Frequency

When a change (e.g., an effect of film) is described in terms of the marginal shift in the distribution of responses, the change so described is the *net change* as a consequence of the various shifts from category to category that might have occurred. As already pointed out, the "internal" changes more completely describe the net effect on the marginal by showing the individual effects that sum algebraically to produce the net effect. In some cases, however, the net effects may be zero because of opposite "internal" effects that cancel each other in their effects on the marginal distribution. Examples of such cancelling effects were very rare in the present film studies, but they are a theoretically possible type of effect that can be measured only in terms of the internal changes.

Marginal Versus "Internal" Effects When Responses Form a Scale of Content

In the illustration used in the preceding section comparing marginal changes with internal changes, it will be observed that the differences in the three responses provided are a mixture of qualitative and quantitative differences. The three ideas expressed are qualitatively different, but at the same time they are along a time continuum as to *when* a great deal of damage would result from air raids on Japan. This is often the case in opinion questions; while in some instances the different responses may represent discrete categories, they frequently represent a *content continuum* along which responses can be graded in degree to which a response differs from one or the other end of the continuum.

A good example of the latter type of question is provided in the same study from which the preceding illustration was borrowed. In this study the main question used to determine the overall effect of the radio program on optimism about the war with Japan was a question asking the men how long they thought the war with Japan would last. The question was of the "open-ended" or "free-answer" type, that is, the men were asked to write in their own best guess as to how much longer they thought the war would last. The answers were coded in six-month intervals—less than six months; six months or more, but less than one year; one year or more, but less than one-and-one-half years; and so forth. Thus the responses can be graded from short to long along the content continuum of estimated length of war, and an individual's change in response, from before to after, can be quantified in terms of the number of steps by which he changed along the content continuum.

In such a case the cross-tabulation of before and after responses, from which "internal" changes can be determined, does not consist merely of *discrete qualitative combinations* of before and after responses. Instead, each individual's change may be completely described in terms of initial level, direction of change (positive or negative), and size of change (number of steps along the single content continuum). This permits several different ways of summarizing the effects obtained, in addition to those already discussed. Thus in the preceding discussion "effects" were describable as net change in the marginal of a particular response, net changes in the marginal distribution of all of the responses, and individual qualitative changes from one category to another. In an item with scaled content, the effect may be described, in addition, in terms of the net per cent who changed by given amounts in a given direction, or in terms of a mean change in number of steps along the content continuum, each of these being expressible as a function of initial level on the continuum.

These measures are illustrated below in the above-mentioned example of the length-of-war question from the study of the radio programs. The results for the control group and one of the four experimental groups are shown below, the length-of-war estimates in the after questionnaire being cross-tabulated against those in the before questionnaire. The numbers in each of the cells below are the numbers of men giving each combination of before and after response.

ESTIMATES OF LENGTH OF WAR BEFORE AND AFTER THE TRANSCRIPTION

CONTROL GROUP

Estimates before, in half-year intervals

		1	2	3	4	5	6	7+	Total after
	1	6	5						11
	2	4	37	5	1	2			49
Estimates	3	1	12	37	7	2			59
after, in									
half-year	4		1	7	11	3			22
intervals									
	5			1	4	17	6	3	31
	6					1	5		6
	7+						2	1	3
Total before		11	55	50	24	24	13	4	181

EXPERIMENTAL GROUP*

Estimates before, in half-year intervals

		1	2	3	4	5	6	7+	Total after
	1	1							1
	2	8	27						35
Estimates	3	1	20	23	2	2	1		49
after, in									
half-year	4		11	26	10	4	1	1	53
intervals									
	5		1	7	6	23	4		41
	6		1		3	5	4		13
	7+			2	1	2	2	6	13
Total before		10	60	58	22	36	12	7	205

* The experimental group used is the one hearing the program giving "both sides" of an issue, as described in Chapter 8.

The marginal change may be measured in terms of a "cutting-point" which dichotomizes the responses and expresses the effect as the increase in percentage falling above or below the cutting-point. For example, "overoptimism" may be defined as estimates of a war of less than one year and the responses dichotomized according to whether they are less than one year or one year or more. The results are:

	CONTROL			EXPERIMENTAL		
	Bef.	*Aft.*	*Diff.*	*Bef.*	*Aft.*	*Diff.*
Estimated less than one year	37%	33%	−4%	34%	18%	−16%

Thus, while only a slight change took place in the control marginal from before to after, a decrease in "overoptimists" of 16 per cent was found in the experimental group. This presumably approximates the results that would have been obtained on a dichotomous question asking the men whether they thought the war would be over in less than a year.

The above measure reduces the effect to a single response category. This may be expanded to show the effect along the entire marginal distribution, as follows:

PER CENT CHECKING EACH RESPONSE

	CONTROL			EXPERIMENTAL		
Response	*Bef.*	*Aft.*	*Diff.*	*Bef.*	*Aft.*	*Diff.*
(1) Under ½ year	6	6	0	5	1	−4
(2) ½ to 1 year	31	27	−4	29	17	−12
(3) 1 to 1 and ½ years	28	33	5	28	24	−4
(4) 1 and ½ to 2 years	13	12	−1	11	26	15
(5) 2 to 2 and ½ years	13	17	4	18	20	2
(6) 2 and ½ to 3 years	7	3	−4	6	6	0
(7+) 3 years or more	2	2	0	3	6	3
	100%	100%		100%	100%	

This shows the changes all along the marginal distribution for the control and experimental group. It can be seen that while only small and inconsistent changes occurred in the control group, the changes in the experimental group were in some cases large and were systematically in the direction of a shift of the distribution to larger estimates, the greatest change in an individual response category being the increase in category (4), a war of one-and-one-half to two years.

It will also be observed from this distribution that the effects in terms of the "cutting-point" as illustrated previously are different according to the cutting-point chosen. A change of −16% was obtained in the experimental group for estimates of less than one year, as shown above, but it can be seen also that the change is −20% for a war of less than one-and-one-half years, and only −5% if the cutting-point is two years.

The effects on the marginal distribution may also be expressed as mean effect for the distribution as a whole.   This is illustrated below.   The response categories are not repeated, but the numbers in the "response" column correspond to the length of the estimate in half-year intervals.[1]

NUMBER OF MEN GIVING EACH ESTIMATE

	CONTROL		EXPERIMENTAL	
Response	Bef.	Aft.	Bef.	Aft.
(1)	11	11	10	1
(2)	55	49	60	35
(3)	50	59	58	49
(4)	24	22	22	53
(5)	24	31	36	41
(6)	13	6	12	13
(7+)	4	3	7	13
Mean (in half-year units)	3.28	3.24	3.38	3.92
Diff.	−0.04		0.54	

Expressed in this way, the results show practically no change in the control group, but in the experimental group the mean estimate increased 0.54 half-year units, that is, a mean increase of about one-quarter of a year.

However, the above expression of the effect in terms of the mean change along the content continuum, and also the other ways of expressing the marginal effects, do not indicate the internal shifts that account for the marginal changes.   The effects can be more completely described by a distribution of individual shifts from "before" to "after."   The individual shifts in the original data presented on page 299 may be described in terms of magnitude and direction of the shifts along the content continuum.   Thus an individual may shift his estimate by zero, one, two, etc., steps, and the direction of his shift may be positive (larger estimates) or negative (smaller estimates).   These individual shifts are shown below.

The mean shift shown below is of course the same as that obtained from the marginal distributions.   However, the mean and the marginal distributions indicate only the net effect of the individual shifts.   They do not distinguish, for example, between large changes among a smaller number of individuals and smaller changes among a larger number of individuals. The distributions below, on the other hand, show magnitude and direction of individual shifts and permit making the distinction between the *number of individuals* affected, the *size* of the individual effects, and the *direction* of the individual effects.   The distribution of "control" changes provides

[1] An exception to this is 7+, which for convenience includes all of the few cases in which the estimate exceeded three years.   These are treated as though all were from three to three-and-one-half years.

DISTRIBUTION OF SIZE OF CHANGE IN ESTIMATE FROM BEFORE TO
AFTER, EXPRESSED IN TERMS OF ONE-HALF YEAR INTERVALS

SIZE OF CHANGE IN HALF-YEAR INTERVALS	CONTROL N	%	EXPERIMENTAL N	%
−3	2	1	2	1
−2	6	3	3	1
−1	26	15	10	5
0	114	63	94	46
1	29	16	67	33
2	4	2	24	12
3			2	1
4			3	1
Mean change	−0.04	100%	0.54	100%

a base for the changes to be expected from question unreliability and causes other than the film. Significant differences between the control and experimental distributions of changes give the effects of the film on frequency, magnitude, and direction of changes.

Net Proportion Who Change

The above distributions provide another way of measuring the effect, namely in terms of the net proportion who change their opinion in a given direction. In the distributions just shown, some individuals are seen to have shifted to smaller estimates and some to larger estimates, while others gave the same estimates in both surveys. The *net proportion who change* to longer estimates is the proportion shifting to longer estimates minus the proportion shifting to smaller estimates, without regard to size of change. Thus in the distribution of changes in the experimental group it can be seen that 67 men increased their estimate by one half a year, 24 increased theirs by a year, 2 by one-and-one-half years, and 3 by two or more years, making a total of 96 who increased their estimates by at least one half a year. Thus 96 of the 205 men, or 47 per cent, increased their estimate. Similarly, 15 of the 205 men, or 7 per cent, decreased their estimate by at least one half a year. Thus the *net proportion who change* to longer estimates in the experimental group is 47 per cent minus 7 per cent, or 40 per cent. This way of expressing the findings is summarized below:

NUMBER WHO CHANGE THEIR ESTIMATE BY ONE-HALF YEAR OR MORE

Direction of change	Control	%	Experimental	%
Decrease estimate	34	19	15	7
No change in estimate	114	63	94	46
Increase estimate	33	18	96	47
Net change (increases minus decreases)	−1%			40%

It can be seen that in the experimental group the net per cent changing to longer estimates was 40 per cent, whereas in the control group, during the same time interval between before and after measurements, there was a net change of only -1%.

It should be clear that the magnitude of the net proportion who change is a function of the fineness of the intervals into which the content continuum is divided. If the free-answer responses in the preceding illustration had been coded in one-year intervals rather than the one-half-year intervals used, a much smaller net change would have been obtained. An examination of the data on page 302 reveals that the net proportion increasing their estimates by at least *one year* in the experimental group is only 12 per cent as compared with the 40 per cent obtained for changes of at least one half a year. Presumably a value even larger than 40 per cent could have been obtained if the intervals could have been made even smaller than half-year intervals. In this particular case, however, a limit was set by the units used by the men in answering the open-ended question —the majority of the men did not answer the question in terms of months but rather in terms of year units and half-year units.

An implication of the dependence of the magnitude of the net proportion changing on the magnitude of the content units is that a more sensitive measuring instrument is provided by a question that permits fine units of change. With a given size sample it may be found that no statistically significant change was obtained merely because the units of measurement were so coarse that few individuals change by the minimal amount measured.

It should be pointed out that the net proportion who change is to some extent independent of the mean change. The mean change is a joint function of the *number changing* and the *size of the changes*, whereas the net proportion changing depends only on the number changing (for a given minimal unit of change). The mean change and net proportion changing may even give results opposite in sign if the changes in one direction are of *larger magnitude* and the changes in the other direction are of *greater frequency*.

Significance Test for Net Proportion Who Change

The test for the significance of the net proportion who change involves estimating the variance of a difference between *mutually exclusive proportions within the same sample*. The before-after results divide each sample into three groups, with the corresponding proportions indicated below:

p_1 = proportion changing positively
p_2 = proportion changing negatively
p_3 = proportion not changing

$p_1 + p_2 + p_3$ = Total = 1

The net proportion who change in each sample is $(p_1 - p_2)$, and the population variance of $P_1 - P_2$ for the experimental and control groups, on the null hypothesis of no difference, may be estimated from the total sample of experimental and control groups combined, as follows:

$$\text{Est. } \sigma^2_{P_1-P_2} = p_{1T} + p_{2T} - (p_{1T} - p_{2T})^2$$

where T indicates that the proportions in the estimate are based on the *total* sample of experimental and control.[2] The estimated S.E. of a difference between the net proportions changing in the experimental and control groups is then:

$$\text{Est. } \sigma_{\text{diff.}-\text{diff.}} = \sqrt{\text{Est. } \sigma^2_{P_1-P_2}\left(\frac{1}{N_e}+\frac{1}{N_c}\right)}$$

The application to the present illustrative data is shown below.

	CONTROL DIST.		EXPERIMENTAL DIST.		TOTAL (POP. DIST.)	
	N	p_c	N	p_e	N	p_T
Neg. change	34	.19	15	.07	49	.13
No change	114	.63	94	.46	208	.54
Pos. change	33	.18	96	.47	129	.33
Total	181	1.00	205	1.00	386	1.00
Net proportion of change		−.01		+.40		+.20

The estimated variance of the differences between positive changes and negative changes in the population distribution is:

$$\text{Est. } \sigma^2 = .33 + .13 - (.33 - .13)^2 = .42$$

The S.E. of the mean difference between the differences between positive and negative changes in the experimental and control samples is therefore:

$$\text{Est. } \sigma_{M \text{ diff.}-\text{diff.}} = \sqrt{\sigma^2_{\text{diff.}}\left(\frac{1}{N_c}+\frac{1}{N_e}\right)}$$
$$= \sqrt{(.42)\left(\frac{1}{181}+\frac{1}{205}\right)} = \sqrt{.00437}$$
$$= .066$$

Difference (exp. minus control) $= .40 - (-.01)$
$$= .41$$
$$\text{C.R.} = \frac{M_{\text{diff.}}}{\sigma_{M\text{diff.}-\text{diff.}}} = \frac{.41}{.066} = 6.2$$

[2] An equivalent formula for computing the sampling variance of the difference between two percentages within a sample is given by S. S. Wilks, "Confidence Limits and Critical Differences Between Percentages," *Public Opinion Quarterly*, 1940, *4*, 322–338.

Thus the critical ratio is 6.2, leaving no doubt that the radio program had a real effect.

Change as a Function of Initial Response

One further refinement may be introduced in order to describe completely the changes produced by the experimental variable. This is the additional information provided by the *initial response* from which the individual changes were made. With this additional information the net effect on the marginal distribution can be completely understood in terms of individual shifts.

An illustration of this additional aspect of the individual changes produced by the experimental variable will not be presented here. This aspect is taken up, however, in the presentation of the findings of the study in Chapter 8, where it can be seen that the initial response was an important factor in the results obtained. With two different ways of presenting the material—giving the arguments for only one point of view versus mentioning the arguments on the other side as well—it was found that the results differed according to the initial stand of the individuals in the audience. This difference did not show up either in the marginal distributions or in the distribution of individual changes when results were computed without taking into account the initial response.

It is partly a matter of definition whether the initial response is regarded as a base for the description of change from initial to final response or whether it is regarded as a population variable which may be one of the determiners of the effects of the experimental variable. In the present research it was generally regarded as a population variable, and a general discussion of effects as a function of initial response is included in Chapter 8. The initial response is introduced as an aspect of the individual change in the present context because of its importance in the interpretation of a *marginal change* when the area represented by the item used is an area with a scaled content continuum. This is discussed in the following section.

The Meaning of a Marginal Change

The frequency distribution of the population on an opinion for which individuals vary primarily in degree rather than in kind may be conceived as a continuous distribution from one end of a *content continuum* to the other. A dichotomous question in this area subdivides the distribution into those falling above and those falling below the "cutting-point" of the dichotomous item. This is easy to visualize in the preceding example of probable length of the war. The population could be distributed along a time continuum as far as their best guess was concerned, and a question such as, "Do you think the war will last at least a year-and-a-half from now?" will merely dichotomize the population at a certain point along the content continuum, as diagrammed below from the before distribution of the experimental sample as shown on page 299.   It can also be visualized,

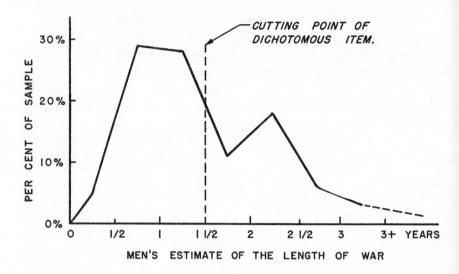

in terms of the results shown previously, that the marginal shift across this cutting-point represents the effects of the experimental variable in only a limited portion of the total sample even though this cutting-point (one-and-one-half years) gave the largest marginal change.   It can be seen from the original data that the net number who *crossed this line* on the content continuum in an upward direction was only 43, whereas the net number who *moved upward* on the continuum was 81.   This is seen by an examination of the data for the marginal distribution on page 301 and for the change of response on page 302.   The total above the cutting-point (codes 4 through 7) before the radio program was 77, and this number increased to 120 after the program, an increase of 43, whereas 96 men increased their estimates and 15 decreased their estimates by at least one-half year giving a net number of increases of 81.

In general, the shift in marginal per cent will reflect the changes only in those members of the population who are *close to the cutting-point*.   This would be seen even more clearly if the question had been, "Do you believe the war will last at least two more years?"   With a question that dichotomized the content continuum at two years the net number crossing this cutting-point in an upward direction would be only 12 out of the net total of 81 who revised their opinions upward.

It is clear in this example that where an area is scaled in content, the marginal per cent of shift with a dichotomous question is a function of (1) the shape of the initial distribution, (2) the location of the cutting-point on the initial distribution, and (3) the distribution of magnitude of changes of individuals at different points along the initial distribution, that is, originating from different initial responses. In the preceding example the shift is maximized at the one-and-one-half year point because, before the program was given, a large portion of the population was concentrated just below that point, and because the great majority of the shifts that did occur were limited to a change of only one-half year. In general, where the individual changes are small in magnitude the cutting-point giving the maximal marginal change will be slightly above (for positive changes) the mode of the initial distribution. Where individual changes tend to be larger, the cutting-point of maximal marginal change will be moved upward (again for positive changes) since the higher the cutting-point the greater the proportion of individuals who can cross it.

Use of a Scale of Items

The preceding discussion of ways of dealing with areas that scale in content has been limited to the situation in which the scale consists of the various response categories to a single question, as in the illustration of the length-of-war question. However, a scale of content may also be formed by asking a series of questions, all in the same content area, and assigning a scale position to each individual according to his combination of responses to the series. A technique for this procedure that was frequently utilized in the Research Branch is described in Volume IV of the present series.

In concluding this topic it should be pointed out that many of the differences in the manner of measuring effects that have been outlined are a function of whether measurements have been made both before and after the experimental variable or whether they are made after only. If the study is carried out merely by measuring a film and control group after the film, the manner in which effects can be expressed is limited. A discussion of the before-after and the after-only experimental designs, together with associated differences in tests of statistical significance, is taken up in Appendix C.

COMPARISON OF THE BEFORE-AFTER
AND THE AFTER-ONLY DESIGN OF
EXPERIMENTS

IN SOME of the experiments reported in this volume, measurements were obtained both before and after the introduction of the experimental variable. In others measurements were obtained only after the experimental stimulus. A comparison of the uses of the before-after and the after-only design of an experiment on opinion change resolves into three major kinds of considerations: statistical and sampling factors, types of analysis that can be made with the data, and effects of the measuring process on the measurements obtained. The *statistical and sampling* considerations arise primarily from the fact that the before-after procedure permits taking correlation between before and after responses into account in the comparison of differences between control and experimental groups. Also, it permits taking initial lack of equating between control and experimental groups into account when these have not been a random selection from the same population. Considerations of *types of analyses* that can be performed arise from the fact that the before-after procedure permits analysis of individual changes and the comparison of effects among subgroups with differing initial attitudes. The remaining consideration above, the *effects of the measuring process* on the measurements obtained, is necessitated by the possibility that making before measurements in the before-after procedure will bias the results obtained in the after measurement. In designing an experiment to measure film effects, all of these considerations are relevant to the decision as to which design to use.

Effects of the Measuring Process on the Measurement Obtained

In all experimental work there is the possibility that the measuring method will interact with the experimental variable in such a way as to make the results obtained nonrepresentative of the effects of the variable outside of the experiment. This possibility should be distinguished from the possible bias in questions and from nonrepresentativeness of measurements that are present both in experimental and in nonexperimental study. The latter possibility applies equally to control and experimental groups and is a general problem of scientific measurement rather than a specifically experimental problem. The specifically experimental problem referred to is that the measuring process may conceal or distort the effects of the experimental variable.

1. PROBLEMS COMMON TO BOTH TYPES OF DESIGN

The "guinea-pig" reaction. In the use of the after-only procedure in the studies of orientation films, the chief potential source of distortion that attempts were made to avoid was the possibility that the measuring process would reveal to the men that they were being experimented upon, with the consequence that they might start discounting the film as propaganda or would give self-conscious rather than "true" responses to the questions. To avoid this possibility, considerable effort was expended in the conduct of the studies to prevent the men from knowing that an experiment was in progress, to prevent any unusual circumstances in connection with the film showings, and to give a plausible rationale for the questionnaire which would conceal its actual purpose.

The "test" reaction. A second kind of distortion that had to be avoided was the possibility that the men would react to the questionnaire as a "test" of what they knew or what was desired in them, so that in answering opinion questions they would give the "correct" response rather than their most representative response. In fact-quiz items this consideration does not apply, but if the entire questionnaire were treated as a test the men might check opinions that agreed with the slant presented in the films although these might not be what they personally believed. To avoid this possibility considerable stress was given, in the administration of the questionnaires, to the importance of honest opinions and the anonymity of the answers. Further, the rationale of the questionnaire as explained to the men was such as to emphasize the importance of the men's expressing their own true opinion. Also the fact-quiz items were placed at the end of the questionnaires to prevent giving the men a "test" approach in their answers to the opinion questions.

Suggesting the experimental variable. Another possible source of distortion that had to be avoided in the questionnaires was the possibility that the questions would remind the men of the film or its contents, so that their answers were representative only of their responses while thinking of the film and would not be representative of their feelings the rest of the time. Thus, as indicated in the analysis of consistency of responses (pages 172–174), the response chosen on a particular occasion has a considerable degree of instability which may very well be a function of momentary considerations on the part of the respondent in making his choice. He may therefore have one answer that he would give if he happened to be thinking of the film but a different answer for the majority of the occasions when he is not thinking of the film. For this reason it was desirable to avoid questions that specifically suggested the film regardless of whether there was any risk of the men's feeling that they were being "guinea-pigged" and giving a "test" set in answering the questions.

2. PROBLEMS SPECIFIC TO THE BEFORE-AFTER DESIGN

All of the above three possible sources of interaction between the experimental variable and the measuring process are applicable to both the before-after and the after-only designs. However, they are especially to be avoided in the *before-after* procedure, in which they not only apply but would if anything be even more likely to distort the results. This is particularly true of the possibility that the men will become suspicious that an experiment is in progress. The administration of two successive questionnaires on much the same content, with a relevant film shown during the interval, would be expected to arouse more suspicion than a single questionnaire that came after the film.

"Sensitization" to the experimental variable. Not only would the before-after procedure be expected to increase, if anything, the difficulties of the sort just described that apply in the case of the after-only procedure, but it also brings new possible difficulties of its own. One is that the "before" questionnaire will "sensitize" the men to the topics to be covered in the film so that their immediate reaction to the film is altered. Thus, if the before questionnaire arouses interest in the topics covered, the men may pay more attention to the material presented in the film. A related possibility is that the combination of the before questionnaire and the film will suggest to the men that they are being "guinea-pigged" *at the time that they are seeing the film* so that it could be discounted as propaganda at that time as well as later when the after questionnaire is being answered.

The "consistency" reaction. Another possibility is that the before-after procedure will stimulate the men to give the same response the second time, so that all changes and effects of variables are minimized. This would be expected to depend somewhat on the rationale given for the second administration and on the time intervening between the two. Rationales suggesting that the after questionnaire was just a "repeat" of the previous questionnaire and the use of a short time interval would both be expected to increase the tendency toward a "consistency reaction." The consistency could be due either to a conscious motive to be consistent or simply due to the absence of a concrete opinion prior to the before questionnaire, which, however, became "crystalized" or established as the respondent's "own opinion" by his being forced to give an answer the first time. Such a tendency toward consistency would be present in both the control and the experimental groups, but its effect would be to minimize the actual degree of change that would otherwise be due to the experimental variable.

A similar factor but one which would lead to diametrically opposed effects would be a tendency to avoid repetition of answers expressed on a previous questionnaire. This possibility is much less likely than attempts at consistency, although such a phenomenon has been observed by Dodd[1] who found Syrian respondents felt that it was important to make their replies "interesting" by varying them from one interview to the next.

In addition to the precautions mentioned earlier with the after-only design, a precaution used in the case of the before-after design was the provision of a convincing rationale for the second questionnaire. In most cases this was handled by making the second questionnaire as different as possible and presenting it as a revised version. The format and paper were different, it was marked "Revised," and additions, omissions and "revisions" were provided by camouflage questions and other questions asked only in one of the two questionnaires. In the administration of the questionnaire, the class leader announced incidentally that some of the men might have taken a similar questionnaire previously but that this was a revised form with different questions. This rationale was designed to cope simultaneously with tendencies to suspect a test on the film and tendencies to try to give consistent answers.

3. COMPARISON OF THE EFFECTS OF MEASUREMENT IN THE TWO DESIGNS

No opportunity was afforded in the studies of orientation films to carry out methodological studies designed to determine the relative effects of the measuring process on the results obtained in the after-only and before-after design. The "applied" nature of the studies forced a policy of using all feasible precautions without determining the extent of the need for the precautions. Thus, the potential distortions listed are merely theoretical possibilities.

A little evidence on the problem was obtained incidentally. The evidence comes from the study of "The Battle of Britain," which was carried out at one camp with the after-only design and at another camp with the before-after design. The samples were comparable to the extent that the men at each camp were new inductees in the first few weeks of basic training. They were not comparable in that the two studies were carried out at different times (about two months apart), the men were receiving different kinds of training (Armored Force versus Infantry), and the populations of the two camps differed somewhat in composition on various demographic factors.

At the end of the "after" questionnaire the men at both camps were asked if they had recently been shown a War Department movie on the history of the war and if so to specify the subject from one of several alternative topics including "the bombing of Britain." They were then asked, "What did you think was the reason for showing this movie to you

[1] In connection with his study: *A Controlled Experiment on Rural Hygiene in Syria* (Oxford Univ. Press, 1934).

and the other men?" This was a write-in question for the purpose of detecting the presence of the feeling that the film was given for propaganda purposes or the suspicion that the film was shown as part of an experiment to find out its effect on the men. The question was designed so as not to suggest either of these ideas to any but those men who had already thought of them. Only a tiny fraction of the men with either design said anything even suggestive of suspicion that an experiment was in progress. The total number of such responses at both camps combined was only five, so comparison of the after-only and before-after is relatively meaningless; for all practical purposes the number was negligible with either procedure. As far as this response is an adequate index, over 99 per cent of the men were unaware of the experiment in either procedure. A weakness of this question for this purpose is that it was phrased in the past tense so that some of the men may have suspected an experiment during the administration of the questionnaire but answered only in terms of what they thought at the time of the film showing. It seems safe to infer, however, that little suspicion of this sort was aroused with the precautions used.

Another result that bears on the relative effects of the two different measuring processes is the relative size of the effects obtained at the two different camps. The general trend was in the direction to be expected from the "consistency" hypothesis—that is, the results at the camp in which the before-after design was used tended to be less than at the camp using the after-only. This is shown below for all opinion items that showed a difference of 8 per cent or more between control and film at either camp.[2]

If the samples at the two different camps could be regarded as equivalent samples from the same population, the above results would show significantly less effect of the film when the before-after procedure is used. The difference in the effects obtained is in the direction expected from the hypothesis that in the before-after procedure the men are stimulated to be consistent in their answers to the questions the second time, either because the men remember their former answer and seek to be consistent or because, having once been forced to give an answer, their opinion tends to be crystalized and repeated.

However, in view of the differences in the samples that were associated with the differences in the procedure, the results must be regarded as only tentative. If the two samples compared had been equivalent, a more definitive answer could be given. Another approach would be to ask, at the camp where the before-after procedure was used, equivalent questions in some cases in the before and after questionnaires and in others only in the after-questionnaire. Unfortunately for this purpose almost all of the

---

[2] The criterion of 8 per cent sets a statistical significance level of about .01 or better at either camp for most of the items. Items with less difference were excluded so the results would not be diluted by comparisons of chance "effects."

SIZE OF EFFECT
(FILM MINUS CONTROL)

Topic of Question	Camp 1 (After-only)	Camp 2 (Before-after)	Diff.
The RAF gave the Nazis their first real defeat	23%	24%	1%
The Nazis failed to conquer England because of determined resistance of British	24	19	−5
RAF had done about best job of fighting in the war	22	11	−11
By refusing to surrender British saved U.S. cities from bombings	19	12	−7
America would produce more war material if U.S. workers worked as hard as British	15	7	−8
Heavy bombings of England by Luftwaffe part of an invasion attempt	14	14	0
U.S. was country that Hitler would have attacked after conquest of England	14	1	−13
America had done little fighting compared with the British	10	4	−6
Nazis probably did not treat conquered countries as bad as radio and press said	9	2	−7
Britain deserves most credit for holding off Nazis while we prepared	8	6	−2
British doing all they can to help in war effort	8	6	−2
Average	13.8%	8.8%	−5.0%

questions that were used only in the after questionnaire at this camp were fact-quiz items. On the fact-quiz items that were asked after-only at both camps no difference was found between the two camps: the mean for significantly affected items at the camp where the design was after-only was *26.8%* and the mean at the camp using the before-after design but at which these particular questions were only in the after-questionnaire was *26.4%*. These results in conjunction with those presented above might be interpreted as indicating that the two samples were alike as far as acceptance of the factual material is concerned but that they differed in their acceptance of the interpretations of the facts. This explanation receives a certain amount of support from the data, in that two opinion items which were asked only in the after questionnaire at the before-after camp conform to the result for other opinion items at that camp, that is, they showed less effect than at the camp at which the after-only design was used.

No definitive conclusion can be drawn from the evidence available at this time. The data suggest that the before-after procedure does minimize the actual effects, but alternative interpretations of the results are not ruled out.

Comparison of the Types of Analysis Possible with the Before-After and the After-Only Procedures

As stated earlier, the before-after procedure has the advantage of permitting analysis of individual changes and determining effects as a function of subgroups of differing initial attitude. One of the major drawbacks of the after-only procedure is the limitation it sets on the detail with which opinion changes can be described. As shown in the earlier discussion of measurement of effects, complete description of effects depends on measuring "internal" changes. With the after-only procedure the description is limited to marginal changes—that is, net shifts in group proportions. The recording of each individual's initial and subsequent response, provided by the before-after design, has a number of related advantages in analysis of the results.

In the after-only procedure the sample may be broken down into subtypes on any variable that cannot be affected by the experimental variable and differential effects can be determined. For example, it is unlikely that a film would have any effects on the years of schooling reported by the individuals, so that differential effects of the film on different educational groups can be determined by a comparison of film and control results among the different educational groups. The same would be true for age, marital status, and similar background variables that would not be affected by the experimental variable unless it motivated the respondent to misrepresent the facts.

However, if the "sorting" variable—that is, the variable according to which the sample is sorted into subgroups—is itself affected by the experimental variable such analyses cannot properly be performed without the before-after design.

1. FILM EVALUATION AS A VARIABLE FOR ANALYSIS

One class of sorting variable is furnished by responses of the men in their direct evaluation of the film. For example, at the end of the experimental questionnaires in the orientation film studies, the men were asked how well they liked the War Department film that had been recently shown at the camp. In order to know the relative effectiveness of the film in changing opinions among men who liked the film as compared with those who did not, the before-after procedure is required because the men who like the film generally have different attitudes to begin with from those who do not like it. Thus the after-only control cannot be used as the estimate of initial response for the two differing groups, and there is no way of identifying in the control group those men who *would have* disliked the film if they had seen it. With the before-after procedure the initial opinions of the members of each group are known so each man serves as his own control. In experience, initial responses generally differed on the attitudes related to the content of the film among men who had different evaluations of the film itself, such as whether they thought it truthful, whether they thought it was for propaganda purposes, and so forth.

It should be pointed out, however, that even with the before-after design, the control is always partly incomplete for any sorting variable based on evaluations of the film. While each man serves as his own control, there is no control on possible *differential effects due to other causes than the film* among the different evaluation subgroups. If it is found, for example, that men who thought the film was propaganda were less changed from before to after by the film than those who did not, it is nevertheless possible that this difference might reflect the differential effect of some outside cause that operates selectively on these two kinds of men. Complete control on outside causes is not possible for the reason already mentioned, namely, that we cannot identify in a control group, which does not see the film, those men who would give the designated evaluations if they saw the film. (See also Chapter 4, p. 96.)

2. INITIAL RESPONSE AS THE SORTING VARIABLE

Another class of sorting variables that require the before-after design is the initial opinion itself in the particular area in which the film has effects. For example, in the analysis of the effects of a film favorable to the British, the question arises as to who was more affected by the film, those already pro-British or those initially anti-British. With the before-after procedure this question is readily answered by sorting the men into subgroups according to initial response and determining the proportion of change on the attitude in these subgroups among film men and among control men. The difference between film and control changes in these subgroups gives the effects of the film in each subgroup. With the after-only procedure, however, there is no way of analyzing for effects as a function of initial level on the same opinion—the men answering positively after the film are a mixture of those who initially would have given the positive response and those who would have been negative but were positively affected by the film.

It might be thought that this disadvantage of the after-only procedure could be offset by sorting the men on a closely related question that was not affected by the film but that did provide a fair index of what the initial attitude had been. Such a procedure, while less precise, could be used except for the fact that well-correlated sorting questions would be the most likely also to be affected by the experimental variable, in which case the subgroups of the sort in the experimental group will not be comparable with those in the control group. In general, whenever the sorting variable is affected by the experimental variable no proper after-only analysis can be made of effects according to subtypes of the sorting variable. This is necessarily true because men who give a particular response because they were affected by the film (or in spite of the film) constitute different groups from those who give the same response but have not been exposed to the film.

Moreover, the after-only procedure cannot properly be used as a basis for fully determining whether or not the sorting variable has been affected by the film. Since it reveals only those effects which produce changes in the marginal distribution of responses, it cannot detect situations in which a film might have opposite effects on different individuals, which fail to show up in the marginal distribution.

3. ANALYSIS TO FIND OUT "WHO CHANGES"

Another advantage provided by being able to identify each individual's change of response lies in the fact that it permits making the analysis of differential effects "in reverse." That is, one can sort into the subgroups according to *change of response* and then examine these subgroups for any related variables that differentiate those affected in one way from those affected in another way or those affected not at all. With data in machine-records form this is often a more efficient method of studying the relation of film effects to population variables.

4. CORRELATION BETWEEN CHANGES

Another type of analysis sometimes desired which cannot be performed with the after-only procedure is the analysis of changes on two different variables as a basis for correlating the changes. For example, a film may have a completely unexpected effect with no obvious relation to the material covered in the film. The presumption is that some interpretation presented or some indirect effect of the material covered accounts for the unexpected result. A source of "leads" to the reason for the unexpected effect is to find out what other changes of response are associated with the unexpected changes. Such correlations may provide important hypotheses concerning the particular part of the film's content which was important or what psychological mechanism was responsible for the unexpected result.

The use of this type of analysis raises the problem of correlation versus causation. The actual concern in most analyses of correlated changes is the discovery of possible *causal* relations, but the analysis is limited to the discovery of correlated changes, and causation cannot actually be identified. However, correlations of changes can be a valuable source of hypotheses and may sometimes serve to narrow the range of possible causal factors. The present concern is that such analyses can be performed with the before-after procedure but cannot be performed with the after-only procedure.

For example, in the after-only film study of the "Battle of Britain," a "boomerang" on men's belief in Russian integrity was found as one of the effects of the film, which did not mention Russia directly or by implication. The hypothesis was formulated that this was due to the release of suspicion of Russia that had been inhibited prior to the film because of a sense of obligation to the Russians for doing all the fighting while America was getting prepared. Thus it was postulated that the main source of the changes in opinions about Russian integrity item would be among men who learned that the British had done a real job of holding off the Axis while we were getting better prepared. It might be expected that an after-only analysis could be made in which the men are sorted according to whether or not they said Britain deserves the most credit for holding off the Axis while we were getting prepared, and the effects on the Russian integrity item then determined separately for the two subgroups, with the expectation that the "boomerang" against Russia would disappear among the "men who did not learn" that Britain deserves the most credit—that is, the men who still named a country other than Britain even after seeing the film.

Such an analysis would be invalid, however. It must be kept in mind that men can have a lessened sense of obligation to Russia as a result of the film *without shifting sufficiently to change their response* from giving the most credit to Russia to giving the most credit to Britain. The very men with the initially *strongest* sense of obligation to Russia are the least likely to change from Russia to Britain, yet they are the most susceptible to the "boomerang" in terms of the hypothesis. Thus the after-only analysis may give just the opposite of the correct result, that is, it may indicate that the "men who did not learn" that Britain had helped hold off the Axis showed the greater "boomerang" against Russia.

With the before-after procedure, however, the hypothesis demands that if the men are sorted according to *initial* obligation to Russia the "boomerang" will be greater among those showing initial obligation, since according to the hypothesis these are the only men who can change as a result of seeing the film. This subgroup cannot be designated in the after-only procedure. Furthermore, the hypothesis demands that men who shift on the obligation item from Russia to Britain will show the "boomerang" whereas men who shift from Britain to Russia or choose Britain on both occasions will show less of this effect. The prediction for the group that chooses Russia both times is ambiguous because it is a mixture of men who did not learn that Britain did its part and men who had an initially very strong sense of obligation to Russia. As it actually turned out, an after-only analysis did give the misleading picture characterized just above, the opposite of that obtained by the before-after finding.

Statistical and Sampling Considerations

As stated earlier, the before-after procedure permits the use of correlation of before and after responses in determining the statistical significance of effects of the experimental variable, as well as the determination of any initial lack of equating between control and experimental samples when these have not been drawn at random from the population. The various statistical and sampling considerations are taken up one by one in the following portion of this section.

1. ADVANTAGE OF CORRELATION BETWEEN BEFORE AND AFTER RESPONSES

When a trend study is being made, the change in response during the time interval can be studied either by use of a "repeat" survey on the same individual or by using two equivalent samples, one for the first and another for the second survey. For a given size of sample, changes in response are generally more reliable with the repeat survey on the same sample because of the correlation of individual responses before and after the time interval. For a given level of statistical significance, smaller changes are significant because of this correlation.

In experimental studies, however, a repeat on a single sample is not sufficient. It is necessary to have a control group as well as the experimental group and the use of changes from before to after in the test of statistical significance resolves into a comparison of the *difference between the before-to-after differences* in the two groups. Since the S.E. of the difference between differences is always larger than the S.E. of the first-order differences, the correlation between before and after responses *may or may not* lead to a statistical advantage for the before-after design, depending on the degree of correlation between before and after responses. This will be made clear in the material that follows.

A convenient procedure for computing the S.E. of the difference between the correlated before and after proportion choosing a particular response in the before-after procedure is to cross-tabulate the before and after responses into a fourfold table as shown below. In the fourfold table below, "positive" is used to signify the particular response category the variance of whose marginal frequency before and after is being determined, and "negative" is used to designate all other responses given to the question.

First Survey

		Negative	Positive
Second Survey	Positive	A	B
	Negative	C	D

$$N = A + B + C + D$$

In the fourfold table the letters A, B, C, and D represent the *numbers* in each of the four subtypes of combination of responses before and after. The proportion positive in the "before" survey is $\dfrac{B + D}{N}$ and the proportion positive in the "after" survey is $\frac{A + B}{N}$. It is obvious, therefore, that the difference between the proportion before and the proportion after is $\frac{A - D}{N}$. The S.E. of this correlated mean difference estimated from the sample is equal to:[3]

$$\text{Est. } \sigma_{p_1-p_2} = \frac{1}{\sqrt{N}} \sqrt{\frac{A + D}{N} - \left(\frac{A - D}{N}\right)^2}$$

If one is merely studying trends, the null hypothesis for the significance of a change from before to after in the sample is that in the population $A = D$ so that $A - D = 0$ and the best estimate of $\sigma_{p_1-p_2}$ from the sample is that:

$$\text{Est. } \sigma_{p_1-p_2} = \frac{1}{\sqrt{N}} \sqrt{\frac{A + D}{N}}$$

$$= \frac{\sqrt{A + D}}{N}$$

And since the obtained difference is $\frac{A - D}{N}$, the critical ratio simplifies to:

$$\text{C.R.} = \frac{A - D}{\sqrt{A + D}}$$

When the correlation between before and after responses is zero, the population values of A and D from the null hypothesis are both equal to NPQ (where P and Q are the population marginal proportions).[4]   There-

---

[3] This formula may be derived simply by the use of the scores 0 and 1, for negative and positive respectively, and applying the ordinary S.E. formula for the distribution of differences between correlated measures, that is:

$$\text{S.E. of meas. diff.} = \frac{1}{\sqrt{N}} \sqrt{\frac{\Sigma \text{ diff.}^2}{N} - M^2_{\text{diff.}}}$$

It may also be regarded as an application of the Wilks' formula for the difference between mutually exclusive proportions in the same sample (see footnote, page 304).   In the present case $\frac{A}{N}$ and $\frac{D}{N}$ are the mutually exclusive proportions whose difference, which is equal to $P_{\text{after}} - P_{\text{before}}$, is being evaluated.   Applying Wilks' formula the S.E. of this difference is:

$$\text{S.E. } \frac{A}{N} - \frac{D}{N} = \frac{1}{\sqrt{N}} \sqrt{\frac{A}{N} + \frac{D}{N} - \left(\frac{A}{N} - \frac{D}{N}\right)^2}$$

[4] If there is no correlation between responses before and after, the expected value for A/N is (P after) (Q before) and the expected value for D/N is (P before) (Q after).   On the null hypothesis, that P after = P before = P, it is obvious that the expected value for either A or D is NPQ.

fore, the S.E. of the difference is equal to $\dfrac{\sqrt{NPQ + NPQ}}{N}$, which reduces

to $\sqrt{\dfrac{PQ}{N} + \dfrac{PQ}{N}}$, the standard form for the S.E. of a difference between independent samples. But to the extent that before and after responses are correlated, $A + D$ will be less than $2NPQ$ and the S.E. of the difference will be correspondingly smaller. In the limiting case of perfect correlation both A and D will be zero and the S.E. of the difference will be zero. Since there is nearly always some positive correlation between before and after responses, and in very reliable questions a fairly high correlation, the before-after procedure on the same sample in trend studies is more efficient in that smaller differences are reliable than in the case of two different samples.

However, in an experiment the significance of a before-after change in the experimental group is usually not the important consideration. Rather, the important consideration is the *comparison of the changes* in the experimental group and the control group. In a before-after study, events other than the experimental variable which intervene between the first and second measurement can produce changes, so that a change in the experimental group may be accompanied by a corresponding change in the control group, indicating that the change in the experimental group was due to factors other than the experimental variable. Thus the test of significance must demonstrate a reliable difference *between the changes* in the experimental group and in the control group.

It should be pointed out that it is not sufficient merely to show that a reliable change occurred in the experimental group but that a reliable change did not occur in the control group. The invalidity of such a procedure is illustrated by the absurd case in which a change of 10 per cent in the experimental group is found to be significant but a corresponding change of 9 per cent in the control group did not quite meet the criterion of significance. In such a case it would be absurd to conclude that the 10 per cent change in the experimental group was due to the experimental variable rather than a trend caused by other variables. Even when a zero change or a difference in the opposite direction is found in the control group, it is not sufficient to demonstrate, by the preceding statistical test, that the change in the experimental group was reliable. The reason for this is that a zero difference or a small but unreliable difference in the opposite direction in the control group, while it fails to prove that a change took place in the control, does not prove that no change took place in the control. The only way to prove an effect of the experimental variable is to prove either (1) that the experimental and control groups (drawn from the same population prior to the experiment) differed reliably *after* the application of the experimental variable, or (2) that the before-after *changes* differed reliably.

In the first form of proof, used in the after-only design or obtained by using only the after measurements in the before-after design, the estimated S.E. of the difference between independent samples is used, namely,

$$\sqrt{P_a Q_a \left(\frac{1}{N_c} + \frac{1}{N_e}\right)}$$

where P_a and Q_a are the marginal proportions in the *combined* "after" samples of control and experimental and where N_c and N_e are the numbers of cases in the control and experimental groups respectively.[5] This test of significance determines whether the two groups, *after the application of the experimental variable*, differ reliably in their responses.

The second form of proof—determining the significance of the difference between the experimental and the control *changes* from before to after—is somewhat more complicated. Since with random sampling the two samples, film and control, are uncorrelated, the correct formula for the S.E. of the difference between the two before-after differences is

$$\sigma_{\text{diff.} - \text{diff.}} = \sqrt{\sigma^2_{M \text{ diff. } e} + \sigma^2_{M \text{ diff. } c}}$$

On the null hypothesis, the before-after response distributions in the control and experimental groups are samples from the same population, and the best estimate of the S.E. of the difference between differences should use the same S.E. of a difference for control as for experimental. The estimate is based in each case on the variance of the before-after difference in the four-fold table of *combined* control and experimental response combinations before and after. However, in the present case the null hypothesis is not that no change took place, but that whatever change took place was not different for control and experimental; that is, in the present case the null hypothesis is that $(A_e - D_e) = (A_c - D_c) = (A_t - D_t)$. Thus the estimate of the S.E. of a difference is

$$\sigma_{p_1 - p_2} = \sqrt{\frac{A_t + D_t}{N_t} - \left(\frac{A_t - D_t}{N_t}\right)^2}$$

Thus the S.E. of the mean difference between the before-after changes in the control and experimental groups is

$$\text{Est. } \sigma_{M \text{ diff.} - \text{diff.}} = \sqrt{\left[\frac{A_t + D_t}{N_t} - \left(\frac{A_t - D_t}{N_t}\right)^2\right]\left(\frac{1}{N_c} + \frac{1}{N_e}\right)}$$

---

[5] This formula differs from the more conventional formula, $\sqrt{\frac{p_1 q_1}{N_1} + \frac{p_2 q_2}{N_2}}$, in which p_1 and q_1 are the marginal proportions in the one sample and p_2 and q_2 are the proportions in the other sample. The conventional formula systematically underestimates S.E. when N's are small; the formula in the text above gives a test exactly equivalent to Chi-square.

While this formula appears complicated, the computation is very simple and in many cases the term $\left(\dfrac{A_t - D_t}{N_t}\right)^2$ is so small that it can be ignored for all practical purposes. The computation is especially simplified if the N is the same for both control and experimental groups.

A consideration of this S.E. of the difference between before-after changes as contrasted with that of the difference between the after-responses, shown on page 321, reveals that the question of which of the two is the more sensitive is a function of the amount of correlation between before and after responses. If the correlation is zero, the expected values for $(A_t + D_t)$ and $(A_t - D_t)$ can be expressed in terms of N_t and the marginal proportions, P_a and P_b, where subscripts a and b indicate "after" and "before," respectively. Thus

Expected $A_t + D_t = N_t(P_a - P_aP_b) + N_t(P_b - P_aP_b) = N_t(P_a + P_b - 2P_aP_b)$

Expected $A_t - D_t = N_t(P_a - P_b)$.

Substituting,

$$\frac{A_t + D_t}{N_t} - \left(\frac{A_t - D_t}{N_t}\right)^2 = P_a + P_b - 2P_aP_b - (P_a - P_b)^2$$

$$= P_a(1 - P_a) + P_b(1 - P_b)$$

$$= P_aQ_a + P_bQ_b$$

Thus the variance of the difference when r is zero is larger by the factor P_bQ_b. In the usual case in which the combined before and after marginals do not differ greatly, the variance of before-after changes will be approximately twice as large as the after-only variance, and the S.E. of the mean difference is approximately $\sqrt{2}$ times as large. This would make the significance of the difference between the before-after changes a less sensitive statistical test than a straight test of the after-only difference—the *mean difference* would average the same over a large number of samples, but the *variability would be greater*, so that a larger difference would be required for a given confidence level.

On the other hand, it can be seen that this disadvantage of the test of differences between before-after changes when the correlation is low can be more than offset by higher correlations between before and after responses. This can be done by applying the formula,

$$\sigma_{\text{diff.}} = \sqrt{\sigma_1{}^2 + \sigma_2{}^2 - 2r_{12}\sigma_1\sigma_2}$$

to the combined experimental and control group data, the null hypothesis being that the before-after changes in the two groups are samples from the same population of changes. In this case the estimated variance of the *difference* between experimental and control before-after changes is:

$$\sigma^2_{\text{diff. in } a-b} = \left(P_aQ_a + P_bQ_b - 2r_{ab}\sqrt{P_aQ_aP_bQ_b} \right)\left(\frac{1}{N_c} + \frac{1}{N_e} \right)$$

where subscripts a and b refer to "after" and "before," respectively, and c and e refer to "control" and "experimental," respectively. This may be expressed as:

$$\sigma^2_{\text{diff. in } a-b} = P_aQ_a \left(\frac{1}{N_c} + \frac{1}{N_e} \right) + \left(P_bQ_b - 2r_{ab}\sqrt{P_aQ_aP_bQ_b} \right)\left(\frac{1}{N_c} + \frac{1}{N_e} \right)$$

Since the first term on the right-hand side is the variance of the after-only difference, we may solve for the value of r at which the after-only and before-after procedures are equally sensitive by setting the second term equal to zero, thus:

If
$$\left(P_bQ_b - 2r_{ab}\sqrt{P_aQ_aP_bQ_b} \right)\left(\frac{1}{N_c} + \frac{1}{N_e} \right) = 0,$$

$$P_bQ_b = 2r_{ab}\sqrt{P_aQ_aP_bQ_b};$$

and
$$r_{ab} = \frac{1}{2}\sqrt{\frac{P_bQ_b}{P_aQ_a}}$$

It can be seen, therefore, that for values of r_{ab} greater than $\frac{1}{2}\sqrt{\frac{P_bQ_b}{P_aQ_a}}$, the before-after procedure is more sensitive than the after-only, because the covariance between before and after scores subtracted is greater than the variance added in by using a distribution of differences rather than single scores. In a typical case in which the combined experimental and control proportions do not differ too greatly before and after, r would have to be over approximately .50 before there would be increased sensitivity by using the before-after procedure. For highly reliable questions, the sensitivity is greatly increased, but such high reliability is likely to be rare for questions on topics subject to experimental change. In the present studies the straight after-only difference was sometimes more sensitive and the advantage of the before-after differences between the changes was generally very slight despite the fact that a sizable gain would have been present if only trend studies were being made.

2. INSURING THE EQUIVALENCE OF NONRANDOM SAMPLES

All of the discussion of statistical considerations in the before-after as compared with the after-only procedure has so far made the assumption that the control and experimental groups have been drawn as random samples from the total population being used in the experiment. If random sampling or its equivalent is not possible, other considerations may be of importance in the statistical problem of determining what size differences between film and control are to be considered outside the possibility of sampling differences.

If some selection variable distinguishes the experimental and control groups such that they represent different populations in terms of some property, two results are possible:

(1) they may show initial differences in responses

(2) they may react differently to experimental and other causal variables—that is, they may *change* differently when exposed to the same causal factor.

The first possibility is important mainly for the after-only procedure, in which the effect of the experimental variable is gauged from a comparison of the two samples after one sample has been exposed to the experimental variable. In this case obtained differences may be due to the initial population differences rather than to the effects of the experimental variable. This possibility is not important with the before-after procedure because the *before measurement* determines any initial population differences, which differences are subtracted out when the effects of the experimental variable are gauged from the differences between the before-to-after changes in the two samples.

The second possibility noted above—selective change in two populations exposed to the same causal factors—is relevant to the before-after design. It is of little importance if no important causal factors other than the experimental variable operate during the interim between the before and after measurements, but since this cannot be entirely ruled out there is the possibility that a *differential change due to outside causes* will be falsely judged an effect of the experimental variable. This possibility is not relevant to the after-only design because changes are not measured—with the after-only design such differences come under the heading of population differences in response at the time of measurement, the first possibility above.

The possibility of selective change is of more importance in a before-after experiment comparing two or more experimental variables with a different sample for each variable. Here different causal factors are applied to different samples, and obtained differences in effect may be selective changes due to population differences if the samples differ in some population property. When the comparison is only between experimental and control samples, selective changes are important only because of causal factors other than the experimental variable. In attitude experiments, however, these are a real possibility.

Relevant and irrelevant selection properties. If the experimental and control groups are not strictly comparable because of some difference in the properties of the populations from which they are drawn, it becomes important to distinguish between properties which are relevant and those which are irrelevant to the experiment.   As an extreme example in Army experiments, the control may be selected from the population of men with even-numbered and the experimental group from the population of men with odd-numbered digits in the last position of their serial number.   This is a population property that is completely irrelevant to the experiment because it is uncorrelated both with initial response and susceptibility to changes in response when exposed to causal factors.   If, however, the control group consists of Air Force personnel and the experimental group is from the Infantry, the population difference may be relevant—that is, it may be accompanied by correlated differences in either initial response or changes in response.   This is always a question that cannot be settled on a priori grounds but rather must be settled empirically.   In many experiments what are conceded *generally* to be important population variables are nevertheless irrelevant for the experiment—the control and film might differ completely with respect to sex, or age, or religion, etc., with no accompanying effect on the results obtained.

In Chapter 6 some experience is cited concerning the relevance of a number of population variables in the present film studies done in the Army.   Except for the variables of education and intellectual ability, few sizable correlations of initial response and population variables were obtained, and again except for these variables, almost no reliable differential changes were obtained for the attitudes and films studied.

Relevance of a selection property is not an absolute matter but is a matter of degree.   The extent to which it is important in an experiment is a function of:

1. the extent to which the initial response or the change in response depends on the selection property;

2. the extent to which the two samples differ with respect to the selection property.

By way of illustration, suppose that a particular response is given by 33 per cent of the men with I.Q.'s below 100 but by 66 per cent of those with I.Q.'s above 100.   Under these conditions the largest degree of initial inequality in response would occur if one sample contained only high I.Q. men and the other only those with low I.Q.   Then there would be a difference of 33 per cent.   If, however, in one sample there were 50 per cent high I.Q. men and in another 60 per cent the difference in percentage giving the response should amount to only 3.3 per cent (10 per cent of the initial thirty-three per cent difference).   Similarly, if one sample has 40 per cent and the other 60 per cent high I.Q. men, the difference in per cent giving the response would be expected to be 6.6 per cent, and so forth.

In general, it can be seen that under the condition of a dichotomous selection property (e.g., "high I.Q. men" versus "low I.Q. men"), the expected difference between the proportion giving the response in the two samples is the *product* of the difference in proportion on the selection property and the difference in proportion on the response for the two selection properties. It will also be observed that the product of these two fractions is quite small except for very large values for the two fractions. When the correlation between the initial response and the selection property is relatively small and the inequality of the selection property in the populations from which the samples are drawn is small, only a tiny difference between the sample means is expected. The same analysis also applies in the case of selective *changes* as contrasted with the above case of selective initial differences. But in the case of selective changes even less correlation between change in response and population properties was found (see Chapter 6).

Use of equating when selection is not random. For some kinds of selection properties, the inability to use a random procedure in selecting samples can be compensated by selecting *equated* samples. In the field of public opinion *surveys* representative samples are generally achieved by *stratifying* the sample to predetermined population composition constants. In experimental studies the experimental and control groups can be *equated* —that is, stratified to the same population-composition values, as a means of achieving equality of the samples on population properties.

The situation in which this equating procedure is most appropriate is when the control and experimental groups necessarily differ in some *irrelevant* population property which is nevertheless correlated with relevant properties. In the film research studies carried out in the Army this situation often appeared to be the case. Since training is carried out *by units* in the Army (e.g., company units or platoon units) the test of a film— to achieve proper realism—was necessarily by units. But if an experiment is limited to a sample, say, of 200 film and 200 control and has to be carried out at the company level, one company would have to serve as control sample and the other as film sample. Further, if the subjects are new recruits, membership in a particular company will have had little time to operate as a causal factor, but local assignment practices may be such that there is a nonrandom difference in, say, the educational background of the two companies. Thus the irrelevant variable of company membership is nevertheless correlated with education—one company having been given a greater share of the better educated. In this case we can administer the experiment to the entire group and afterward select two equated samples for analysis—one from each company—and overcome the difference in composition on the important population property of education.

This procedure was generally followed in the Army film studies reported in the present volume, partly because it was felt that for new recruits company membership was for the most part an unimportant population property, relevant only because of correlated differences on relevant properties. However, it was never established that company membership was not an important variable in its own right, even for men with only two or three weeks' membership.

Use of Unit Variance with Random Units Rather than Random Individuals

As indicated earlier, a frequent reason for nonrandom sampling is that the experiment must be administered to units rather than individuals. This may be required for purposes of realism—where the variable is used outside of the experiment with units rather than individuals. Or, it may be required for practical reasons, as when a limited number of camps or cities can be visited—a random sample of 100 members of the U.S. population would require traveling to just about 100 different locations. In such a case the population units may often be randomized and the statistical tests made in terms of the obtained variance among means of units rather than responses of individuals. This is a very efficient procedure if a sizable number of units is possible. If unit differences are really irrelevant selection properties, this fact will show up in the smallness of the variance of their means. If selection properties are relevant and units in the control sample can be paired with similar units in the experimental sample on the basis of important population properties, the distribution of pairs of mean differences will accordingly provide an even more sensitive significance test.

It should once more be pointed out that equating of samples is more likely to be of value—even if its exact value cannot be determined—when the experimental design is after-only. Correlations of population variables with initial responses may be found fairly often, but correlations with changes would be expected to be less frequent. More often the correlation with initial response would be expected to remain much the same in the final response—but with a shift in the overall level. But in either case the population differences must be large and the correlations large before much advantage from equating is expected.

Summary of Comparison of Two Procedures

A general conclusion from the various considerations discussed is that neither the before-after nor the after-only procedure has all the advantages or disadvantages, and the one that is most useful for a given study depends on the purpose and the methodology that can be worked out. The most important advantage of the before-after procedure is the more complex analyses and more complete description of effects that it provides. Probably its main disadvantage is the greater opportunity for the measuring process to bias the results obtained, but this may well be completely avoidable with the proper methodology. While the before-after procedure is generally more sensitive in measuring trends or changes occurring during a time interval, greater sensitivity is not guaranteed in a controlled experiment, in which the outcome depends on a comparison of second-order differences between control and experimental groups. In the latter case the relative sensitivity depends on the reliability of the questions—with low reliability the after-only procedure is the more sensitive. The before-after procedure, however, has a definite advantage when the control and experimental samples cannot be drawn at random from the same population and therefore differ on some population variable that may be correlated with the measurements. In such a case spurious "effects" may be obtained with the after-only procedure which may merely reflect population differences, whereas the before-after procedure takes initial differences into account.

"REGRESSION" IN THE ANALYSIS OF EFFECTS OF FILMS

I N SEVERAL places in the present volume reference has been made to the phenomenon of "regression." Allowance for this phenomenon was of particular relevance in the analyses reported in Chapter 8, where opinion changes were examined in relation to men's initial opinion. The purpose of the present appendix is to give a somewhat fuller treatment of various aspects of regression, particularly as they apply in experimental studies of changes in qualitative variables.

The general concept of regression has been more or less familiar since Galton's application of the term to the tendency for the children of very tall or very short persons to *regress* toward "mediocrity"—that is, to be closer to average height than were their parents. A similar phenomenon is found in the case of the extreme values encountered when one is dealing with test scores or scales of opinion, that is, individuals who obtain the extreme scores—either the very high or the very low—will, when retested, always tend to regress to less extreme positions. The reason for this lies in the fact that all tests, attitude or opinion scales, etc., are subject to a certain amount of unreliability. With any imperfectly reliable measure, the group getting the highest scores contains not only those who really belong in the highest category, but also some who were erroneously classified as belonging in this category because of chance errors of measurement. Since the chance errors will not necessarily occur in the same direction in a retest, the scores of this high group will tend to average lower in the retest. This does not imply a "law of averages" that invariably follows good luck with bad—it is merely an implication of the fact that the individual's average performance is always the most likely result.

The tendency of extreme scores to regress toward the average is of great importance when one is analyzing the effects of an experimental variable on those with varying initial positions, because of the artifact that is introduced if the phenomenon is not controlled.[1] A good example of this artifact has been pointed out by McNemar in his criticism of studies of the effect of environment on IQ.[2] In these studies children with low initial

---

[1] Thorndike, R. L. "Regression Fallacies in the Matched Groups Experiment," *Psychometrika*, 1942, *7*, 85–102.

[2] McNemar, Q. "A Critical Examination of the University of Iowa Studies of Environmental Influences upon the IQ." *Psychol. Bull.*, 1940, *2*, 63–92.

IQ scores were given special training and then retested. An average improvement in retest score was found, but it was subsequently pointed out by McNemar that improvement would be expected in this initially low-scoring group simply because of regression due to the presence of a certain amount of unreliability in IQ measurement.

As with test scores, it is the element of chance in opinion measurement that accounts for the regression of opinions toward the "average" opinion in a retest. Opinion questions are never completely reliable—chance factors of the moment account for errors of measurement when a question is asked the first time, and similar chance factors account for shifts of response when the same question (or a related question) is asked at a later time. If one focuses attention on the group which gave the most extreme answer in the first questioning, one can expect that a certain proportion will "regress," in a second questioning, to a response that is less extreme in the population as a whole. This phenomenon of regression toward the mean in comparing "test" and "retest" results for opinion is well illustrated in the cross-tabulation of estimates of length of the war, used as an illustration for other purposes in Appendix B. The results for the control group, which was subjected to no experimental variable during the interim between the first measurement and the retest, are reproduced below. As in the previous illustration, the numerical code stands for the estimated length of war in half-year units. For convenience of presentation, all estimates of over three and one-half years have been combined into one class interval which is coded below as "7+."

Despite the fact the N's involved are very small, an almost perfectly consistent progression of regression is found from the lowest initial score to the highest initial score. At the extremes, men with the lowest initial score (1.0) regressed to 1.5 in the retest, and men with the highest initial scores (7+) regressed to 5.5 in the retest. But, furthermore, without exception all groups regressed in the retest to a value closer to the mean of 3.2; and in general the relative amount of regression is proportional to the degree of initial deviation from the mean of the group.

This result—that those with moderately high and moderately low scores regressed as well as those with extreme scores—illustrates the fact that although regression is most conspicuous at the extremes it is also present in some degree for all scores that deviate initially from the mean. Except for the extent to which test and retest measures correlate, the most probable value in the retest for any individual is the mean value of the group as a whole. Since the correlation is not perfect, all individuals initially deviating from average tend, as a group, to come a little closer to average in the retest.

It is obvious that an artifact would be involved if we concluded from the results presented that those initially low in their estimate of the length of war increased their true estimate and those initially high decreased their true estimate. Rather, the results are interpretable in terms of the un-reliability of anyone's estimate at a given point in time. Without any real change of opinion a person makes a different guess depending on chance factors of the moment, and the greater the degree of chance in-volved, the greater the regression.

Estimated Length of the Remaining War with Japan in Half-Year Intervals

Initial Estimate (before)

		1	2	3	4	5	6	7+
	1	6	5					
	2	4	37	5	1	2		
Retest (*after*)	3	1	12	37	7	2		
	4		1	7	11	3		
	5			1	4	17	6	3
	6				1		5	
	7+						2	1
Mean est.		1.5	2.2	3.1	3.9	4.5	5.7	5.5

$N = 181$

Regression		+0.5	+0.2	+0.1	−0.1	−0.5	−0.3	−1.5

In the illustration that has been given, the responses are scaled with numerical scores and the usual conception of regression toward the *mean* of the scores applies directly. That is, the responses have an average in the usual sense, and averages on the retest can be computed for each of the subgroups of original response. This conception is not quite as apparent when responses are completely qualitative rather than being measured in scalar units. But even in the case of qualitative designations the same expectation of regression is equally applicable. Suppose, for example, that the above results are dichotomized, using as "cutting-point" the smallest estimate recorded, namely, less than one-half year, which was scored as "1" in the preceding breakdown. The cross-sort of responses then becomes:

Initial Estimate (before)

		Less than one-half year	One-half year or more	
Retest (after)	One-half year or more	5	165	
	Less than one-half year	6	5	
	Total	11	170	181
	% Regression	45%	−3%	

With this breakdown the regression may be measured as *per cent who regress*, and it can be seen that of the 11 men with estimates of less than one-half year, five, or 45 per cent, regressed to larger estimates in the retest, whereas only 3 per cent of the 170 with initially longer estimates shifted to less than one-half year.

If "cutting-points" for dichotomization are made successively at higher estimates along the length-of-war continuum, it would be expected that successively fewer of the men with smaller estimates would regress to higher estimates and successively more of the men with higher estimates would regress to smaller estimates. This merely describes, in terms of percentages above or below a certain value along the continuum, the same relation previously shown for mean values of the different subgroups of initial response. The percentages actually obtained at the different "cutting-points" are shown below.

PER CENT WHO REGRESS:

"Cutting-point" between	To higher estimates	To lower estimates
1 and 2	45%	3%
2 " 3	21	7
3 " 4	8	18
4 " 5	4	17
5 " 6	1	53
6 " 7+	1	75

It can be seen that the proportion who switch to the category of longer estimates progressively decreases as the dichotomy is made at longer and longer estimates, whereas the proportion who switch to the category of smaller estimates increases. In general, the proportions switching to the opposite category would tend to be equal at the "cutting-point" which dichotomizes the total sample into two equal-sized groups, i.e., with a 50-50 split. Such a dichotomy is not actually possible with the categories used in the above illustration, but the theoretical point can be obtained by plotting the above percentages who regressed as a function of the proportion of the total group included on a given side of the cut-point, i.e., as a function of the percentile point corresponding to each of the different answers. The first category above—less than one-half year—includes 11/181 of the sample, or 6 per cent; the second category includes 66/181, or 36 per cent; and so forth. The results plotted in this way are shown in the figure below. It will be noted that the two curves cross the 50-percentile line at about the same level, indicating that with a 50-50 split the propor-

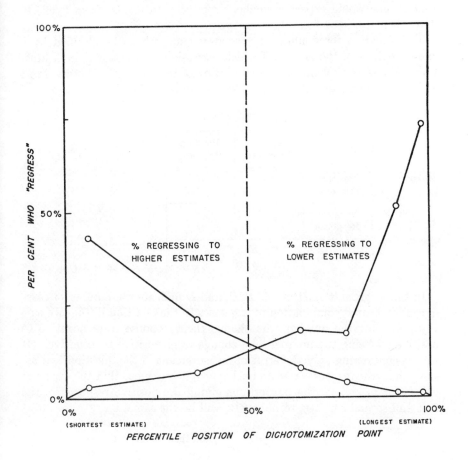

PERCENTILE POSITION OF DICHOTOMIZATION POINT

tions regressing in the negative and positive direction are approximately
equal.

The figure shows the per cent who regress to the opposite response of a
dichotomy, as a function of the "cutting-point" chosen for the dichotomy.
The responses shown in the figure were initially obtained in scale units of
length of time and for purposes of illustration have been dichotomized at
the various possible "cutting-points." But the same sort of relation between per cent regressing and the "cutting-point" of the dichotomy is expected in the more usual case with qualitative responses, in which the
"cutting-point" is determined by the wording of the question.

Suppose, for example, the question had been, "Do you think the war
will be over in less than one-half year?" One would then expect a fairly
high proportion of those saying "yes" to this question to regress to "no"
in a repeat survey, but very few of the "no" responses to regress to "yes"
because most of the initial estimates fell above this point. But if the
question had been, "Do you expect the war will be over in less than two
years?" one would expect a smaller proportion to regress from "yes" to
"no" then regressed from "no" to "yes."

The situation for qualitative responses can perhaps be clarified by a
closer analysis of the factors of which regression is expected to be a function. Below is a schematic representation of the correlation between test
and retest with a dichotomous qualitative question.

First Survey

		Negative Response	Positive Response	
Repeat Survey	Positive Response	A	B	$p_2 = \dfrac{A + B}{N}$
	Negative Response	C	D	

$$p_1 = \frac{B + D}{N} \qquad N = A + B + C + D$$

In the diagram, the letters A, B, C, and D indicate the number of cases
in each indicated combination of responses to the question in the two surveys, A being the number who change their response from negative to
positive, D being the number who change from positive to negative. If
we are considering only the error of measurement in the question and assume that true responses remain unchanged, it is obvious that the expected
values for p_1 and p_2, the proportions giving the positive response in the
first and second surveys, respectively, will be the same, i.e.,

$$p_1 = p_2 = \frac{B + D}{N} = \frac{A + B}{N}, \text{ and therefore } A = D.$$

Therefore, it can be seen that if only errors of measurement are being considered the number who regress to each of the two opposite responses in a retest will be the same (i.e., A will equal D), and therefore the *proportion* of those giving a particular initial response who shift to the opposite response is a function of the initial division of opinion and the relative size of A or D. The proportion of those initially negative who shift to positive is

$$\frac{A}{A + C}$$

and the proportion of those initially positive who shift to negative is

$$\frac{D}{D + B}$$

Since $A = D$, the relative size of the *proportions* "regressing" for each initial category depends on the relative sizes of $(A + C)$ and $(D + B)$. Now if the coefficient of reliability, r, is measured in terms of point-correlation,[3] then:

$$\frac{A}{A + C} = p (1 - r)$$

and

$$\frac{B}{B + D} = q (1 - r).$$

Thus it can be seen that the per cent regressing from negative to positive or from positive to negative can be expressed as a function of p, the proportion choosing the positive response, and r, the reliability of the question as expressed in terms of point correlation.

The regression of qualitative responses to the other response in the dichotomy is completely analogous to the regression of quantitative scores toward the mean. By using 0 and 1 scores for absence and presence, re-

---

[3] Point correlation is often called the "phi-coefficient": it is Pearson r using 0 and 1 scores for absence and presence, respectively, of the qualitative trait.

$$\text{If} \quad p_1 = p_2 = p, r = \frac{B/N - p^2}{pq} = \frac{\dfrac{Np - A}{N} - p^2}{pq} = \frac{p - p^2 - \dfrac{A}{N}}{pq} = \frac{pq - \dfrac{A}{N}}{pq}.$$

Solving for A gives $A = Npq (1 - r)$. Since $A = D$, D is also equal to $Npq (1 - r)$, and since $(A + C) = Nq$ and $(B + D) = Np$,

$$\frac{A}{A + C} = p (1 - r)$$

$$\frac{D}{B + D} = q (1 - r)$$

spectively, of the qualitative trait it can be shown that the mean of the scores is p, and that considered as groups those initially negative, all with initial scores of 0, and those initially positive, all with initial scores of 1, both regress toward the mean, which is p, the proportion of positive responses in the population.

In view of these considerations, it is not surprising that in the dichotomy of the estimated length of war at the two-year point there was a regression of 34 per cent among the men guessing a war of two years or more. The question was a fairly unreliable one, and only about one man in four selected a response of two or more years initially. The fact that only 11 per cent regress in the experimental group therefore constitutes evidence that the communication was effective in reinforcing the expectation of a long war by preventing 23 per cent of those initially expecting a long war (of 2 years or more) from regressing.

The importance of a control for such regression due to unreliability of the measuring instrument is obvious here. If one had merely measured the experimental group before and after the administration of the experimental variable, one might make the mistake of assuming the -11% net change was a negative effect of the communication, rather than the effect of regression due to unreliability, coupled with a sizable positive effect of the communication. For the experimental group *as a whole*, the phenomenon of regression does not affect the conclusion, because regression in a negative direction is offset by regression in a positive direction and any significant overall shift in one direction or the other reflects a true change rather than an artifact of regression. In the present illustrative experiment the overall net change in the control group was only -1%, which is well within chance expectation. Thus the net change of 39 per cent between the before and after measurements in the experimental group is a quite accurate representation of the overall effects of the program because in this case there was no appreciable change due to other causes, so that before and after measurements on just an experimental group would have been adequate for the overall evaluation. However, since this outcome can rarely be accurately predicted in advance, a control is generally needed simply to check on the possible overall shifts due to other causes. In any case, the point to be emphasized here is that in order to break down the results into subgroups of differing initial level, the control group is an absolute necessity in order to determine the effects of regression.

A simple example may be used to illustrate the type of false conclusion that can be drawn from data if the errors of measurement and the consequent regression are ignored. Consider the following cross-tabulation of before and after responses which were obtained in a control group in one of the orientation film studies:

Question: "Do you feel that the British are doing all they possibly can to help in the war effort?"

FIRST-SURVEY AND REPEAT-SURVEY RESPONSES (TWO WEEKS LATER)
IN A CONTROL GROUP

		First Survey		
		− (no)	+ (yes)	Total
Repeat survey	+ (yes)	40	308	348
	− (no)	57	37	94
	Total	97	345	442

It will be observed that about the same number of men originally saying "no" changed to "yes" (40) as changed from "yes" to "no" (37). But it is also observed that the number originally saying "no" is much smaller to start with (97) than the number saying "yes" (345). If we mistakenly treat all of the changes as real changes of opinion, we get the interesting conclusion that a much larger proportion of the "no" group changed their opinion than of the "yes" group. In fact, 41 per cent of the 97 men originally saying "no" changed to "yes," whereas only 12 per cent of the initial 345 "yeses" changed to "no." This finding might even be generalized in terms of an explanatory concept: it might, for example, be postulated that the majority opinion has much more effect on the minority group than vice versa. In line with this, it might be said that the group opinion exerts a force on the dissenters, causing many of them to align themselves with the group opinion whereas only a small fraction shift away from the group opinion.

This reasonable-seeming hypothesis would receive ample "verification" from other sources if the same interpretation were made of similar data. This follows from the fact that a repeat on any question whatsoever, provided there is error of measurement, will give the same picture as in the above illustration. Solely on the basis of error of measurement, the number of individuals who shift from negative to positive will be expected to be the same as the number who shift from positive to negative. This has already been seen to be a necessary consequence if p_1 and p_2 remain the same. It can perhaps be made more meaningful by realizing that whether an individual is a "true positive" or a "true negative," and whatever the frequency of errors for either designation, it will be just as likely that his two responses will be positive first and negative second in the successive surveys as that they will be negative first and positive second. And if the *number* of positive-negative pairs is approximately the same as the number of negative-positive pairs, *the proportion changing will necessarily be larger for whichever response was initially in the minority.*

Treating the changes in this way as entirely due to the errors of measurement, the marginal per cent of positive responses is seen to "regress" toward the group proportion, in each of the two subgroups of initial response. Thus the group of individuals initially giving the negative response regresses from 0 per cent positive to 42 per cent positive, and the group initially giving positive responses regresses from 100 per cent positive to 88 per cent positive, both groups shifting toward the overall value of 78 per cent positive. If the question had zero reliability, both groups would regress to 78 per cent positive on the retest, which would be a shift involving 78 per cent of those initially negative and a shift of only 22 per cent of those initially positive.

This illustration is chosen as an obvious example of a spurious conclusion that can be drawn because of failure to attend to the errors of measurement in the opinion question used. A similar false conclusion could be drawn if one had used before and after measurements on a single group that was exposed to the film between the two measurements. With the present opinion item no significant effect of the film was obtained in the before-after study, so the film-group results were very similar to the control-group results just shown. But if one ignored regression due to unreliability, one might conclude that the effect of the film was to shift both groups in the opposite direction—making the anti-British more pro-British and make the pro-British more anti-British, the former being the larger "effect."

This obviously spurious example shows clearly the effects of ignoring regression—i.e., the effects of ignoring chance error of measurement—in opinion study. Probably few analysts would draw the spurious conclusions drawn here for illustrative purposes. However, in more complex attempts to analyze opinion changes, the regression factor may enter in a disguised form that leads to spurious conclusions due to failure to consider the involved effects of errors of measurement.

In experiments with the effects of films on opinions, as in most studies of opinion changes, it is often desired to study factors related to a given opinion change by means of analysis of the effects as a function of predisposing background variables, as a function of initial opinions related to the opinion that changed, and as a function of related changes in opinions. The effects are expected to be indirect results of the interaction of the material presented and numerous human variables not subject to the experimenter's control. Special analyses have sometimes been used in an attempt to get at the effects of those elusive variables as causal factors, not by manipulating them and observing the changes produced, but by measuring their extent in each individual and comparing individuals who differ with respect to these variables. In performing such analyses it is particularly important to control for errors of measurement, to prevent phenomena due to regression in selected groups from being attributed to the variables under investigation.

The members of the Experimental Section found a number of examples in which their own earlier attempts to analyze opinion change as a function of other opinions and other opinion changes turned out to be subject to artifacts due to regression. An example of the kind of artifact encountered is illustrated in Appendix C in the discussion of the advantages to analysis of the before-after procedure. In order further to illustrate the effects of neglecting errors of measurement in a complex analysis of opinion change, another illustrative example is provided below. The example and the data are fictitious, but they illustrate the problems involved. Suppose that one of the orientation films had made the point that the League of Nations failed because America refused to become a member. Suppose further that the film produced an increase of 10 per cent, from before to after, in the number holding this belief and that the control group as a whole showed a 0 per cent change in frequency of expressing this belief. The analyst might be interested in whether the film differed in effectiveness among those of differing education, and since the control showed no change might concentrate his attention on the before-after changes in the experimental group. A hypothetical outcome in the analysis might be as follows in response to the question:

"In your opinion, did the League of Nations fail because America refused to become a member?"

| | | LESS WELL EDUCATED *Before* | | | | BETTER EDUCATED *Before* | | |
		No	*Yes*	*Total*		*No*	*Yes*	*Total*
After	*Yes*	20	20	40	*Yes*	25	35	60
	No	50	10	60	*No*	25	15	40
	Total	70	30	*N = 100*	*Total*	50	50	*N = 100*

The analyst might look at these results and note that among those initially opposed to the idea (i.e., those "no" before), 25/50 or 50 per cent changed to "yes" among the better educated, whereas only 20/70 or 29 per cent changed from "no" to "yes" among the less well educated. Similarly among those initially favoring the point of view only 15/50 or 30 per cent of the better educated went from "yes" to "no" whereas 10/30 or 33 per cent changed from "yes" to "no" among the less well educated. Thus on both counts the better educated were more affected than the less well educated: many more of the "no" responses changed to "yes," and fewer of the "yes" responses changed to "no."

The hypothetical analyst might be a little puzzled, however, by the fact that the marginal change in each case is 10 per cent; that is, the less well educated shifted from 30 per cent "yes" to 40 per cent "yes" and the better educated shifted from 50 per cent "yes" to 60 per cent "yes." The difficulty is that the initial response is correlated with the variable being examined—that is, the less well educated have fewer facts and tend to give a "patriotic" response exonerating the United States. The less well educated initially say "yes" in only 30 per cent of the cases whereas 50 per cent of the better educated believe initially that America's refusal led to the failure of the League. We therefore expect a smaller proportion of the "yes" responses and a larger proportion of the "no" responses to *regress* among the less well educated. Until we examine the same breakdown in the control group, we do not know how many regress in the various subgroups and cannot conclude anything about differential changes among those initially opposed and those initially favoring, and the results as expressed in the preceding paragraph are meaningless. All we may conclude is that there was a 10 per cent shift in the marginal proportion saying "yes" in each group. We may further express this shift in terms of the "effectiveness index" to take account of the initial differences in the marginal proportions. Without examining the control results, even these calculations are risky because there may have been a differential change due to other causes in the two educational groups. Such a possibility is readily taken into account by examining the control results for effects of other causes. Further, with the control breakdown available, individual cells in the before-after analysis can be examined, and conclusions may be drawn as a function of the initial position of the members of the samples. What the control adds is the result to be expected, due to all other causes, and it includes as one of the important "other causes" the effects of regression due to errors of measurement.

INDEX

A

Acceptance of communication, as factor influencing opinion change, 98, 164ff., 174f., 194ff., 269f.

After-only experimental design, *see* Experimental design

AGCT, *see* Army General Classification Test

Alternative presentations, 6, 120–146
   commentator vs. documentary study, 130ff.: experimental design, 132ff.; results (audience evaluation, 134ff., opinion change, 137ff.)
   evaluation of existing products, 120f.
   film-strip vs. sound motion picture, 121ff.: experimental design, 123ff.; results, 126ff. (for men of different intellectual ability, 126f., for particular presentation devices, 128ff.)
   introductory vs. review exercises, 141ff.: experimental design, 142f.; results, 143ff. (for men of different intellectual ability, 144f., relation to motivation, 144ff.)

Applied research, 6, 9, 257ff.; practical value of theoretical studies, 279

Army General Classification Test, 30, 147ff. *See also* Intellectual ability.

Attitude, *see* Opinion; Opinion change

Audience evaluation, 11f., 80–119, 249; as variable in analysis, 314; attempts to infer effects from, 93f.; authenticity of material, 81, 87ff., 135ff., 215ff.; general interest films, 103ff., 108ff.; in comparison of commentator and documentary radio transcriptions, 134f.; interest in films and radio transcriptions, 81, 85f., 95ff., 104ff., 134f.; interpretation of, 86; methodological considerations, 102f.; of programs presenting "one side" and "both sides," 215ff. (effects of omission of important argument, 216ff.); orientation films, 82ff. (criticisms by men, 88ff.); polygraphic recording, use in, 104ff. (as basis for interviews, 106f., comparison with questionnaires, 109ff., 117ff., instructions, 105f.); relationship to effects of film, 11, 80f., 94ff., 257 (methodological considerations, 95f); research methods, 82ff., 95f., 104ff.; skepticism concerning communication, 98ff.; suggestions of men for improving films, 92f.

Audience participation, *see* Participation

Authenticity, men's opinions concerning, 81, 87, 135ff.

Awareness of measurement, 14, 25, 27

B

Baseline for measuring percentage changes, 284–292

"Battle of Britain, The" (film) 21–50; checks on possible "boomerangs" in, 46ff.; content and objectives, 21ff.; criteria of effectiveness, 22ff.; effects on information (delayed, 184, immediate, 39ff., 42, 55); effects on motivation (delayed, 199f., immediate, 44ff.); effects on opinion (comparison of immediate and delayed effects, 184ff., delayed, 184ff., immediate, 33ff., 42f., 55ff.)
   experimental evaluation of: long term effects (design, 183f.); short term effects (administration, 30ff., design, 25ff., sampling, 29f.)

Before-after design of experiment, *see* Experimental design

Behavioral measures, *see* Criteria of evaluation

"Boomerangs," checks on possibility of, 46ff., 316ff.; definition, 23

"Both sides" vs. "one side" of argument, *see* Controversial arguments, presentation of

C

Camouflage items, 25, 27, 311

"Ceiling" effects, 60, 65ff., 284f.

Chi-square test, in analyzing effects, 296ff.

"Commentator" radio transcriptions, *see* Alternative presentations, commentator vs. documentary study; Radio transcriptions

study, 228ff.; relationship to intellectual ability, 240ff.; relationship to motivation, 231, 238ff.; results, 233ff. (interaction with difficulty, intellectual ability and motivation, 241ff., with different degrees of motivation, 238ff., with materials of varying difficulty, 236f.); summary of study, 263ff.

Personal history items, 25, 28, 30, 147

Polygraphic recording of interest, see Audience evaluation; Interviews, group

Population variables, see Variables

Predisposition, 168, 192ff.

"Prelude to War" (film): content of, 52; effects of, 55ff.

Presentations of arguments, order of, see Controversial arguments, presentation of

Pretest, function of in preparing communication, 203; qualitative, 26; quantitative, 26f.

Program analyzer, see Audience evaluation, polygraphic recording, use in

Propaganda, 81, 87ff., 92, 98ff., 131, 135ff., 221, 224; operational definition of, 275ff.

Q

Questionnaires, 82f., 107; construction of, 25ff.; pretesting of, see Pretest

R

Radio transcriptions, 69f., 130ff., 201ff. See also Alternative presentations, commentator vs. documentary study.

Realism of testing conditions, 15f., 29ff., 123ff., 234, 244f., 252, 327

"Regression": in analysis of film effects, 222ff., 329ff.; relationship to reliability, 330ff.

"Rehearsal," as factor in participation, 243ff., 264

Reliability, relationship to regression, 330ff.

Research design, 150; summary of, 247ff. See also Experimental design.

Review exercises, see Alternative presentations, introductory vs. review exercises

S

Sampling considerations: equating experimental and control groups, 30; equating of non-random samples, 323f.; unit sampling vs. individual sampling, 29, 327

Scales of items, 26, 61ff., 223

Selection ceiling, 197. See also "Ceiling" effects.

Selection effects, 66, 290ff. See also "Regression"; Self selection.

Self selection, 16, 252

"Sensitization," 310

"Short-time" vs. "long-time" effects, see Temporal effects

Significance tests: average effectiveness index, 289; chi-square for "internal" changes, 296f.; net proportion who change, 303ff.; with before-after procedure, 317ff.

"Sinking in" period, 71f.

Skepticism of films, see Audience evaluation, skepticism concerning communication

"Sleeper" effects, 71, 182, 188ff. See also Temporal effects.

Slide-film, see Film-strips

Specific coverage, 69ff.

Specificity of effects, 53ff., 61ff. See also Transfer of effects.

"Stability" of opinion: relation to intellectual ability, 172ff.; relation to lapse of time, 173ff.

Supplementary exercises, see Alternative presentations, introductory vs. review exercises

T

Temporal effects, 28, 182–200, 251; hypotheses to explain, 189, 197ff.; methodological implications, 200; on factual information, 184; on "informed" and "uninformed" opinion, 190ff.; on opinion, 184ff.; relation to initial position, 190ff.; relation to intellectual ability, 190ff.; summary, 273ff.

"Test" reaction, 309

Theory, role of, in communication research, 8f., 179f.

Training films, 14f., 121ff., 141ff., 228ff.

Transfer of effects, 43, 53ff., 61ff., 129

Transfer of training, 244, 265

U

Unit sampling, see Sampling considerations

V

Validity of opinions: distinction between "informed" and "uninformed" opinion, 166ff.; relation to effects of films, 168ff.

THE SOCIAL SCIENCE RESEARCH COUNCIL was organized in 1923 and formally incorporated in 1924, composed of representatives chosen from the seven constituent societies and from time to time from related disciplines such as law, geography, psychiatry, medicine, and others. It is the purpose of the Council to plan, foster, promote, and develop research in the social field.

CONSTITUENT ORGANIZATIONS

American Anthropological Association
American Economic Association
American Historical Association
American Political Science Association
American Psychological Association
American Sociological Society
American Statistical Association

PERSPECTIVES IN SOCIAL INQUIRY

CLASSICS, STAPLES AND PRECURSORS IN SOCIOLOGY

Jenks, Edward. **The State and The Nation.** 1919

Judd, Charles Hubbard. **The Psychology of Social Institutions.** 1927

Kelsen, Hans. **Society and Nature:** A Sociological Inquiry. 1946

Lange, Frederick Albert. **The History of Materialism:** And Criticism of Its Present Importance. 3 vols. in 1. 1879-1881

Le Bon, Gustave. **The Psychology of Peoples.** 1924

Lewis, George Cornewall. **An Essay on the Influence of Authority in Matters of Opinion.** 1849

Lewis, George Cornewall. **A Treatise on the Methods of Observation and Reasoning in Politics.** 2 vols. in 1. 1852

Lowell, Abbot Lawrence. **Public Opinion in War and Peace.** 1923

Maine, Henry Sumner. **Village-Communities in the East and West.** 1889

Merton, Robert K. and Paul F. Lazarsfeld, eds. **Continuities in Social Research:** Studies in the Scope and Method of "The American Soldier." 1950

Michels, Roberto. **First Lectures in Political Sociology.** 1949

Ogburn, William Fielding and Alexander Goldenweiser, eds. **The Social Sciences and Their Interrelations.** 1927

Park, Robert Ezra. **The Collected Papers of Robert Ezra Park.** 3 vols. in 1. 1950/52/55

Plint, Thomas. **Crime in England:** Its Relation, Character and Extent as Developed from 1801 to 1848. 1851

Ranulf, Svend. **The Jealousy of the Gods and Criminal Law at Athens.** 2 vols. in 1. 1933/34

Ross, Edward Alsworth. **Social Psychology:** An Outline and Source Book. 1912

Small, Albion W. **General Sociology.** 1905

Studies in Social Psychology in World War II: Vols. I, II, and III. 1949

Sutherland, Alexander. **The Origin and Growth of the Moral Instinct.** 2 vols. in 1. 1898

Tarde, G[abriel]. **Social Laws:** An Outline of Sociology. 1899

Teggart, Frederick J. **Prolegomena to History.** 1916

Thomas, William I. **Sex and Society.** 1907

Von Wiese, Leopold. **Systematic Sociology.** 1932

Ward, Lester F. **Applied Sociology.** 1906

Wirth, Louis, ed. **Eleven Twenty-Six:** A Decade of Social Science Research. 1940

Wright, R[obert] J[oseph]. **Principia, Or Basis of Social Science.** 1875